SYLVIA PLATH

SYLVIA PLATH

The Shaping of Shadows

Al Strangeways

Madison • Teaneck
Fairleigh Dickinson University Press
London: Associated University Presses

Associated University Presses
440 Forsgate Drive
Cranbury, NJ 08512

Associated University Presses
16 Barter Street
London WC1A 2AH, England

Associated University Presses
P.O. Box 338, Port Credit
Mississauga, Ontario
Canada L5G 4L8

The paper used in this publication meets the requirements of the American National Standard for Permanence of Paper for Printed Library Materials Z39.48-1984.

Library of Congress Cataloging-in-Publication Data

Strangeways, Al.
Sylvia Plath : the shaping of shadows / Al Strangeways.
p.   cm.
Includes bibliographical references and index.
ISBN 0-8386-3735-3 (alk. paper)
1. Plath, Sylvia—Criticism and interpretation. 2. Women and literature—United States—History—20th century. I. Title.
PS3566.L27Z9137   1998
811'.54—dc21   97-51189
                                                                       CIP

PRINTED IN THE UNITED STATES OF AMERICA

Contents

Abbreviations

CP   Sylvia Plath, *Collected Poems,* ed. Ted Hughes (London: Faber, 1981).

JP   Sylvia Plath, *Johnny Panic and the Bible of Dreams and Other Prose Writings,* ed. Ted Hughes (London: Faber 1975).

J   Sylvia Plath, *The Journals of Sylvia Plath,* ed. Frances McCullough and Ted Hughes (New York: Ballantine-Random House, 1982).

LH   Sylvia Plath, *Letters Home: Correspondence 1950–1963,* ed. Aurelia Plath (London: Faber, 1975).

Acknowledgments

Thanks to my family, friends, and colleagues for their unstinting financial, academic, and moral support throughout the writing of this work. I am grateful for the bursary provided by the University of the West of England, which allowed me to complete this work, and for the travel fellowship awarded by the Ball Brothers Foundation at the Lilly Library, which enabled my encounter with the Plath archives. Thanks to the librarians at Smith College Rare Book Room and the Lilly Library, who made the archive digging such an enjoyable and profitable experience. My thanks to Jim Davies for his initial and continued support and encouragement. Jean Grimshaw's insight into psychoanalysis and her comments on chapter 3 were immensely helpful. Thanks also to Jean Gooder for her careful reading of, and comments on the whole manuscript; to Debbie Johnson, Alan Brown, Chris Ryder, Ann Hancock, Shirley Foster, and above all to Kate Fullbrook for her persistence, painstaking re-readings of the work, and consistent belief in my aims. This work is for Andrew, who probably will never read it all, but without whose unfailing practical and moral support, it would neither have been finished, nor, indeed, started.

* * *

Letters Home by Sylvia Plath. Selected and Edited with Commentary by Aurelia Schober Plath. Used by permission of Faber and Faber Ltd.

Unpublished poetry and prose by Sylvia Plath used by permission of Faber and Faber Ltd., The Lilly Library, Indiana University and Mortimer Rare Book Room, Smith College.

Some material in chaper 3 originally published as "'The Boot in the Face': The Problem of the Holocaust in the Poetry of Sylvia Plath," by Al Strangeways. *Contemporary Literature*, Volume 37 Number 3 (Fall 1996): 370–390. Used by permission of The University of Wisconsin Press.

SYLVIA PLATH

Introduction:
An Intellectual Background

I wrote my first poem . . . when I was eight-and-a-half years old . . . and from then on, I suppose, I've been a bit of a professional.
—Sylvia Plath, interview, 1962

If I must be pestled to death
Let it be with knowledge.
—Sylvia Plath, draft of "Years," 16 November 1962

Fascination with Plath's personality and the events of her private life directs and sustains most accounts of her work. Identifying the significance of any poem with the poet's experience or consciousness is always, however, open to question, because, in Jan Montefiore's terms, "it is the poems which are available to us, not the poet's mind."[1] Additionally, and specifically in Plath's case, although (like all poets) she utilized such "personal" material in her poetry, she also saw herself very clearly as part of a poetic tradition and was proud of her intellect and of her academic background. Neglecting the central impact of both her intellectual training and her relationship with literary tradition cannot fail, then, to lead to an unbalanced and incomplete account of Plath's poetry, as, indeed, much of what is central and often most controversial in her work is clarified through examination of the influences of her literary and academic history.

This study of Plath's work consequently will utilize many previously unexamined documents (including her academic essays and her often heavily marked collection of books) held by the two major archives at Smith College and the Lilly Library, Indiana University, archives which have attracted much attention, but whose contents, with the exception of her later drafts, are generally examined in depth only by Plath's biographers. I will attempt to redress the balance of critical approaches to Plath's work by assessing the impact on her poetry of her intellectual and literary

13

(rather than biographical) history, in terms of her often anxious dialogue with literary Romanticism, in the light of her relationship with contemporary political debates, and in relation to her struggles with what was becoming, in the 1950s, the new religion of psychoanalysis. This will show that the general critical divisions between Plath's critics (into, for instance, those who applaud and those who denigrate her work as "sincere," or those who biographicalize and those who abstract her writing) are in fact reflected in and stem from Plath's own conflicts about her relationship with the discourses with which she is in dialogue.

An Intellectual Approach to Writing

Plath was closely involved in academia, either as a student or a teacher, for all but the last five years of her life. She was both a compulsive and a competitive scholar throughout her academic career, writing extensive longhand notes for classes she both taught and attended.[2] Her letters to her mother (even taking into account the fact that Plath tailored her information to meet her perception of her mother's needs) are suffused with information about her A grade average and the extreme conscientiousness with which she approached her studies, to the extent of getting highly emotional about a science course with which she was having difficulty. Even after leaving the academic world in summer 1958 (after a year of teaching at Smith College), Plath continued to write detailed academic-style notes on subjects that interested her poetically. A notebook (undated, but appearing to have been written in late 1958) survives, containing notes on bulls, stones, saints, and frogs, pertinent to poems she wrote in late 1958 and 1959, such as "The Stones" and "The Bull of Bendylaw."[3]

A similar kind of conscientiousness also characterized Plath's approach to her writing, which, from an early age, she considered a profession, declaring in an interview in 1962 that

> I wrote my first poem, my first published poem, when I was eight-and-a-half years old. It came out in *The Boston Traveller* and from then on, I suppose, I've been a bit of a professional.[4]

Throughout her career, her letters to her mother are conscientious in the tallies they keep about how many poems and stories she had published and how much money she earned from them. In her journals, as well, Plath's competitiveness and professionalism comes out in her frequent comparisons of her own literary output with that of contemporaries: in January 1959, for one example among many, she directly compares her perceived laziness with Adrienne Rich's publishing success (J 292).

Attention to Plath's academic background is, therefore, not only illuminating, but crucial to the understanding of her poetry because her academic and intellectual pursuits formed such a large and important part of her life that they are ultimately inseparable from her poetic activities. Such an examination is useful in two ways. First, it highlights an important conflict which underlies all of Plath's poetry, between intellect and emotion, or objectivity and subjectivity, although, as will be seen, the distinction between these terms is less than absolute. Second, such an examination helps elucidate the ideas (in terms both of broad impressions and of specific appropriations) that helped shape Plath's poetry. These influences, as the following chapters show, are not simply literary, because as a liberal arts student at Smith College, her intellectual training also encouraged the critical and interdisciplinary study of many other subjects. Other than literary and creative writing classes, Plath studied European history in her first year, politics and religion in her second year, physical science in her third (interrupted) year, and nineteenth-century history of European ideas on her return to the third year. The idea of undergraduate study providing a general liberal arts education was institutionalized in America; as such, the connections between the disciplines Plath studied were emphasized and reflected in the prospectus descriptions which, for example, show that French literature was examined in order to study "the literary, historical and cultural background of France," and that the religion course considered the relation of the western religions to "the problems presented by scientific thought, nationalism and an industrialized society."[5] Plath clearly embraced this interdisciplinary approach by using texts from one course to write papers for another: she used Nietzsche's *Thus Spake Zarathustra,* a set text for her second-year religion course, when writing an essay two years later for her intellectual history course. She continued in this way at Cambridge: referring, for instance, to Aldous Huxley, Eric Fromm, and Freud in an essay on Plato's *The Republic,* quoting Blake's poetry in an essay on Locke, and referring to Nietzsche in an essay on Blake and Lawrence.[6]

SUBJECTIVITY AND OBJECTIVITY

Although the terms "emotional women" and "intellectual," or "subjective" and "objective," do not stand in isolated and clear opposition to each other (it is perhaps more useful to see them as describing the two ends of a continuum), they warrant such detailed probing in Plath's case not only because of her own struggles with their connotations, but because it is within, or more precisely at the limits of this continuum that much debate about her status and worth as a poet takes place. Plath's own apparent privileging of one extreme, that of the emotional or subjective, has encouraged both the intense interest in her life and the biographical readings of her poems. In terms of this extreme, she is frequently characterized as hysterical, intense, and egotistic by supporters as well as detractors. At the other limit of the continuum, her intellectual and academic talents, while not in question, are usually regarded as marginal, perhaps even inimical to her poetic talents, and are generally examined only as a way of explaining the careful formality of her poetry up to and including much of *The Colossus* (1960). Critics tend to see this conscientious poetic apprenticeship as the only manifestation of Plath's intellectual skills, viewing the evidence of such skills as merely characterizing her compulsive desire to succeed, and perceiving her as decisively breaking free from their restrictions in the powerful *Ariel* (1965) poems (written between 1962 and 1963). Joanne Feit-Diehl's attitude is characteristic of this tendency: writing about Plath's conflict between her desires to gain access to Romantic tradition and to express her feminine "bodily ego," she views the final poems as "a release" from the former and writes about "the final free flight of 'Ariel', 'Lady Lazarus', and 'Fever 103°'."[7] The powerful hold of this view of Plath's career at least partly stems from Ted Hughes's consistently held position: his description of her method of writing poetry until the *Ariel* poems, poring over her father's thesaurus, is not easy to forget,[8] and neither is his compelling contention that in the quickly written late poems, she shook off all such intellectual constraints.[9] Such a view establishes an erroneously stable separation between the intellectual and the emotional so that Plath appears, at different stages of her career, either as a conscientious academic or as an unconstrained goddess of intensity. It fails to take into account the impact of her academic studies throughout her career and leads to the banal pigeonholing of her pre-*Ariel* poems as all intellect and no emotion, and those post-*Ariel* as mythic statements by a woman possessed, abandoning all conscious poetic craft. Yet, as I will show, Plath's intellectual background and academic studies played a central role in shaping all her poetry: these studies were not simply formal exercises to be gone beyond like the strict villanelles of the poetry she schooled herself to write while she was a student.

To simplify Plath's poetry into the opposing extremes of being either the result of a conscious intellectual and market-driven desire for poetic success or the unconscious subjective out-pourings of a woman possessed ignores Plath's own conscious struggles with ideas of subjectivity and objectivity in relation to her work (struggles which, most notably, influence her treatment of history and psychoanalytic theory, explored in chapters 2 and 3, respectively). These conflicts are rooted in Romantic literary tradition (explored in more depth in chapter 1), and are most famously characterized in Wordsworth's axiom, that poetry can be "the spontaneous overflow of powerful feelings," yet take "its origin from emotion recollected in tranquillity."[10] Critics have also fallen into similar extremes with Wordsworth, often quoting the first part of his formula and ignoring its qualification, yet it is worthwhile to note that Plath was familiar with the complete dic-tum, quoting its second part in a letter to her mother in October 1955, to express her desire to pause and reflect on the whirl of her experiences in her first term at Cambridge (LH 184).

As with his attitude toward the progression of Plath's writing, Hughes's view of her relationship with what she read is widely accepted. He describes her reading as real to her in a way he thinks of as unlike most other poets, declaring of "The Eye-Mote," a poem Plath wrote in 1959, that while the literary and mythic figures to which she refers may appear overliterary, they were, in fact, an integral part of her emotional life.[11] Hughes perceives Plath's reaction to her literary readings as purely emotional and subjective, and indeed, Plath herself appeared to concur with this straightforward view. Five years before she wrote "The Eye-Mote," while an undergraduate at Smith College, Plath described the subjective appeal of her academic literary studies, writing, in 1954, in an introduction to an essay on the death of God in Dos-toevsky's *The Brothers Karamazov,* that she became "dynamically involved" in the writer's concerns, and that she felt in tune with his themes of dualism and conflict.[12] Such personally grounded introductions preface many of Plath's academic essays throughout her years at Smith. In a paper written in 1951 on Edith Sitwell's poetry, Plath's preface describes how she came by chance on the collection, *The Canticle of the Rose,* in a bookshop, and could not put it down, so entranced was she by Sitwell's poetry. Plath ex-plains that she included this autobiographical detail in her preface to emphasize her belief that poetry should be "judged primarily by its emotional impact."[13] In the same year, Plath wrote an essay on *The Cherry Orchard* in which she makes the same point about the primacy of the emotional impact of literature more vehemently, stating that the meanings of the play lie "closer to the inarticulate mist of tears than to the lucid realms of reason."[14] Her attitude is rooted in traditional Romantic ideas of the value and effect of literature, which, as I explore below and in the next chapter, are not themselves unproblematic.

Just as Plath studied other, nonliterary subjects at Smith, so these personally grounded introductions to her academic essays are not confined to literary subjects: a book report written in 1950, on Jacques Barzun's study, *Darwin, Marx and Wagner* (1947), is prefaced in a similarly personal way, emphasizing Plath's distinction between subjective appeal and "abstract theories":

> I have learned to accept Darwin, Marx and Wagner, not as isolated and almost abstract teachers of equally isolated and abstract theories, but rather as human beings in the proper setting of their times . . . I have not only become more aware of the tenets of mechanical absolutism in the latter nineteenth century, but I have also been interested to learn about the swing to pragmatism of Will [sic] James at the beginning of the twentieth century.[15]

Plath's idiosyncratic use of such introductions not only for literary essays, but for other work as well, implies that it was not just the study of literature that appealed to her in this intensely subjective way. These introductions (which she dropped from her essays at Cambridge) also attest to something more important than her wish for her tutors to see how personally involved she was in her studies. First, they strongly indicate that Plath felt it necessary to try to explain the preeminence of the emotional and sensual value of poetry over its intellectual worth; and, second, that she felt it important to distinguish between the subjective and objective or the personal and intellectual in all her academic work. However, this last extract is characteristic of the difficulties Plath faced in making such a distinction. In this preface to her essay, Plath blurs the very distinction she tries to set up by writing about things which would fit well in the "analytic" body of her book report: about, for instance, the impact Barzun's book made on her understanding of history. In her essay on Sitwell, as well, after declaring that the appeal of poetry is primarily sensual rather than intellectual, Plath spends the rest of the piece trying to explain in intellectual terms the emotional impact of the poetry, analyzing in great detail, as she does in most of her essays on poetry, the auditory and sensual appeal of rhythm and rhyme.

So, while Plath's prefaces were designed to separate her subjective response from her intellectual analysis proper by stating the subjective impact of the topic and getting it out of the way, in fact the very reverse is true. Such introductions highlight the subjective content of the "objective" analysis and confirm the impossibility of any clear separation of intellect and emotion, or subjective response and objective analysis in these essays. The project of "objective analysis" Plath attempted in these essays was a New Critical one, an approach which originated during the late 1920s and which was still powerful in both the British and American academies in the 1950s. David Lehman provides a concise overview when he reflects that

> the New Criticism taught two generations of students how to read works of literature, what terms to use in their analyses, what characteristics to value (irony, paradox, complexity, and ambiguity), what to disregard (the intentions of the writer, the impact of the work on its readers), and which periods of English literary history were most deserving of careful study (the metaphysical poets of the seventeenth century were in, the poets of the Romantic movement were out).[16]

Plath's own struggles with subjectivity and objectivity are therefore rooted in a broad contemporary critical debate about the means and purposes of both the study and the production of literature. So, while her self-conscious introductions can, to a certain extent, be viewed as the academic confusions of a young undergraduate, unsure of how much subjectivity is allowed in analytic essays, the consistency with which these introductions occur throughout all four and a half years of Plath's undergraduate work and intellectual maturation at Smith implies that the subjective-objective problem was central to her thinking about both academic and creative writing.

New Criticism and the Debate

This subjective-objective conflict in Plath (as in many of the educated members of her generation) is, then, informed both by Romantic tradition and by the New Criticism (itself informed by Romantic theories of literature), which was the prevalent standard by which literature was judged. Plath's library contained most of the seminal texts of both the American New Criticism of Cleanth

Brooks and Robert Penn Warren, and its English counterparts and precursors in the theories of I. A. Richards and (to a lesser extent) F. R. Leavis.[17] The entrenched power of the literary approach of New Criticism in the postwar years may be viewed in wider terms: its interest in unifying apparently irreconcilable antagonisms responded to wider cultural needs of the period. As Terry Eagleton notes:

> New Criticism's view of the poem as a delicate equipoise of contending attitudes, as disinterested reconciliation of opposing impulses, proved deeply attractive to sceptical liberal intellectuals disorientated by the clashing dogmas of the Cold War.[18]

Such an approach was concerned with reconciling traditional literary and philosophical conflicts such as those between material and spiritual, cerebral and sensual, form and content. T. S. Eliot's proposition that a post-Elizabethan "dissociation of sensibility" between the cerebral and the sensual had occurred was a powerful (if somewhat contradictory) reworking of the traditional Romantic valuing of the literary work as an organic whole, reconciling apparent dualities.[19] Plath's awareness of and intellectual involvement in such debates is clear. In her copy of Brooks and Warren's *Understanding Poetry: An Anthology for College Students* (a prize she gained at high school in 1947 for "excellence in English expression"), she marked their exhortation that "a poem should always be treated as an organic system of relationships"[20] and writes "bravo" next to Brooks's statement in *The Well Wrought Urn,* that

> the common error that besets our criticism . . . [is that] it conceives of form as the transparent pane of glass through which the stuff of poetry is reflected, directly and immediately.[21]

Yet, in contrast to this desire of the theory's proponents to recognize the reconciliation of the emotional and the intellectual in the "substitute religion" they saw literature as providing, the New Criticism was itself engaged in a struggle with these terms. On the one hand, while literature was viewed as an emotive use of words (and requiring an almost mystical response) in contrast to the everyday "scientific" use of language, on the other, objectivity was perceived as having a necessary place in criticism—with the right tools a critic would be able comprehensively to account for the affects of poetry. Analysis was an objective pursuit; literary meaning, as Terry Eagleton notes, was, certainly for the more formally rigorous American New Critics, public and objective, inscribed in the very language of the text, not a question of some putative ghostly impulse in a long-dead author's head, or the arbitrary private significances a reader might attach to his words.[22]

The power of the poem was paradoxically perceived, then, as primarily emotional, but also objective and universal, capable of elucidation and analysis through a "scientific" approach. Indeed, the work of the poet, according to the English critic I. A. Richards (who, although the proponent of literary criticism as a "science," was generally less rigorously formalist in his approach, and more interested in the psychological aspects of the creation and communication of literary meaning), was to struggle with the emotional and cerebral. Plath marks Richards's statement in her copy of *Practical Criticism* that "from the technical point of view, indeed, the poet's task is constantly (though not only) that of finding ways and means of controlling feeling through metaphor."[23] Plath placed the New Criticism's precursor, T. S. Eliot, among her poetic "gods," and it must be assumed, also read his criticism (although none of his critical texts survive in Plath's library collections at Smith College and the Lilly Library). Eliot, too, centers his critical debate on questions of subjectivity and objectivity—not only in terms of his assertion of the dissociation of sensibility (thought and physical feeling), but in relation to the subjectivity of the writer. He writes in his famous essay, "Tradition and the Individual Talent":

> the poet has, not a "personality" to express, but a particular medium, which is only a medium and not a personality, in which impressions and experience combine in particular and unexpected ways . . . poetry is not a turning loose of emotion but an escape from emotion; it is not the expression of personality, but an escape from personality.[24]

Yet, as Patrick Parrinder asserts, both Eliot and Richards's work are characterized by inherent tensions around the questions of objectivity and mysterious subjectivity. He writes of Eliot that "His criticism is as notable for its dark and pregnant hints about the mystery of inspiration as it is for demanding that the study of poetry should become an intellectually rigorous pursuit," and of Richards that he "seemed intent on denying the mythic potency of art in the very act of asserting it."[25] Plath's ambivalence about subjectivity and objectivity, then, reflected the attitudes of the contemporary academy. In this period, before the rise of Structuralism (which, with its more extreme and theoretical versions of formalism, moved the debate away from the foregrounding of such empirical interests), such issues were of immense importance. Plath was certainly aware of, and perhaps somewhat confused by this critical climate when, in an interview in 1958, she declared in relation to her interest in lyric poetry, that the sensuous aspects of imagery and sound with which she enjoyed working in her poetry were currently out of fashion.[26] The importance of this debate for Plath lies not only in the confusion it appears to elicit in relation to her perception of poetic fashions, but also because the terms of the debate implicitly inform her treatment of the two most controversial subjects of her poetry (explored in later chapters): her personalized appropriation of the Holocaust and her attitude toward the extreme and nihilistic transcendence she depicts in her late poems.

Sensual and Cerebral as Framework

The impact of this debate on Plath is apparent in the fact that such terms, describing the life of the mind and the life of the emotions, appear for her to form a framework, not only for thinking about her position as a writer, but also as evaluative terms which she applied to a far broader area. For much of her adult life, in all her different types of writing (academic essays, journal entries, letters), Plath frequently treats these terms, intellectual and emotional (or sensual), as a linked pair, stressing the importance of each at different times. She writes of Auden, for instance, in an undated Smith undergraduate essay, that his poetic appeal was sensuous, but still intellectual:

> even in his most lucid/lyric moments he seldom ignores a cerebral content, even in the face of a tempting and attractive form.[27]

Similarly, in other academic work at both Smith and Cambridge, for example, she bases her approval of the Unitarian Church on her perception that it provided an intellectual rather than emotional appeal to the individual, and, conversely, commends the poets Blake and De Quincey specifically on the grounds of their anti-understanding, pro-experience philosophy.[28] In the very different context of a letter to her mother, written in 1955, these terms emerge again, this time in an evaluation of the impact on her of the Lincoln Memorial in Washington, which she describes as impressing her "emotionally and intellectually most of all."[29] As in her description of the appeal of Auden's poetry, Plath here sees a need for a balance between intellectual and emotional appeal, with the cerebral aspects of this joint appeal, finally, privileged. Yet in the context of her attitude toward her own poetry (as with her attitude toward the writing of Blake and De Quincey), such a privileging appears reversed. During her year of teaching at Smith (1957–58) her concerns center on the constraints the intellectual process of analyzing literature put on the production of her own writing. At the start of the year, in November 1957, she complains in a letter to her brother:

> I don't like talking *about* D. H. Lawrence and about critics' views of him. I like reading him selfishly for an influence on my own life and my own writing. (LH 330)

Toward the end of her year at Smith (after she had made the decision to leave teaching), in a poetry reading and interview in Springfield in April 1958, she declares that the intellectual approach to poetry she pursues in the classroom conflicts with her own writing.[30] Such a clear privileging of the emotional over the intellectual sources of her poetry was not, however, stable as later, during the period in which she produced the *Ariel* poems (on which her reputation as goddess of unmediated intensity generally rests), Plath wrote public analytic reviews of both poetry and historical biography with obvious relish: in 1962, she edited an American poetry supplement for *Critical Quarterly;* in 1963 she reviewed Donald Hall's influential collection, *Contemporary American Poetry* for BBC radio; and in late 1962 she writes to her mother of her satisfaction with the reviewing work she undertook for the *New Statesman* throughout that year.[31]

Woman and "Poetess"

Plath's struggle with the relative value of objectivity and subjectivity is not confined to poetic theory, but is bound up in, and foregrounded by her broader anxieties concerning her perception of herself as a woman, intellectual, and poet, anxieties which, as the following chapters show, are integral to the form and content of her poetry. Plath was proud of her intellect and yet, strongly influenced by fifties' ideas about women, she felt that intellectuality was, in some ways, unfeminine. In 1956 she wrote an article about the position of women at Cambridge University, in response to a *Sunday Mirror* piece, "Guess Where It's Heaven To Be A Girl" (which proposed that Cambridge was a "heaven"

education // unfeminine

for its female undergraduates because of their minority status, and their resulting social opportunities). Plath's response to this article outlines her conception of the difficulties surrounding women's position. Women at the university, she declared, were pressured either to conduct themselves like "those bluestocking Cambridge women who brood in the University Library until closing time" or to behave like mindless "girls," and she wonders whether "this drastic split in the functions of a whole woman (matter versus mind, one might say)" stems from a male or a female inadequacy. She concludes by declaring a need for a change in the male attitude which would allow a more complete development of a woman's personality, so that she could maintain "her female status while being accepted simultaneously as an intelligent human being."[32] Such issues were clearly central for Plath at this time, because in the same year she writes to her mother in a letter from Paris that, certainly in terms of English attitudes, such an ideal acceptance of "both functions of a whole woman" was far from common practice: to be viewed as truly "feminine" a woman must avoid having ideas or opinions.[33] The "ideal" woman, in men's eyes, was solely capable of subjective response, unable to engage in intellectual, rational thought: women, as the prejudice ran, were closer in some way to nature than to culture.

Yet, while in broadly cultural terms Plath saw such an ideal as resulting in an imbalance in the "functions of a whole woman," in terms of her attitude toward the female writer, she appears to subscribe to this traditional perception of femininity. In a letter to her mother, she disparages the writers Dorothy Parker and Sara Teasdale in strictly gender-related terms, as "abstractionist man-imitator[s]," focusing her criticisms on their perceived lack of tenderness and groundedness in reality, which, Plath implies, makes them essentially untrue to their femininity (LH 277). Plath thought of herself not just as a writer, but as a specifically *female* writer, and a female writer for her needed to be, in some way, positioned closer to nature than culture: male writers, she assumes, were positioned closer to culture, and therefore allowed to be somewhat more "abstractionist" than women. In a similar vein to her criticisms of Parker and Teasdale, Plath also censures Virginia Woolf, a writer she admired strongly, but saw as deficient because of her "unnatural" childless state. Woolf, Plath declares in her journal, is "too ephemeral, needing the earth," and asserts that having children brings depth to a woman's writing (J 166). Two years later, in 1959, in more detailed criticism of Woolf, Plath writes in a similar vein that *The Years* is superficial and dull because of its lack of a sense of feminine fertility and the resulting absense of grounding in everyday details (J 305). In an interview in 1962, Plath again returns to her belief in the importance, as a female writer, on the groundedness afforded not only by childbearing, but also by domestic detail.[34] So, while Plath believed the "whole woman" consisted of both the intellectual and the sensual, she saw creativity for women as somehow linked to childbearing, to a stereotyped version of the natural, in opposition to the intellectual. Her ideas stemmed not only from 1950s attitudes toward women, explored at the time by Betty Friedan in *The Feminine Mystique* (1963),[35] but from their historic and mythic backing in traditional Romantic literary ideals: ideals with which, as the next chapter shows, Plath was in an uneasy dialogue.

Examination of Plath's intellectual history, then, clearly relates to elucidation of her poetry—not only in terms of her struggle with ideas of intellect and emotion, but also in relation to her appropriation of the material she studied as a student. The examination of "Ariel" (1962) in the next chapter, for instance, shows both her response to her literary and intellectual past, here in the form of D. H. Lawrence's short story "The Woman Who Rode Away," and also how Plath uses her intellectual past to explore the conflict between intellect and emotion outlined above, in terms of confronting her attraction to the anti–intellectual ideas (especially in relation to women) that Lawrence embodies in his story. Before such a close study of influences is embarked upon, however, the factors which inform Plath's relationship with such influences should be explored.

ANXIETIES OF INFLUENCE

"Who Rivals?"

Close textual work on Plath's poetry in relation to her literary and academic history is helpful in the light it can throw on her dialogue with such histories: how far her poetic appropriation of other writers and ideas was a careful placing of herself in a tradition, and how far a struggle for subjectivity within that tradition. Harold Bloom's psychoanalytic-based theories of anxiety about such a placement of the poet-subject are useful in this respect. Plath was very conscious not only of her intellectual abilities, but also of her position as a writer in relation to past and present writers. Her attitude toward such writers can be divided into a number of broad and necessarily schematic categories: heroes and heroines beyond criticism (including Yeats, Pound, Eliot, and Dickinson); writers to whose lives Plath was drawn (again Yeats, Dylan Thomas, Woolf, James); writers she consciously analyzes and "uses" (Lawrence, Woolf, James); rivals, mainly contemporary, Plath criticized and praised circumstantially (Bishop, Lowell, Rich, Sexton, Snodgrass, Starbuck, Swenson, Wilbur, and again, Woolf); those she discovered through teaching, academic study, or the encouragement of Ted Hughes (Lawrence, Yeats, Eliot, Hopkins); and those she met socially, a group which consists of most of those listed above who were living. Both Plath's journals and her letters to her mother contain repeated references to the writers listed above (as well as to Hughes, who, Margaret Uroff argues convincingly, should be viewed as Plath's main poetic influence[36]). A statement Plath made in her journal on 28 March 1958 while she was teaching at Smith is characteristic of the complexity of her attitude toward her own self-placement in the writerly tradition. She declares:

> Ted is right, infallibly, when he criticizes my poems and suggests, here, there, the right word—"marvelingly" instead of "admiringly," and so on. Arrogant, I think I have written lines which will qualify me to be the Poetess of America (as Ted will be the Poet of England). Who rivals? Well, in history, Sappho, Elizabeth Barrett Browning, Christina Rossetti, Amy Lowell, Emily Dickinson, Edna St. Vincent Millay—all dead. Now: Edith Sitwell and Marianne Moore, the ageing giantesses, and poetic godmother Phyllis McGinley is out—light verse: she's sold herself. Rather May Swenson, Isabella Gardner, and most close Adrienne Cecile Rich—who will soon be eclipsed by these eight poems: I am eager, chafing, sure of my gift, wanting only to train and teach it—.(J 211)

The swift movements in tone, between irony, self-deprecation, and self-confidence, testify to the complexity of Plath's attitude: her contemplation of respected writers is both an anxious clearing of the ground for herself and a confidence-boosting placement of herself in a tradition—in this case, of female poets.

Questions such as these, surrounding originality and history, concerned Plath throughout her adult life. A letter in 1951 from her teenage correspondent, Eddie Cohen (in which Cohen declares his belief that no one, including Plath, has had an original thought for several thousand years, but that it is the presentation and application of ideas that matters), implies the existence of an ongoing debate about issues of originality of thought and expression.[37] Eleven years later, in an interview for the BBC in 1962, Plath publicly examines her anxieties about originality and tradition in respose to her interviewer, Peter Orr's question about the impact of writing under the burden of the past. Plath talks of the burden placed on a young poet by English universities' coverage of a far longer period of literary history than their American counterparts, and describes her experiences at Cambridge:

> Young women would come up to me and say "How do you dare to write, how do you dare to publish a poem, because of the criticism, the terrible criticism, that falls upon one if one does publish?" And the criticism is not of the poem *as poem*. I remember being appalled when someone criticised me for beginning just like John Donne, but not quite managing to finish like John Donne, and I first felt the full weight of English Literature on me at that point.[38]

Plath's statement is, in many ways, remarkably Bloomian in its description of the burden of the past (of course, as W. Jackson Bate notes, such anxieties are far from new,[39] just as theorizing influence is not new—yet Bloom's theories are, as will be shown below, particularly applicable to Plath). Bloom describes his theory of the "anxiety of influence" in Freudian terms, declaring that he sees "the story of intra-poetic relationships . . . as parallels of family romance."[40] He uses the scenarios and terminology of Freudian psychoanalysis to examine a traditional aspect of literary criticism, the "strong" poet in relation to "his" precursors, a relation Bloom sees characterized by a sense of "anxiety" in the ephebe or young poet, as being a "latecomer," and so needing to find some way of being "original." The poet, Bloom declares, does this by writing poems which are misreadings and so revisions of his precursors, thereby creating space for his "originality." In his struggle for individuality, the poet is writing against the monolithic power of all those poets who have written before him. Plath relates feeling the "paralysing" sense of literary history under which, Bloom asserts, all strong poets labor. She also directly depicts, in her reference to John Donne, a crude example of the primary "revisionary ratio" Bloom names *clinamen* and describes as:

> a corrective movement . . . which implies that the precursor poem went accurately up to a certain point, but then should have swerved, precisely in the direction the new poem moves.[41]

Although Plath asserts that, while she is aware of certain influences, the end result, the poem, is complete unto itself, that it should be criticized "as poem" (a typically New Critical concern), Bloom maintains that such a denial ("poets tell me they don't have it, whatever it is"[42]) is in fact characteristic of the original anxiety.

Bloom and Plath

Bloom's theorizing of influence is particularly useful in Plath's case for a number of reasons. Bloom credits Nietzsche and Freud as the prime influences on his theory. Plath's thinking was also strongly affected by the theories of these two figures (as chapters 2 and 3 show). Also, Bloom declares that his intention to concentrate on poets in the Romantic tradition stems from the fact that "as poetry has become more subjective, the shadow cast by the precursor has become more dominant."[43] Plath's poetry is often both unashamedly subjective and lyrical and, as the next chapter shows, she places herself broadly in this tradition; on both counts, she would appear to respond to a Bloomian approach. In addition, many feminist approaches to women's writing (approaches encouraged in Plath's case by, among other things, her view of herself as a *female* poet) are concerned with questions similar to those Bloom addresses about the influence of the past. Adrienne Rich, writing in 1971 about female poets and the poetic tradition in "When We Dead Awaken—Writing and Re-Vision," declares,

> We need to know the writing of the past, and know it differently than we have ever known it; not to pass on a tradition but to break its hold over us.[44]

The need Rich describes, "to know the writing of the past . . . differently," while stemming from different origins, is very close to Bloom's description of the (patriarchal) system of general poetic influence, which, as he states,

> always proceeds by a misreading of the prior poet, an act of creative correction that is actually and necessarily a misinterpretation.[45]

While Bloom certainly does not share Rich's feminist agenda, the similarity between these two statements indicates the way feminist critics have been able to actively use and revise his theories (some of whose revisions are explored below). Finally, Bloom's theories are useful in the response they enable to the limited nature of much criticism of Plath's poetry. Bloom sets up a scenario that emphasizes the psychological importance of a poet's literary, as opposed to biographical history, writing in his introduction to the first of his tetralogy of books expounding this theory: "That even the strongest poets are subject to influences not poetical is obvious even to me, but again my concern is only with *the poet in a poet,* or the aboriginal poetic self."[46] His theories are potentially useful in Plath's case as a way of exploring images of the "family romance" as applying not only to Plath's real family, but also to her literary family. In *The Burden of the Past and the English Poet,* Bate describes the problems associated with the temptation of critics to personalize and thus reduce any description of writer's anxieties about writing:

> if, as biographers, we are considering writers like Coleridge or Keats, we dissolve their inner anxieties about what the poet is still able to do, within other, more personal forms of reductionism: Coleridge was struggling with opium or his neuroses generally; Keats was having trouble with Fanny Brawne or memories of his dead parents.[47]

Biographical critics of Plath (the most crass of whom is David Holbrook, but others are noted in later chapters) base their approach to her work on the reductive belief that the intensity of her poetry is solely and incontrovertibly rooted in her personal response to the physical experiences of her life. Bloom's theories (with their acknowledged debts to critics such as Bate) posit the possibility that such personal and subjective intensity is not necessarily tied only to biographical worries, but may also be the result of other, literary and cultural anxieties.

Yet Bloom's theories fall into a number of traps. In specific relation to Plath, he does what numerous critics do and sees Plath's mature poetry as existing at one end of the subjective-objective continuum outlined earlier. Describing her late poetry as emotionally manipulative and lacking craft, he writes,

> Poetry relies upon trope and not upon sincerity . . . Hysterical intensity, whatever its momentary erotic appeal, is not an affect that endures in verse.[48]

For Bloom, sincerity does not make a poem; indeed, by his apparent self-contradiction, he appears to imply that "sincerity" on its own can work against itself and make a poem merely manipulative of the feelings of the reader.[49] Bloom views Plath as only one among a group of what he terms the "School of Resentment," which includes other female poets such as Adrienne Rich and Alice Walker. In many ways the "aesthetic of resentment" Bloom so disparages (yet does not explore in relation to Plath[50]) appears remarkably close to, or perhaps an extreme example of his own aesthetic of the production of poetry (Oedipus and Laius at the crossroads—the ephebe resenting the power of the father poet). Yet, it appears also that in other ways Bloom's final ironic statement about Plath's poetry—that his own paradigm of criticism does not enable him to judge the poetry of this group of women writers—may well be true.[51]

To return to Plath's own expression of her "anxiety of influence" in the 1962 BBC interview: in her description of the criticism of her "Donne-like" poem, she situates this anxiety of influence not purely within the poet (as Bloom would have it), but outside, in the criticism of the community. Also, she is very specific in describing her sense of inadequacy before the "full weight of English Literature," not as a young poet, an "ephebe," but as a female poet; it is "young women" who ask her how she "dare" write or publish (and again, as seen in the description of the "Donne-like" poem, the anxiety is situated outside the poet, "the terrible criticism that falls upon one if one does publish"). So on several related points, Bloom's theories, while opening up interesting avenues of thought, are not sufficient to account for certain aspects of Plath's "anxiety of influence"; most notably those related to her gender and the link between internal and external poetic pressures.

Frank Lentricchia asserts that it is in Bloom's denial of the importance of external pressures on poets ("There is no social dimension to what we do"[52]) that the central weakness of his theory lies. He declares that Bloom's confinement of interest to "the poet in the poet" (noting, but then ignoring any consideration of the sociohistoric dimensions of the production of literature) is unrealistically systematic, writing:

> Of course, all of his stress on voice, on struggle and historicity seems to be absolutely and by intention, contained by his sense of literariness as a kind of domain that we can consider apart from its social setting: I find that a problem. Another element of this problem is that Harold says that he's interested in the relations of "strong" poets to one another. Where this really comes from is that Harold's education—like a lot of our education—ignores the fact that writers at 18 or 19 (especially modern writers) don't necessarily think of their relationship to Milton and Aristotle: they exist within a visible and palpable market of contemporary writers. That level of struggle has to be taken care of.[53]

Plath was very conscious of her "market"—not only earlier in her career, when, as cited above, she compares her poetry to that of her female contemporaries, but also much later, when she was writing the *Ariel* poems, which critics like to see as very different from her earlier self-conscious and market-led poems. In 1962 Plath writes to her mother that these poems would "make my name" (LH 468), an equally market-orientated observation. Plath's conscious "professionalism" about her poetry forms one of the roots of her sense of direct rivalry toward and anxiety about other contemporary poets. She writes in her journal of her recognition that her anger toward more successful writers (especially those she knows or those who write about similar experiences) stems from her desire for "the world's praise, money and love" (J 325). Bloom's lack of recognition of the social and financial pressures on the poet, his desire to isolate "the poet in the poet" and study this on its own, is not only unrealistically systematic, it also narrows the application of his theories. Jacqueline Rose, for instance, writes of an "anxiety of influence" she perceives operating on Plath in a way Bloom would be unlikely to approve.

> Her books on culture and politics . . . are at least as relevant as those books of literature . . . which have received so much more attention—anxiety of influence as much a cultural-political as a literary effect.[54]

Such broad cultural-political influences are treated in chapter 2, although, because of the nature of the specific topics explored, the Bloomian framework I use in the rest of the work is less directly appropriate here, forming the background to, rather than the terms of the discussion.

Post-Bloomian Feminist Theory

The most obvious result of Bloom's denial of the sociohistoric aspect of the production of literature, however, is that in ignoring social conditions he ignores gender. As Sandra Gilbert and Susan Gubar write in *The Madwoman in the Attic*, their classic feminist study of nineteenth-century women novelists which uses a revised Bloomian approach:

> A woman does not "fit in" [to Bloom's theory] . . . Bloom's male-orientated theory of the "anxiety of influence" cannot be simply reversed or inverted to account for the situation of the woman writer.[55]

They posit instead an "anxiety of authorship." Female writers are not so much anxious about their ability to write something original, they are anxious about their ability to write at all. Because of this more primary anxiety, Gilbert and Gubar perceive women writers as cherishing their female precursors as allies rather than worrying about them as rivals. Women writers are, in this somewhat naive formulation, in a positive rather than anxious relationship with their female precursors. Certainly Plath felt some positive aspects of being part of an, albeit limited, female writerly tradition. In the journal entry cited above, Plath's listing of her "rivals" in the female tradition enables her to move from a mode of apprenticeship to her (male) poetic master, Hughes, to being "chafing, sure of my gift." Elsewhere in her journals, Plath writes more explicitly of the positive impact of the female tradition, stating of Woolf (and indeed, reflecting the earlier writer's concept of the relationships of "sisterhood"), that "Her novels make mine possible" (J 168), and seeing women writers as acting like "godmothers" to one another, declaring that Elizabeth Bishop's poetry surpasses that of her godmother, Marianne Moore (J 319).[56]

Yet such feminist revisions undertaken by the likes of Gilbert and Gubar, Alicia Ostriker, and Joanne Feit-Diehl do in fact appear to be a simple reversal of Bloom's theories and oversimplify considerably Plath's attitude toward her place in literary tradition.[57] Such oversimplification becomes apparent when confronted with a poem by Plath such as "The Disquieting Muses" (1957). In this poem, influenced both by De Chirico's painting of the same name and, more crucially (as the next chapter shows) by De Quincey, the speaker describes her female muses, not as supportive "grandmothers," but in fairytale terms of powerful and ugly uninvited godmothers at a christening, in whose oppressive shadow the daughter develops (CP 75). The muses are blank-faced and enigmatic rather than supportive, and the daughter's relationship with them is characterized not by feelings of comfort and supportiveness, but by a sense of awful and fearful pride in her oppression:

> But no frown of mine
> Will betray the company I keep.
>
> (CP 76)

In her journals as well, while Plath occasionally views female writers such as Woolf as allies, her frequent attacks both on Woolf and on contemporary women writers implies the existence of an equally anxious relationship with the female literary tradition. She writes, for instance, in unpleasantly perjorative terms about outstripping Isabella Gardner and Elizabeth Bishop (J 189). Adrienne Rich is the writer Plath attacks most frequently, perhaps because she sees her as closest in experience and poetic style to herself. Plath writes, in one example among many, of "sitting" on better poems than any of Rich's that she has read (J 218). Conversely, male writers, while sometimes seen as rivals, figure more frequently in her journals as allies: again, perhaps, because Plath sees them as more different from herself, more distant and less threatening, and perhaps because she held such male "masters" in greater esteem.

In addition, in her poems, Plath figures her "family romance" of poetic influences in terms very similar to the traditional patriarchal scenario Bloom describes. Her muses are female and she has ambivalent feelings of desire and fear regarding their power and coldness (most notably when they are connected to images of the moon in poems such as "The Munich Mannequins" [1963]). The powerful precursor is a more shadowy figure, and generally male (as in "Full Fathom Five" [1958] and "The Colossus" [1959]). Plath's conscious interest in this traditional aspect of the "family romance" is also shown in her heavy markings of Ernest Jones's book *Hamlet and Oedipus,* which concentrates on the literary and mythic history of expression of the Oedipal rivalry with the father.[58] Plath may also have been fascinated with the patriarchal scenario that forms the basis of Bloom's theory because in her life, she was married to a poet and saw herself in the position of apprentice to his poetic mastery, writing, as I noted above, that Hughes is "infallibly right" in his suggestions for her poetic improvement. The importance of sociocultural reasons in Plath's affirmation of her husband's poetic preeminence are evident when, in a letter Plath wrote to her mother in February 1957, she denies any sense of rivalry between them and declares her pleasure in Hughes achieving publishing success before her, seeing this as making it easier for her to celebrate when she gains a publisher (LH 297). This speculation is further supported by Plath's combining of the imaginary and real, literary and biographical "family romances," in her conflation of the father and the husband in poems such as "Daddy" (1962) and "Man in Black" (1959), a conflation Hughes also recognizes in his previously uncollected poem, "Black Coat," a reflection on the composition of "Man in Black," in which the speaker describes his partner's observations of him during a walk by the sea, and his subsequent realization of, "How as your lenses tightened / He slid into me."[59]

Gilbert and Gubar, do, to a certain extent, note this conflicting side to their optimistic feminist reversal of Bloom's theory and revise their argument, writing, in *No Man's Land—The War of the Words (vol. 1)*,

> Allegiance to literary fathers does not inevitably sweep away the longing for literary mothers; anxiety about literary mothers does not always lead to desire for literary fathers. Indeed for all its flaws, Freud's model is useful precisely because it implies such a range of reaction to (literary) parentage.[60]

Yet there are problems even with this revision. Gilbert and Gubar, although referring to Freud as the inspiration for Bloom's paradigm, appear not, in their revision, to confront the centrality of the *unconscious* nature of the poet's anxieties which Bloom describes. Bloom frequently states that the anxiety of influence and its resulting defenses (revisionary ratios) are not conscious struggles for the poet. He describes his criticism, for example, as "the art of knowing the *hidden* roads that go from poem to poem."[61] The roads are hidden not only from the reader (as is traditional), but also from the poet. Bloom, for instance, writes, characteristically, about Hart Crane,

> with his palpable assertions of Whitmanian influence, but with the poetry's enormous and not-so-covert struggle against the abominable Eliot.[62]

In other words, Bloom distinguishes between writers with whom poets align themselves, and writers from whom they cannot escape (or, in terms of Plath's intellect-emotion conflict, writers whom their literary descendants objectively appropriate, and writers who are uncontrollably rooted in the psyche). Gilbert and Gubar appear to ignore this second group of precursors in their revision. They write, for instance,

> Metaphorically speaking, as Bloom has shown, male literary history functions like a biological family, albeit a socially constructed one . . . for women, however, female genealogy does not have an inexorable logic because the literary matrilineage has been repeatedly erased, obscured, or fragmented. Thus when the woman writer "adopts" a "mother" like Mrs Gaskell, or an "aunt" like George Eliot, she is creating a fictive family whose romance is sufficient to her desire . . . even

in the unprecedented presence of female literary history, women do not engage in the kind of purely agonistic struggle that Bloom describes.[63]

While it is certainly true that a female writer's relation to her literary past is usually less secure (even Bloom admits, as Feit-Diehl notes, that "women may now be inheriting power and making it their own. Only women can create the necessary discontinuities to break effectively from the past"[64]), this does not mean that she has no inescapable precursors (male or female), or that she cannot "adopt" male writers, just as Crane, in Bloom's view, "adopts" Whitman. In Plath's case, as the next chapter argues, not only does she write, as it were, from under the burden of inescapable precursors she rarely acknowledges (such as Thomas De Quincey), she also (and this may be partly due to her academic background, where learning from "masters" is the norm, and partly because of her pragmatic desire to write poetry that will sell, which leads her to "adopt" well-respected authors as models) consciously and selectively uses aspects of male and female writers (both past and contemporary). Woolf is mentioned frequently in her journals in this respect. More often, however, the "master" is male (perhaps a result of her drive for marketability), as can be seen in, for instance, a journal entry when she debates the relative merits and drawbacks of Lawrence, Henry James, Joyce Cary, J. D. Salinger, and Jack Burden as potential masters to help her write a "terrific novel" (J 156). This distinction between the types of literary influence brought to bear on Plath is an important one because the resulting anxieties, between "mastering" and "being mastered by" one's antecedents, are also evident and play a crucial role in her relationship with other discourses (historical and psychoanalytic, for instance, which are explored in chapters 2 and 3, respectively).

In addition to (and partly as a result of) Gilbert and Gubar's lack of discussion of unconscious anxieties in their revision of Bloom,[65] they fail to apply their theories to a discussion of primary texts. Where they do refer to texts, it is generally only to note what the writer is consciously saying about her influences, not to examine the actual workings of influence in the texts. Although Bloom's six revisionary ratios do occasionally appear fanciful, the strength of his paradigm of criticism is precisely that he can usefully apply these ratios to a discussion of literary texts. While Gilbert and Gubar's argument is an interesting and necessary exploration of how female writers consciously feel about their place in the literary heritage, the restriction of their discussion to conscious intention and the resulting lack of any detailed examination of how "anxiety of influence" is exhibited in the writers' work, makes their revisions of Bloom, finally, of limited practical use.

Plath, Woolf, and Haworth

An example of this ultimate limitation in Gilbert and Gubar's revision of Bloom can be found in their interesting discussion of Virginia Woolf's first published work—a description of and meditation on a pilgrimage she undertook to Haworth in 1904. They note Woolf's obsession with the physical details of her female precursors, that she

> lingered lovingly on the display cases that contained "the little personal relics, the dresses and shoes of the dead woman."[66]

and observe that this "literary voyeurism" has its dark side; that it "focuses on the relics of an emphatically 'dead woman'."[67] Woolf's emphasis on the "deadness" of her admired female predecessors brings to mind Plath's expansion on her comment about her literary place that Gilbert and Gubar cite, declaring how many of her rivals for the position of "poetess of America" are dead. Yet perhaps a more interesting parallel is that of Plath's own visit to Haworth and the poem and short story which came out of it. Plath visited Withens in the summer of 1956, while staying with Hughes's parents in Yorkshire. The visit inspired a newspaper article,[68] a short story, and several poems, the most obvious, "Two Views of Withens," written that year, and "Wuthering Heights," written several years later in 1961. Her journal entry about the visit is surprisingly reminiscent of Woolf's essay on the same subject. Plath lists the Brontë memorabilia, and writes:

> They touched this, wore that, wrote here in a house redolent with ghosts ... The furious ghosts nowhere but in the heads of visitors and the yellow-eyed shag sheep. House of love lasts as long as love in human mind—Anger jolts like heartburn in the throat. (J 148)

Plath not only engages in the same loving recreation of the Brontës' memorabilia that Gilbert and Gubar draw attention to in Woolf's essay, but she is also similarly ambivalent toward the "ghosts" which appear, in Plath's piece, as both the ghosts that haunted the Brontës and the ghosts of the Brontës that haunt Plath. Such ghosts have their existence only through the minds of the people there, and Plath appears angry about her recognition of this on two counts—one, that their existence is so precarious, dependent as it is upon a human mind to inhabit; and two, that the ghosts are inhabiting her mind. This ambivalence toward her female predecessors continues into a story and poem Plath wrote in this period. Immediately after the entry above (in the published journals) and while still in Yorkshire, Plath writes some notes for a prospective short story, "All the Dead Dears," completed in 1956 or 1957, which appears to have been inspired by her meeting with Hughes's mother.[69] In her notes she describes the Yorkshire setting and the theme of the powerful effect of ghosts on a woman who "*almost* has second sight. Begin—'I saw an angel once'—'my sister Miriam'—" (J 148). Plath also wrote a poem with the same title, "All the Dead Dears," in 1957. Both story and poem explore the ambivalence of the relationship between the living and dead and appear to comment on the specifically literary relationship between an "ephebe" and her precursors. In the story "All the Dead Dears," it is significant that it is the sister who returns as a ghost to Mrs. Meehan, that Mrs. Meehan only "almost" has second sight, and that the characters see themselves as less substantial than their memories, their collective history. They appear discussing the past, the Great War,

> calling up the names of the quick and the dead, reliving each past event as if it had no beginning and no end, but existed, vivid and irrevocable, from the beginning of time, and would continue to exist long after their own voices were stilled. (JP 178)

The stories they share are described as "the fugue of family phantoms" (JP 182); ghosts are mixed with stories and memories in a way that resembles Gilbert and Gubar's description of Woolf's blurring of the boundaries between a writer's self and her writing. For the Meehans and their friends, the past, in the form of these ghosts, memories, and stories, is inescapable, and indeed, Mrs. Meehan is held in a certain amount of awe due to her ability to gain direct entry to the past. Yet the story's title connotes an ambivalence toward this past—"All the Dead Dears" implies not only affection but also pity, and perhaps even a certain amount of scorn for those who inhabit the past. This ambivalence recurs in the poem of the same name. Here, though, the female forebears (or precursors) appear in a more threatening way, reaching "hag hands to haul me in" (CP 70). In addition, the ambivalence is emphasized when the speaker declares,

> All the long gone darlings: they
> Get back, though, soon . . .
>
> (CP 71)

The living can despise or pity these dead, but they and their power are inescapable.

So, as Gilbert and Gubar note in relation to Woolf's essay, "Haworth: November 1904," it is useful to explore Plath's conscious attitudes toward her female literary forebears. Yet this exploration of the conscious anxiety of influence is not something in which Bloom uses his theories to engage—perhaps because the (exclusively male, with the exception of Dickinson) poets he deals with appear less consciously or openly concerned with their place in literary tradition. A Bloomian analysis of these two pieces would concentrate, therefore, more on the (denied) debts they have toward the Brontës' work. The short story "All the Dead Dears" may be viewed as a misprision of Emily Brontë's *Wuthering Heights,* including as it does similar themes such as neighborliness, ghosts, storytelling, and the power of the past in the present. Its structure is also similar—like *Wuthering Heights* it is set in Yorkshire, leads us directly into contemplation of characterization from an opening with "I," sets up a narrative contrast between the later otherworldly happenings and an initial grounding in realistic domestic description, and the chronology of the narrative moves from present to past. In both stories, "Nellie" is the name of the manipulator of narrative time. Brontë, in *Wuthering Heights,* places the power of the past (in the form, for instance, of Cathy's ghost) in the primitive, or in nature; on the moors around the Heights rather than in the manicured surroundings of the Grange, and always outside the Heights (Cathy knocks on the window, Heathcliff roams the moors hoping to contact her). Yet in "All the Dead Dears," the ghosts are not confined to the primitive world of the Yorkshire moors. Their entry into the Meehan's house implies that culture as well as nature is accessible by the ghosts of the past. History, Plath appears to be saying, is more pervasive and powerful than Emily Brontë recognized. The ephebe, therefore, "corrects" her precursor, in what Bloom would call a *tessera:*

> reading the parent-poem as to retain its terms but to mean them in another sense, as through the precursor had failed to go far enough.[70]

Bloom's patriarchal paradigm of literary influence, then, needs revision (or perhaps misprision) to be usefully applied to Plath. It needs to take into account her sense of gender, her relation to contemporary as well as past poets, the similar workings of cultural as well as of literary influences, and Plath's positive and conscious, as well as anxious and unconscious feelings about her influences. Yet the strengths of this theory are, as I have shown, many. Not only does Plath's keen desire to place herself in poetic tradition express itself in terms of her subjective-objective conflict (whether her relation to her antecedents is an objective and reasoned placing of herself in a literary tradition or an uncontrollable subjective struggle for individuality within that tradition), but also, in broader terms, the roots of Bloom's theories share concerns central to Plath: ideas of individualism and struggle explored in the theories of Freud, Frazer, Jung, Nietzsche, and the Romantics will all be examined in later chapters and will show that any balanced appreciation of Plath's poetry needs to confront, not only her perception of her biographical "family romance," but also the integral nature of her cultural and literary "family trees." This study of "anxiety of influence" in Plath's poetry, therefore, while based upon Bloom's theorization, uses his approach selectively: it concentrates, rather, on Plath's dialogue with the concepts behind it, so allowing the complexity of her own conscious and unconscious desires and anxieties to be seen, and showing the broadness of the literary, political, and social foundations out of which she wrote, and on which her poetry rests.

1

Romantic Anxieties

> It is that synthesising spirit, that "shaping" force, which pro-
> lifically sprouts and makes up its own worlds with more inven-
> tiveness than God which I desire.
>
> —Sylvia Plath, 1956

Much of what is most striking and troublesome in Plath's poetry
becomes clarified when analyzed in relation to its literary context
of Romanticism. Plath's connection to Romantic tradition is, however, usually treated incidentally; either to explain her unnerving
extremes of subjectivity or to ally her with the post-Romantic
school of Yeats.[1] This narrow treatment of Plath's Romanticism
conceals the profundity of her debt to, and struggles with, this
extended tradition. Many of Plath's central conflicts (explored in
later chapters), such as her struggles with individualism, her
anxieties about the uses of poetry, her victim/master ambivalence,
and her interest in the extremes and intensities of the unconscious, are rooted in Romantic concerns and influenced by Romantic versions of conflict.

It is important to regard Plath's poetry in its Romantic context
both because of her own desire to see herself as part of a tradition,
and because of the frequency with which her poems directly al-
lude to other key Romantic works.[2] As Bloom notes, however,
when such influences operate for the poet, they invariably involve
anxiety about the precursor, so Plath's placements of herself
within Romantic literary traditions also involve a struggle to establish her own subjectivity amid such strong literary antecedents.
These struggles are exhibited both within individual poems and
in themes which occur across Plath's corpus of work.

The history surrounding definition of the term Romanticism
is, as Gareth Griffiths notes, complex, leading to a "confusion
... [which] seems only to be deepened by further attempts at

definition," so for the purposes of this study, I will attempt to circumvent such difficulties in two ways.[3] The discussion of Plath's debts to and struggles with Romanticism will be limited to and defined by an exploration of four "case studies" (William Blake, D. H. Lawrence, Emily Brontë, and, most significantly, Thomas De Quincey), four Romantic writers from different periods and in often quite diverse Romantic traditions, with whom Plath shared many central concerns.[4] In addition to this focusing of scope, the study of Plath's Romantic affinities can be helpfully set against the background of her own general perceptions of Romanticism.

Because of the critical preferences of her era (a period which is characterized by its privileging of the newly rediscovered metaphysical poets often at the expense of the early Romantics), Plath did not, either at Smith or at Cambridge, study the canonical Romantic writers as a group. As a result of this, perhaps, she generally uses the term "romantic" only in its popular, demotic form, such as in her criticism of a Cambridge friend who, in 1956, she describes as pedestrian because of the romantic aspect of his otherwise admirably rational personality (J 127). More frequently, Plath uses the term to comment adversely on her own poetry, although in describing her poetry as "too romantic," she often uses the term in direct opposition to its literary historical meaning. For instance, she writes to her brother, Warren, in 1958, that many of her published poems are "too romantic, sentimental and frivolous and immature," and not immediate or grounded enough (LH 343), and regularly returns to this debased use of the term in her journals, consistently viewing "romanticism" in her poetry as a limitation (J 199, 298). Indeed, in August 1952, she writes with all the knowingness of a young poet rejecting a central tenet in Romanticism's treatment of the imagination— inspiration—declaring that it is simply a part of the illusion the writer creates about "writing work" to bypass the reader's concern that the writer can intentionally "reach inside and yank my heart because he wants to keep his pot boiling" (J 54–55). Yet many of Plath's journal entries show her strong adherence to Romantic ideals about the importance of the mysterious creativity of the imagination. She writes, for instance, in February 1956 about her dread that her imagination will fail her by not developing to its fullest extent, leaving her with only

that photographic mind which paradoxically tells the truth but the worthless truth, about the world. It is that synthesising spirit, that "shaping" force, which prolifically sprouts and makes up its own worlds with more inventiveness than God which I desire. (J 110)

While such exuberance may be merely the self-conscious self-modeling of a young poet, the frequency with which this attitude toward the centrality of the writer's godlike imagination occurs in her journals shows that certain Romantic notions were central to Plath's view of herself as a poet. In 1951 she describes nature as only coming into being through the consciousness of the observor (J 28), and in 1958 she declares her desire to "master" what she sees and make it her own (J 182). Indeed, if Romanticism broadly connotes stylistic experiment, an extreme commitment to the exploration of the artist's inner self, an attempt to reconcile inner vision and external experience ("man" and nature), and a struggle with perceived corruptions that subjugate both society and the individual, then Plath's poetry is clearly a voice in the Romantic tradition. I examine different aspects of this voice in relation to the four case studies below. The section dealing with Blake explores Plath's conscious modeling or legitimizing of her ambivalence toward the central dualities of her work through one of the more popular canonical Romantic writers of her time. The Lawrence case study analyzes "Ariel" as a product of Plath's deeper debt to, and therefore more profound anxieties about this late-Romantic's treatment of the individual's relation to the world. Emily Brontë's landscape poetry is examined in terms of its prefiguring of Plath's own feminine post-Romantic ambivalence toward Romantic attitudes towards nature. Finally, De Quincey's unique position in Plath's literary "family tree" as her most powerful Romantic precursor is proposed.

WILLIAM BLAKE: ADOPTED "MASTER"

William Blake is an often suggested influence on Plath's poetry: Arthur Oberg sees *Ariel* as part of a "romantic imagist tradition extending back and beyond the official Romantic poets to Smart, Blake and Clare." Edward Butscher describes "the intense surreal, Blakean confessionalism of the *Ariel* poems," and declares that "it was her brilliant willingness to carry this confessional material into a surrealist realm . . . that brought her to William Blake, that defined her as a modern apocalyptic poet with a tradition"; Gordon Lameyer writes more glibly in biographical terms that "she could not stick to the golden mean, nothing too much, but was always anxious to experiment in extremis, with Blake, to find out what was 'enough' was by indulging herself in 'too much'."[5] Yet while Blake is an often proposed influence on Plath, such critics do not explore his impact in any depth.

Plath's own awareness of the effect Blake's writing had on her late work is demonstrated in an interview recorded for the BBC in 1962. Asked by her interviewer, Peter Orr, about writers who have influenced her, Plath names only Dylan Thomas, Yeats, and Auden, whom she puts very clearly in her past (as poets she read at university), but comes to rest on Blake, who she sees as characterizing her current interest in history, her general tendency to "go backwards."[6] Yet even before this late period, when Plath acknowledges Blake as a new figure in her literary history (and in which Plath wrote the poems that critics such as Butscher and Oberg broadly class as Blakean), Blake figures in a number of significant ways in Plath's writing. In her short story "The Wishing Box" (1956), a tale ostensibly about dreams but implicitly about the creative imagination (the dreams are described as "meticulous works of art"), Plath places Blake in a prominent position, opening her story with the protagonist's husband, Harold, and his description of his most recent dream in which he was discussing manuscripts with Blake (JP 48). In comparison to his jealous and inadequate wife, Harold is a proficient dreamer or imaginer (synonyms for the artist), and Blake stands as an emblem for the imaginative artist, a literary colossus, either by whom the husband is inspired or with whom he is potentially equal. In 1955, the year before she wrote "The Wishing Box," Plath arrived at Cambridge and, it appears, encountered Blake academically for the first time. As she noted in the BBC interview, the study of literature in American universities was confined, with the exception of Shakespeare, to the moderns such as Auden and Eliot; in contrast, literature courses at Cambridge seemed to end, as Plath noted in a letter to her mother, with the Romantics and Victorians, writers who, in England, were viewed as "modern" (LH 186).[7] She dated her copy of his work *The Portable Blake* "1955" (an American edition: it appears she bought it before she arrived in England, although this is more probably because its editor, Alfred Kazin, was her Smith College final year mentor, than because of any relevance it had to her American degree courses, of which Blake formed no part).[8] An essay Plath wrote on Blake at Cambridge survives at the Lilly Library,[9] and she answered a question on him in her final exams in 1957 (LH 315). Plath also shared her interest in Blake with early Cambridge acquaintances, noting in her journal on 6 March 1956 of a conversation with the Cambridge friend mentioned earlier, that they talked about mysticism and Blake, and how strongly the friend admired Blake (J 127). More significantly, perhaps, was the enthusiasm Hughes felt for Blake—in April 1956, Plath concludes a letter to her mother by mentioning Blake as one of the poets she and Hughes "love together" (LH 234). Indeed, during this period, (1955–57) Blake served as a touchstone, whose aphorisms Plath quoted in letters to her mother, describing the unfocused whirl of her first term at Cambridge using the Blakean reasonings "You can never know enough without knowing more than enough" and "The road to excess leads to the palace of wisdom" (LH 203). Although Plath's interest in Blake may have initially stemmed from a desire to fit in (discussing him with colleagues she admired, and following Hughes's example in adopting him as a favorite poet), the regularity with which Blakean motifs appear in her writing from 1956 until 1963 implies that her interest was, if not at first spontaneous, consistent. Indeed, the influence of her contemporaries (most notably Hughes) on Plath's conscious adoption of Blake is emphasized by the placement of him in "The Wishing Box." The story's male protagonist, Harold, is modeled on Hughes, to the extent, at least, that both fictional and real artists dreamed of red foxes (LH 244). And just as Blake was Hughes's favorite poet whom Plath was keen to adopt, in "The Wishing Box" Blake's exclusive position as the successful male artist's literary colossus leads, alternatively, not to adoption, but to the wife's jealousy and despair.

It was in the Cambridge period, shortly after meeting Hughes, that Plath wrote her most obviously Blakean poem, "Pursuit" (1956), which, she declares privately, is dedicated to Hughes (J 116). Indeed, in writing about it to her mother, Plath is explicit about her debt to Blake. She writes, on 9 March 1956, of her satisfaction with a new "batch" of poems, and declares that "Pursuit" is

> influenced by Blake, I think (tyger, tyger) . . . [about] the terrible beauty of death, and the paradox that the more intensely one lives, the more intensely one burns and consumes oneself; death here, includes the concept of love, and is larger and richer than mere love, which is part of it. (LH 222)

"Pursuit" is too overtly sensationalist and too obviously modeled on Blake's "The Tyger" to be effective and, as Uroff notes, over-ambitious in its attempt to demonstrate that "passion is destiny."[10]

Yet it is an interesting poem because of Plath's treatment of two Blakean motifs, which became central to her work: the ambivalence toward the creative and destructive properties of fire, and the broad idea of contraries.

Fire

The panther at the center of "Pursuit" is identified with fire, both fascinating and terrifying. His blood courses in his veins like fire, and he leaves in his wake "charred and ravened women" who were "kindled like torches for his joy." The speaker describes herself as a burning signal in her flight from the panther, an ambiguity in her attitude toward the panther that reaches a climax at the end of the poem, when her retreat from "such assault of radiance" to "the tower of my fears" appears not only useless (as the panther continues to track her), but also a cowardly retreat from light to darkness. Plath's awareness of the ambivalence of fire, in its figuring of the creative and destructive properties of both passion and creativity, informs her description of the poem to her mother. She goes on to write of its epigraph (from Racine's *Phèdre, "Dans le fond des forets votre image me suit"*) that a possible alternative would be from Yeats:

"Whatever flames upon the night, Man's own resinous heart has fed." The painter's brush consumes his dreams, and all that. (LH 223)

The powerful appeal of this emblem of fire is evident in the fact that later in the same letter Plath applies similar imagery directly to her own life, writing that she is "being refined in the fires of pain and love." Plath was fascinated by Blake's depiction of fire both as associated with creative distinction, yet also destructive. In her copy of his work, she stars and marks, for instance, a line from his poem "The Golden Net," "To be consumed in burning Fires,"[11] and underlines his aphorism in *The Marriage of Heaven and Hell,*

As I was walking among the fires of hell, delighted with the enjoyment of Genius, which to Angels look like torment and insanity.[12]

Like Blake, Plath saw fire as an emblem of some special torture, singling out the creative and risk-taking artist from the rest of humanity.

In her later work, Plath goes further in this Blakean appropriation by feminizing the emblem—specifically identifying it with women who were different from other women, saints such as Joan of Arc or witches who were burnt at the stake—in poems like "The Times are Tidy" (1958), "Witch Burning" (1959), "Wuthering Heights" (1961), and "Getting There" (1962).[13] Plath's fascination with Joan of Arc is partly due to the powerful influence the figure had in post-war Europe and America, spawning, as Marina Warner notes in *Joan of Arc: The Image of Female Heroism* (1981), a new output of creative reconstructions of the woman's life. Plath writes home of the impact of two films about Joan of Arc: in March 1954, she describes her powerful emotional response to a silent French film of the temptation of St. Joan (LH 135); the next year, during a Christmas trip to Paris in 1955, Plath writes of Charles Péguy's "Jeanne D'Arc," which she saw at The Comedie Française, declaring that it was "exquisitely moving."[14] Later, in her teaching year at Smith in 1958, Plath writes of her nightmares about Joan's death at the stake, engulfed in smoke and flames (J 226). Yet nine days earlier, on 5 May, she writes of her wonder at, and fascination with, the firelike effect of wearing a pair of red stockings (prefiguring the ending of "Witch Burning" written a year later) (J 221).

Plath's fascination with the martyrdom of Joan of Arc forms one focus of her interest in witches. In her copy of Margaret Mead's popular and influential book, *Male and Female: A Study of the Sexes in a Changing World* (1952), Plath annotates Mead's description of the social influences on societies' perception and persecution of witches:

> Sorcerers, witch-doctors and black magicians appear and disappear through history and in different cultures. The *witch* remains as a symbol so deep she seems to resist dethronement . . . The figure of the witch who kills living things . . . is a statement of human fear of what can be done to mankind by the woman who denies or is forced to deny childbearing, child-cherishing. . . . Religious experience and religious leadership may be permitted to one sex alone and the *periodic outbreak of vision in the wrong sex* may be penalized. A woman my be branded a *witch*, a man an *invert* [Plath's emphasis].[15]

This extract neatly illuminates not just a reason for Plath's interest in the emblem of the witch, but a central conflict in her attitude toward the witch-figure she treats in her poetry. Nothwithstanding Plath's connection of women's poetry with childbearing (noted in the introduction), the witch as visionary (or poet) appears as essentially childless, reflecting the conflicting demands, noted also by her contemporary and perceived "rival," Adrienne Cecil Rich, of motherhood and creativity. Rich writes:

> to write poetry or fiction, or even to think well . . . a certain freedom of mind is needed . . . to be a female human being trying to fulfil traditional female functions in a traditional way is in direct conflict with the subversive function of the imagination . . . there must be ways . . . in which the energy of creation and the energy of relation can be united."[16]

Mead also touches on these conflicting demands, noting that the definition of the witch was partly a social, patriarchal one (the witch being someone whose powers were not considered "natural," that is, allied to childbearing), but implying that vision requires chastity, further emphasizing the conflict with which Plath's poetry struggles, between bodily/emotional life and disembodied transcendental vision. This connection between saint and witch, emphasizing the power of social attitudes toward the strong woman and misfortune, informs the not conventionally religious Plath's motive behind her copious notes on the female saints, especially St. Therese (although it should be noted, in relation to the wider implications of critical attitudes toward Plath's "courting" of misfortune and extreme experiences, that she feels distaste for St. Therese's thirst for bodily mortification, writing, when reading St. Therese's autobiography, of the "horrid self-satisfied greed for misfortune which in its own way is perverse as greed for happiness in this world"[17]). So while the witch often appears as a positive figure, affirming the power of women in contrast to society's constraints (which society then labels them as witches), Plath is ambivalent about the dual nature of such a singling out. In her mostly unmarked copy of Christopher Fry's play *The Lady's Not for Burning* (a play with whose eponymous protagonist Plath may well have identified, as both shared a scientist father, and the death by drowning of the protagonist's father reflects the mythic cause of death Plath ascribed for her own parent), Plath marks the witch Jennet's comments about her fate of being burnt at the stake:

> My heart, my mind
> Would rather burn. But may not the casting vote
> Be with my body. And is the body necessarily
> Always ill-advised?[18]

The Cartesian duality of body and mind was often at the forefront of Plath's mind (reflecting earlier-noted dualities of intellect and emotion, earth-mother and blue-stocking), to the extent that in February 1957 she describes her own morality as "the commitment to body and mind" (J 153). As a result, in her poems which deal with fire and women, Plath is ultimately ambivalent toward fire on two linked levels: as both destructive and creative, and as something that the mind desires but that the body fears. The ambiguity of Plath's figuring of fire and the witch/saint is crucial to recognize, because it is bound up in her complex attitude toward transcendence—the transcending figure is often witch-like and the moment of apotheosis is often accompanied by fire imagery.

Contraries

An important way Plath was to deal with such ambivalences was through Blake's assertion of the creative importance of unresolvable contraries, expressed, for instance, in his celebration of the "fearful symmetry" of "The Tyger," which Plath double-marked in her copy of his work.[19] She also annotates Blake's most concise explanation of the notion in *The Marriage of Heaven and Hell:*

> Without Contraries is no progression. Attraction and Repulsion, Reason and Energy, Love and Hate, are all necessary to Human existence.[20]

In Kazin's introduction as well, Plath marks the editor's declaration that:

> Blake did not believe in a war between good and evil; he sees only the *creative tension* presented by the *struggle of man to resolve the contraries.* [Plath's emphasis]

and annotates this statement with a reference to the later Thomas Mann's similar perception that man is "lord of the counterpositions."[21] It is her awareness of the literary history of such contraries that enabled her own ambivalence toward such subjects as female literary creativity and transcendence to achieve expression. Indeed, if Blake's most famous expression of Contraries was in the striped tyger of his most well-known poem, Plath's own consciousness of the creative tension found emblematic expression in the striped bees of drudgery and of creativity of her late poems.

In other, later poems scattered throughout her career, such as

"The Eye-Mote" (1959), "Magi" (1960), and "Mystic" (1963), Plath continues to recall Blake in her treatment of fire imagery and dualities. In "The Eye-Mote," fire signifies the singling-out of the speaker that the visionary moment connotes, yet is also the focus for the poem's resulting ambivalence toward such an experience. Plath foregrounds the poem's debt to Blake: the prominent final line in the second stanza, which introduces the experience, "Horses warped on the altering green" (CP 109), recalls the refrain in Blake's "The Echoing Green," whose last line, "On the darkening Green," she marks in her copy of his work.[22] Plath drew the situation of "The Eye-Mote" from a real incident in 1956, when she had to have a splinter surgically removed from her eye. She recalls, in a detailed and melodramatic letter about the incident to her mother, having it removed under local anaesthetic, and describes how she rambled on about the new vision Oedipus and Gloucester in *King Lear* gained by losing their sight, but that she would rather have sight and new vision, and how, after she recovered, the world looked "shining as Eden" (LH 229–30). "The Eye-Mote" explores this idea of "new vision"; not vision into the future, but seeing the present in a different way, exploring Blake's perception, which Plath marked, in "The Mental Traveller, "For the eye altering, alters all."[23] Just as the fire refines the speaker in the more famous "Fever 103°," so, too, in "The Eye-Mote," the fiery abrasion of the cinder scrapes away false perceptions to leave the pure center—to the extent that the speaker's universe becomes centered around the cinder. Such moments of altered vision of the present lead, the poem apparently suggests, to understanding. The final stanza is one of new realization, as the speaker declares that she needs to reclaim her past in order to escape from "this parenthesis" in which she is trapped. Yet, just as Plath is ambivalent toward the emblem of fire, so the final stanza may be read not as a new awareness (of the need to regain history) born of the visionary experience, but a backing away from experience and vision altogether, returning to the childlike innocence of her past. This alternate desire to retreat from the assault of new vision is supported in the opening of the poem, where the speaker describes herself as "Blameless as daylight." In addition, the last two stanzas of the poem move away from the surreal descriptions of the visionary moment to more naturalized imagery describing the physical action of removing the splinter. The poem, then, ends in a position of ambivalence toward innocence and experience, toward the benefits of visionlessness and vision.

Neglecting Plath's Blakean attitude toward the necessity of both poles of any duality leads to oversimplification of Plath's poetry. For example, Joyce Carol Oates's misjudgment of Plath's balanced ambivalence about innocence and experience leads her to accuse Plath of unrealistically and immorally privileging the silent innocence of the child above the difficulties of the social and communicating world. Oates writes of "Magi":

> It is, in effect, a death sentence passed by Plath on her own use of language, on the "abstractions" of culture or the literary as opposed to the physical immediacy of a baby's existence. . . . Plath is saying here, in this agreeable-mannered poem, that because "Good" and "Evil" have no meaning to a six-month-old infant beyond the facts of mother's milk and a bellyache, they have no essential meaning at all—to anyone.[24]

Certainly "Magi" is about childhood innocence. It strongly echoes Blake's "Infant Joy" in its description of the necessary losses when the child is socialized and consequent valuing of the time of innocence. Certainly Plath esteemed and was attracted by such childhood innocence. Much earlier, in 1950, she unfavorably compares the social structures of the world with a presocial primitivism, concluding: "Almost, I think, the unreasoning bestial purity was best" (J 12). Yet it is crucial to note her double qualifications, "almost" and "I think." Plath does not, as Oates would contend, assert that the state of childhood is better than adulthood. While she values the short period of childhood innocence, like Blake, Plath also perceives the necessity of its contrary and consequent socialization and experience. The unattractive images of abstraction and socialization in "Magi" are accordingly those of the school room ("chalk," "multiplication table," "papery"), implying that the six-month-old child *will* become schooled, but not before her time. Indeed, examination of Plath's journals shows the strength and consistency of her commitment to the necessity of experience (and so opposition to the state of mute innocence Oates sees celebrated in "Magi"). She writes in July 1957, for instance, in one of many journal references to the idea, about an innocence that develops out of experience—"No garden before the fall, but a garden hand-made after it" (J 169)—and much earlier, in 1953, declares her belief in the Yeatsian attitude toward creative life as a spiralling gyre of experience, in opposition to the "final repetitive circle" which is innocence (J 75).

Even in her very late poetry, Plath returns to Blake. "Mystic" echoes Blake's style, combining the interrogative mode with the poetic modes of innocence and surrealism in the speaker's search for a mythic framework through which to cope with the intense sensitivities resulting from visionary experience. These sensitivities are most crucially to the "civilised" or industrialized world. While the poem opens with oppressive natural images, its climax describes the oppression of the postindustrial world: "The chimneys of the city breathe, the window sweats" (CP 269), using imagery strongly reminiscent of Blake's "London." (Plath returned frequently to focus on such traditionally Romantic concerns about the relation between the individual and the industrialized world, as the section on De Quincey and the next chapter show.) The speaker asks, in self-consciously simplistic response to the oppressive sensitivity resulting from vision: "Once one has seen God, what is the remedy?" In search of a framework or "remedy," the bulk of the poem is spent discarding traditional frameworks, such as Christianity, individual or community memory, Christian pantheism, retreat from the world, the fairy tale, and even passion. Yet, while Blake famously found such a personal mythic framework, in "Mystic," Plath ends almost where she began (asking "Questions without answer"), recognizing that the only framework able to contain the visionary experience is, for the speaker, a stoic awareness of continuing life: "The heart has not stopped."

Ultimately, however, the impact of Blake on Plath's poetry is not as extensive as it first appears. Certainly much of her surreal imagery reflects that of the earlier poet, and Blake addressed many issues which were of literary and social importance to Plath. Yet Blake was a popular figure for many writers of her generation, and his "influence" (her direct allusions to Blakean phrases, motifs, and themes) may have been a carefully constructed affair, designed to establish her poetic voice in terms of the legitimately canonical tradition Blake represented. In Bloom's terms then, Blake did not so much deeply influence Plath, but was more superficially adopted by her.[25] In other words, Blake was a then currently popular focus for Plath's general Romantic interests which could be equally well represented by other canonical Romantic writers (Blake's "contraries," for instance, find reflection in Keats's "negative capability," or indeed in the later Yeats's "quarrel with oneself"; the idea of poetry as an antidote to mechanization is equally clearly expressed by many early Romantics). Notwithstanding the general sweep of Blakean imagery and themes in Plath's poetry, it is with other writers, often coming out of different Romantic traditions, with whom Plath is in more direct dialogue, and with whose work her own poetry struggles to establish a voice. Indeed, it is with one of Blake's heirs, D. H.

Lawrence, whose ideological similarities with Blake she noted—comparing them in a Cambridge essay and fiercely annotating, in support of Lawrence, Kazin's often derogatory comparisons between the two in her copy of *The Portable Blake*[26]—that Plath's struggles with Romantic traditions are more compellingly expressed.

D. H. Lawrence and "Ariel"

"Ariel" (1962), usually viewed as one of Plath's most fully achieved works, is generally read as a celebration of energy. Its climax is variously perceived as an achievement of either suicide or rebirth, or both. This division reflects Plath's own unresolved ambivalence in "Ariel," not between the crude choices of life or death, but in a Romantically rooted conflict between desires for a mindless subsumption in the universe, or an intellectually willed individuality within it. Calvin Bedient writes of two angles of this conflict: "Loving the freedom of nonbody, the romantic yet instinctively shuns its lack of intimacy . . . The romantic would happily melt time into aboriginal timelessness, but not if that meant (as it would) deliquescence of space."[27] That this is the focus of the ambiguities in "Ariel" becomes clear when the poem's debt to D. H. Lawrence's tale "The Woman Who Rode Away" is recognized. In "Ariel," Plath uses her intellectual background to confront her attraction to the Romantic privileging of emotion over intellect expressed by one of its most extreme late adherents, Lawrence.

Plath clearly viewed Lawrence as a potential literary master. A year after her consideration of *Women in Love* as a possible model for her first novel (J 156), Plath writes, in 1958, that she learns about expressing the grounded physicality of life from him (J 199). Indeed, Perloff, in "Angst and Animism," argues that Plath's poetry is situated in the tradition of angst and animism of ecstatic poets that found twentieth-century expression in D. H. Lawrence. In addition to Lawrence's literary charisma, Plath was, like many of her educated contemporaries, strongly attracted to his attitude toward the importance of the instinctual passions and their subsequent effect on relationships. In May 1952, she explicitly relates her own thoughts about love relationships to Lawrence, meditating on the ideal result of passion as a charged equilibrium of two autonomous individuals and declaring "D. H. Lawrence did have something after all" (J 42).[28] In her copy of his *Selected*

Essays she underlines his description of the subjective/objective split in "Man":

> The blood also thinks, inside a man, darkly and ponderously. It thinks in desires and revulsions, and it makes strange conclusions. My blood tells me that there is no such thing as perfection. . . . Man finds that his head and his spirit lead him wrong. We are at present terribly off-track following our spirit, which says how nice it would be if every-thing was perfect, and listening to our head, which says we might have everything perfect if we would only eliminate the tiresome reality of our obstinate blood being.[29]

In terms both of imagery and theme, Plath appears to concur with Lawrence's beliefs. In her poetry, the imagery of blood is closely linked to all that is living, creative, and natural as opposed to the cold white perfection of her moon trope. In an essay on Plato, written at Cambridge for her moralists course, she, like Lawrence, concludes that "man's" desire for perfection is incompatible with creative life, resulting in "death by stasis."[30] In an essay she wrote on Lawrence for the same course in 1957, Plath appears keen to demonstrate her sense of fellow-feeling with Lawrence's brand of post-Nietzschean Romanticism. She writes of his short story:

> "The Woman Who Rode Away" existed in "deadness within deadness." . . . She was dead and she rode away to be reborn. . . . This is her rebirth . . . she becomes aware of the cosmic circles not by knowing but by growing spontaneously identified with them. And she is a "living sacrifice." Living where once she was dead. But nevertheless a sacrifice.[31]

The resonances between Plath's commentary on the story and "Ariel," written five years later, are striking. The situations are similar—a woman on horseback is riding toward some sort of new experience or rebirth, away from a feeling of deadness. Plath describes the rebirth of the woman in Lawrence's story as "involv-[ing] no personal love"; in "Ariel," too, personal love is dispensed with—"The child's cry dies in the wall." The rebirth in both texts is into some sort of macrocosmic consciousness. Even the descending moisture Plath quotes from Lawrence's story appears at the end of "Ariel" as the morning dew. The similarities between Lawrence's tale and "Ariel" do not end there. In both Lawrence's story and "Ariel," the woman is stripped bare and white in preparation for her rebirth, and her rebirth or sacrifice in both cases is signalled and accompanied by the entrance of the sun. Beyond these direct similarities, the subjective/objective theme identified by Plath in Lawrence's story (that the figure experienced this macrocosmic consciousness "not by knowing but by growing spontaneously identified" with it) is, as I showed in the introduction, a central concern for Plath. So "Ariel" appears to be a very Laurentian poem, dealing with a woman's return to her creative bloodbeing—a sort of mindless subsumption in nature taking the form of self-sacrifice to the sun. The sensual and emotional simply triumphs over the intellectual; the individual returns to immanence, sacrificing individuality for diffusion in something greater.

Yet Sandra Gilbert, who also sees "The Woman Who Rode Away" as an important text for Plath, argues a strong case for Plath's opposition to Lawrence's celebration of female sacrifice in his tale.[32] Indeed, a year after writing her Cambridge essay, Plath describes her conflicting feelings toward Lawrence, "Why do I feel I would have known and loved Lawrence. How many women must feel this and be wrong!" and goes on to say that reading Lawrence, whose vision, she perceives, is at once similar and yet very different from her own, she believes she "can be itched and kindled to a great work" (J 196). Plath defines her conflicting feelings toward Lawrence by the fact that, as a woman, her sense of fellow-feeling with the adamantly male writer, while powerful, must be only provisional. She describes her strong sense both of connection to, and of divergence from Lawrence's vision as a *creative* struggle, and it is this struggle which informs "Ariel." Certainly Lawrence addresses many of Plath's concerns, such as the conflict for women between the emotional and the intellectual, yet his conclusion was simply that woman should return to nature, deny the mind and any form of individualism.[33] It seems unlikely that Plath, in "Ariel," would merely replicate Lawrence's mythology, given that she was adamant about the importance of intellect and individuality for a woman. Closer examination of "Ariel" and its drafts shows that while Plath does not necessarily resolve the emotional-intellectual conflict she sets up in the poem, she uses Lawrence's terms for her own purposes, confronting the attraction she feels for Lawrence's mythology, and moving beyond it.

Plath's attraction to Lawrence's mythology focuses on three linked, Romantically based tenets, all of which she confronts in "Ariel." These are: Lawrence's authoritarian ideas about the necessity for individual subsumption into some larger power as an escape from destructive individualism; his ideas of woman as closer to nature than man; and the importance he placed on living "blood-being" as opposed to the cold perfection of the mind. Examination of Plath's drafts of "Ariel" shows even more clearly than the final poem both her references to Lawrence's expression of these attitudes in "The Woman Who Rode Away" and her reworking of them.

Individualism and "Will"

Lawrence's belief in the importance of giving up personal will was reflected in other persuasive critical writing of the time: for instance, in T. S. Eliot's theorizing of the poet's place in a monolithic tradition in "Tradition and the Individual Talent," described earlier. While Plath saw the attraction of such a potentially authoritarian situation (in the sense that the individual is worth less than the order in which she or he exists),[34] individualism was for her, as for most Americans, a central ideological commitment. In the first surviving draft of "Ariel," Plath immediately questions Lawrence's position, opening her poem by describing how she is becoming one with the horse, which she describes as "Crude mover whom I move."[35] While Lawrence strips his "woman who rode away" of any individual "will," in "Ariel" the figure's will is not submerged in that of the horse, but powerfully combined with it. Further on in "Ariel," Plath more explicitly reworks Lawrence's tale. Plath's speaker becomes bare and white, like the woman before her sacrifice in Lawrence's story, but a draft shows her as a fiery white Lady Godiva—her nakedness is power rather than defenselessness, and the fire imagery connects her to Plath's frequent depiction of the powerful woman as a persecuted witch or saint. Yet Plath's revision of Lawrence is not a straightforward reversal of his rejection of individual will. Her draft of the climax of the poem:

> In the sun
> One white melt, upflung
> To the lover, the plunging
> Hooves I am.[36]

recalls the image of the sacrifice in Lawrence's story—the woman is killed when the sun reaches an icicle hanging in the cave. Yet, while Plath's figure (unlike Lawrence's) retains both her identity, her "I am," and her seat on the horse, she is also "upflung / To the lover," somehow also merging with, and powerless in comparison with, some "other." These seemingly exclusive meanings reflect a central Romantic conflict between a desire to be in complete communion with the world, to obtain some intuitive "macrocosmic consciousness," yet also to retain some sort of intellectually conscious individual identity, which Plath, too, fails to resolve. Such a conflict is also linked to the traditional Romantic struggle with ideas about the position of the poet, most neatly summed up in Wordsworth's preface to *Lyrical Ballads*—whether "he" is a "man speaking to men," or positioned on a superior level, in a less democratic relationship with his readership: a division between, broadly, poetic democracy and poetic individualism, which is also apparent in Plath's attitude toward her position as writer, noted in chapter 2. The conflict "Ariel" explores, between individualism and immanence, is heightened and made more crucial because of the speaker's gender.

Femininity and Nature

Plath's ambivalence toward questions of intellectual will and individualism stems from, and is reflected in her treatment of gender in "Ariel." She was, as I note in the introduction, ambivalent about many aspects of traditional attitudes toward femininity, not least the idea that women were in some way closer to nature than men—an idea persuasively expressed by Rousseau, and finding power in many later versions of Romanticism. In "Ariel," the ambiguity of the climax (whether it figures a selfless subsumption in nature or a willed identification with it) is emphasized by the ambiguity of the figure's gender. The speaker of "Ariel" is at times very clearly a woman, at other times quite androgynous. In a draft of the poem's climax, Plath is more explicit about the androgyny of the speaker, describing him or her as, more actively, "*foaming* to wheat, a glitter of seas." Both phrases are ambiguous. The first implies some sort of ejaculatory movement, but also contains overtones of female fertility in the form of wheat; the second, while perhaps connecting the sea with femininity, also contains, in the word "glitter," overtones of a barren male image of superficial attractiveness Plath uses in other poems such as "Gigolo" (1963) and "Death and Co" (1962). The speaker later describes herself in phallic terms, shooting at the sun, revising Plath's simplistic view of female passivity before the male sun in the earlier "Two Sisters of Persephone" (1956). Plath, then, moves away from any simplistic analogy of female = nature by unsettling the gender symbolism of the speaker. While it is unclear how far the speaker's movement is toward a willed androgynous identification with the

cosmos, it is manifestly not simply a movement of female subsumption into it.

"Blood-being"

Plath's destabilizing of Lawrence's attitudes toward will and gender in "Ariel" focuses on the Romantic privileging of emotion
over intellect, nature over culture. Such a privileging is relatively
straightforward for a male in the Romantic tradition, his intellectual capacities being generally already accepted as central to his
masculine subjectivity. As Plath recognized, for a female already
supposedly at the mercy of her emotions, such a stance is more
problematic. While it appears that Romanticism's privileging of
the "feminine" (in terms of sensibility, closeness to nature, and so
on) empowered women, as Richardson argues, in fact it worked
in the opposite way: "The Romantic tradition did not simply ob-
jectify women [by conflating them with nature]. It also subjected
them, in a dual sense, portraying woman as subject in order to
appropriate the feminine for male subjectivity."[37] The central ambiguity of "Ariel," then, lies in the fact that while celebrating physical (as opposed to intellectual) life in the joy of movement, it casts
off the very emotions and sensual physicality that is typically set
against the cold life of the mind. In her first draft, Plath's imagery
of such a casting-off of physical and emotional life is more explicit
in her description of the blackberries which try to impede her
journey.[38] The blackberries with their "sweet blood mouthfuls" of
juice and their hooks (or "nets" in the draft) are metaphors for
both love and life. They are creative, "multiplying." Their blood
is the blood of primitive life, and their hooks recall the hooks in
"Tulips" (1961), which are the loving smiles of her family trying
to return the speaker to life, away from the sterile white calm of
emotional deadness. So the speaker's journey in "Ariel" cannot
be a journey toward the "blood-being" which Lawrence acclaims,
because the love and sensuality of such a state have been cast off
by the speaker. This movement may be viewed as an exploration
of the ambiguity of life, an ambiguity Plath reflects in her ambivalence toward the creative and destructive properties of fire (noted
with reference to Blake), and to which she returned in "Kindness"
(written four months after "Ariel" in February 1963), describing
the unstoppable "blood-jet" as poetry (CP 270). To *express* life
(blood/creativity/poetry), one must spill it and so lose it. Yet the
cluster of ambiguities in "Ariel," in Plath's treatment of Lawrence's
ideas about will and gender as well, implies that the movement in

"Ariel" (away from the "blood-being" it apparently celebrates) works more to unsettle the Romantic opposition of intellect and emotion, just as it destabilizes the opposition of male and female. In utilizing the structure, themes, and imagery of "The Woman Who Rode Away" in "Ariel," Plath enacts a kind of Bloomian revision of Lawrence's tale, questioning her own attraction toward Lawrence's Romanticism, and exploring the instability of the terms of her conflicts between intellect and sensual emotion, and between a Romantic individualism and an equally Romantic yearning for communion with the external world. In questioning Lawrence's Romantic beliefs about femininity and nature, Plath echoes Emily Brontë, whose poetry stems from a different strand of literary Romanticism: less from a Blakean, visionary Romantic tradition, and more from the nineteenth-century's Romantic poet of choice, Byron.

EMILY BRONTË: FEMALE IDENTITY AND MOTHER NATURE

While, as the introduction noted, Plath is in an anxious relationship with Emily Brontë's *Wuthering Heights,* Brontë's landscape poetry appears as a positive reinforcement of Plath's own struggles with the traditional Romantic attitude toward nature. It is not known whether she read Brontë's nature poetry: Brontë does not figure in Plath's list of "poetesses" with whom she felt in rivalry (J 211), and the only mention of her at all in Plath's journals is in relation to her visit to Withens (the setting for *Wuthering Heights*) and Haworth (J 148, 300–301). Yet Brontë's impact was large, to the extent that Plath, when pregnant with her second child, told her mother that if it were a girl she would name her Megan Emily after Dickinson and Brontë (LH 407). Plath's visits to Yorkshire (the Hughes family's home county) left her fascinated by the barren landscape of moors which form the powerful backdrop to Brontë's writing. In April 1957, just before the start of her Cambridge Tripos exams, Plath writes to her mother of the inspiration provided by the setting of *Wuthering Heights* when describing their summer vacation plans to visit the Yorkshire moors (LH 308). The moors also inspired Plath to write several poems: "The Snowman on the Moor" (1957); "Hardcastle Crags" (1957)—probably the poem whose notes are in her journals (J 149) immediately after her description of Withens; "Two Views of Withens" (1957); and "Wuthering Heights" (1961). In these poems, as in much of her other landscape poetry, Plath's attitude toward nature echoes that of the earlier poet, an attitude which finds its focus in both poets' ambivalence toward Romantic views of nature and nature itself.

Nature as Alien

Both Plath and Emily Brontë are generally more comfortable when nature is viewed as alien to humanity.[39] A. E. Dyson notes that Plath "was more at home when she sensed behind nature its naked inhospitability to man," and many of her landscape poems describe the comfort found in an alien and hostile nature.[40] In "Two Campers in Cloud Country" (1960), relief and freedom is provided by the perception that the "rocks offer no purchase to herbage or to people" (CP 145). In "Stars Over the Dordogne" (1961), the speaker is more explicit, declaring that "There is too much ease here; these stars treat me too well," and finding relief and comfort in drinking in "the small night chill like news of home" (CP 166). In "Watercolour of Grantchester Meadows" (1959), the gentle picture-perfect scenery is disturbed by the speaker's perception in the ominous last lines, that "in such mild air / The owl shall stoop from his turret, the rat cry out" (CP 112). Stevie Davies notes Emily Brontë's similar attitude toward landscape, "For Emily . . . the moors mean rest, clement on the very verge of annihilation."[41]

This ambivalence toward nature which both Plath and Emily Brontë share (and which is characterized by their expression of the comforts found in a nature which is alien to humanity), stems from their awareness of the dangers to poetic subjectivity the traditional comforts of nature held. In Brontë's "Shall Earth No More Inspire Thee," for instance, while nature, as the speaker of the poem, appears benign and able to "caress" and "soothe" the poet, who is wandering "in regions dark," the dominant sense is of a nature able to overpower the poet's "wayward will," denying the equality of "dwelling" together that nature proposes. In the fifth stanza such power becomes more sinister, when "nature" states "I've watched thee every hour" and that she knows her power "To drive thy griefs away."[42] The very fact that the only voice in the poem is that of nature—the poet is effectively voiceless—implies that the "regions dark" in which the poet wanders provide more hope of identity than nature's apparently benign, yet oppressive powers. The comforts and powers of mother nature are then, positioned in direct conflict with the poet's voice, will and identity. Several of Emily Brontë's other poems enact a similar battle between poet and nature. In "The Night Wind," the wind disturbs the solitary night (and the height of the poet's imagination) to tempt the poet, or force her to its will:

> O come, it sighed so sweetly
> I'll win thee 'gainst thy will.[43]

"The Night is Darkening Round Me," while a Gondal poem, nevertheless also returns to this conflict between nature and the subject's will: here the speaker is not only initially bound by nature, but finally loses her will to it, as the hypnotic refrain develops from "cannot go" to "will not go."

Plath also explores the ambiguous power of nature's ability to provide comfort or to annihilate the individual self, in a poem which she situates in clear relation to Emily Brontë: "Wuthering Heights." The work opens with a direct statement of this ambiguity, in a desire for the warming yet destructive fire, as the speaker describes the horizons surrounding her as precariously leaning "faggots" (CP 167). From this awareness, the speaker moves immediately to meditate on the traditional Romantic sense of inability to grasp or connect with this alien nature, as she describes the apparent solidity of the horizons dissolving as she moves toward them. In this first stanza, however, Plath also raises what is to become the central struggle of the poem—the struggle to assert her own subjectivity within such an impinging environment. When the poem opens, the speaker is at the center of this threatening landscape, ringed like a witch at the stake by the faggotlike horizons. Yet, by the end of the stanza, as she steps forward, the solid horizons have dissolved and the speaker appears implicitly to dissolve in the landscape as well. Throughout the poem, the speaker tries to approach the hostile nature of the moors on her own terms by an increasingly extreme use of personification, using the poetic device to try to achieve some kind of stable subjectivity, through the assertion of her own identity. The sheep are described as "dirty wool-clouds," their eyes as cosmic mail-slots or in "grandmotherly disguise." Yet the final metaphor points out the fruitlessness of such a project—the sheep are only "disguised" by the speaker's personification. As the poem progresses, the use of personification gathers pace and becomes more extreme. In describing the deserted houses, the doorsteps are depicted as moving, the lintel and sill "have unhinged themselves," the air "remembers" the past inhabitants and "rehearses them moaningly." The sky "leans" and the grass "is beating its head distractedly." Such a glut of personification appears to be fighting against the speaker's sense that she is dangerously close to being submerged in the nature upon which she tries to impose her poetic will. The wind is all powerful and dangerous to her as it tries to sweep away her warmth and life. Any sense of real connection to the landscape (the sort of connection that the Romantics were keen to forge) appears achievable only at the expense of individual subjectivity, at the expense of life. The speaker emphasizes this point by noting that if she tries to examine too closely the heather on the moor she would be in danger of lying down and dying among it. The speaker's feeling of dispossession in this landscape, being "unrooted" or "the one upright / Among all horizontals"—unlike the sheep, not knowing where she is—can, then, be remedied only by accepting her total identification with this landscape, and so her loss of individuality. Just before she withdraws to the safety of "narrow" female domesticity offered by the valley (a retreat which reflects that at the end of other poems such as "Finisterre" [1961] and "Hardcastle Crags" [1957]), this sense of dangerous submergence in the landscape reaches a climax when the speaker describes the grass as "beating its head distractedly" because it is not strong enough to survive "in such company," frightened as it is of the darkness around it (CP 168). The "company" for whom the grass is too delicate may well be that of the hostile moors, and the speaker imposes her own feelings on the action of the grasses. Yet the ambiguity of the "whose company" leaves an added implication that it is also the speaker's company for whom the grass is too delicate, implying a stronger connection between speaker and nature than is desired. It is this final realization that leads the speaker to her rejection of such a mother nature in favor of the alternative, civilized, female landscape offered by the lights of the valley which "gleam" comfortingly like coins in a purse. Plath expresses a similar sense of finality in "I Am Vertical," written six months before "Wuthering Heights," in March 1961. Here the options are more clearly stated: achievement of nature's "motherly love" is seen as impossible—either nature is alien or connection with nature leads to loss of subjectivity and so to death.

Romanticism and Gender

The similarity between Plath and Emily Brontë's poetic perception of a nature hostile to humanity is founded on shared difficulties with their relation, as female writers, to traditional

Romantic attitudes toward "mother nature" and toward the project in which these attitudes are rooted, a desire to renew the bond between "man" and "mother nature." The difficulties both poets share in their approach to nature stem from a problem inherent in Romanticism (and central to Plath's struggles with Lawrence's vision): the implicit masculinity of the Romantic poet-subject. As Alan Richardson argues, while Romanticism privileged the "feminine" qualities of natural, intuitive feeling, such a privileging was, in effect, no more than a colonization of the feminine by the traditionally rational male subject "when androgyny functions as another manifestation of the male poet's urge to absorb feminine characteristics his (or his protagonist's) female counterpart stands to risk obliteration."[44] An example of the profound influence of this implicit masculinity of the Romantic poet-subject shows itself in the similar ways in which both Plath and Brontë's work was initially received. Both writers' work has, to some extent, been debased by the posthumous "romanticizing" of their lives. For both, this was initially (and unintentionally) conducted by a close relative, who was also, at the time, a more established writer. The ways in which Ted Hughes and Charlotte Brontë contend with the character of their respective relatives' work bear some scrutiny. Both Charlotte Brontë and Ted Hughes esteem Emily's and Plath's work in a similar way, as poetry full of an implicitly masculine feeling, and unlike that which women usually write. Charlotte recalls her first reading of Emily's poetry, and her conclusion that:

> these were not common effusions, nor at all like the poetry women generally write. I thought them terse, vigorous and genuine.[45]

Plath also reports in a 1956 letter to her mother in the early stages of her relationship with Hughes that "Ted says he never read poems by a woman like mine" and that he perceived in them a raw power and richness unlike that of her female contemporaries (LH 244).[46] Yet in contrast to this, Charlotte struggles to apologize for Emily's sensibility in *Wuthering Heights,* which she admits may appear "a strange and rude production" to many who "will hardly know what to make of this rough strong utterance, the harshly manifested passions."[47] Similarly, Hughes, in his extensive reordering of *Ariel* for publication, and in his removal of the "nasty bits" in his editing of Plath's *Journals,* also appears to be discomfited by the very raw strength of emotion he celebrated earlier,[48] an emotional intensity implicitly acceptable only in terms of the male subject's colonization of feminine feeling. Such difficulties

were, in both Plath and Emily Brontë's cases, eased by their inad-
vertent mythologizers' resort to describing each poet's writing as
Romantically "inspirational." Brontë declares that neither of her
sisters were highly educated: "they had no thought of filling their
pitchers at the well-spring of other minds; they always wrote from
the impulse of nature, the dictates of intuition," and more specifically of Brontë's characters in *Wuthering Heights,* "Having formed
these beings, she did not know what she had done."[49] Hughes
starts his article with a similarly extreme statement about Plath's
literary skills, asserting that her poetry "escapes ordinary analysis" because of its powerful psychic aspects—shifting responsibility
for the art away from the artist by denying the writer's active
mind and craft, and affirming a patriarchal gender division which
places femininity on the side of the unconscious and irrational.

Certainly Romantic tradition is itself in conflict between ideals
of the poet as vessel of inspiration (most famously described by
Coleridge as an aeolian harp[50]) or as the triumphant source of
"his" poetry (seen in, for instance, Wordsworth's preface to *Lyrical
Ballads*[51]). This conflict is inherent in Romanticism's dual privileging of both individualism and the mysterious power of art. Yet
for the female Romantic poet, the conflict is potentially fatal to
her poetic identity, and both stems from and affects her treatment
of the traditional Romantic centralizing of nature. Margaret Homans describes the resulting difficulties the Romantic strengthening of a traditional link between nature and woman created for
nineteenth-century female poets:

> When nature is Mother Nature for Wordsworth, she is valued because
> she is what the poet is not . . . [female Romantic poets] cannot be
> docile daughters of Nature because they know it is all too possible to
> pass from continuity to identification and thence to a loss of their
> own identity.[52]

This problem of a gendered dyad is at the root of both Plath and
Brontë's landscape poetry. The difficulty for both exists in the
dualism between "mother nature" and "speaking subject" or
"man." If woman is Nature, she is other to the poet: silent, imma-
nent, lacking subjectivity and so poetic identity. The Romantic
project, of reactivating the bond between self and nature (subject
and other), appears, for a male poet, achievable through an individualistic assertion of subjectivity. For a woman poet, already
traditionally identified as "other," on the other side of the dyad,
such a connection to nature could only deny her position as a

speaking subject, a poet. Indeed, such concerns were also shared
by Plath's contemporary, Adrienne Rich, who, in 1974, writes in
"From an Old House in America,"

> I am an American woman:
> I turn that over
>
> . . . .
>
> Hanged as witches, sold as breeding-wenches
> my sisters leave me
> I am not the wheatfield
> nor the virgin forest[53]

Rich's concerns reflect Plath's, not only in her awareness of the
metaphoric impingement of nature on her identity, but in her
specific awareness of the relation between the two mutually exclusive categories into which a woman must fit (witch or breeding-
wench) and the two attitudes toward nature as either submitting
or dangerous to man (wheatfield or virgin forest).

   In her early poetry Plath attempts to celebrate the traditional
Romantic positioning of nature and woman. "Two Sisters of Persephone" (1956), for example, adversely compares the barren, intellectual activity of one woman with the sensual identification with
nature of the other. Yet such a simple identification with nature,
an almost Laurentian celebration of mindless fertility, is an exception in Plath's poetry. More generally, she recognizes the problem-
atics of such an identification between women and nature, and
her resulting ambivalence toward nature results either in the celebration of an alien nature or in the depiction of a landscape which
is secondary to the speaker. In both these strategies Plath's poetry
echoes that of the earlier poet, Emily Brontë.

Personalized Landscapes

   Although landscape figures prominently throughout Plath and
Emily Brontë's oeuvre, it is rarely the subject of such poems. Several critics, such as Robin Grove and Rosalind Miles, have noted
this absence of landscape as subject in Brontë's work.[54] Similarly,
in Plath's poems, landscape rarely figures as the subject. In Plath's
case, her exclusion of a generalized nature as the subject of her
landscape poetry is generally perceived as either due to her poetic
narrowness, her egotistical subjectivity, or to her personal psychological problems in establishing boundaries between herself and
the external world.[55] Yet, by viewing Plath as a late-coming Ro-

mantic, this narrowness is more usefully explored in terms of dialogue with the "motherliness" of nature, a problem relating to the dual character of the mother (as both comforting but also potentially annihilating the daughter's identity), which finds echoes in her more direct treatment of "the mother," explored in chapter 3.[56] Rather than simplifying Plath's relation to nature by perceiving her as simply taking to its extreme the traditional Romantic privileging of individual emotion over external perception (expressed by Wordsworth's dictum that "The feeling therein developed gives importance to the action and situation and not the action and situation to the feeling"[57]) and replacing the traditional "spirit of place" with her own spirit, it is important to recognize that Plath's difficulties with nature and the spirit of place make the very distinction between "her spirit" and "that place" problematic, if not impossible.

In "Finisterre" (1961), for example, it is not simply that the speaker becomes her own spirit of place because the obvious option, the towering statue of "Our Lady of the Shipwrecked," is looking away from humanity. The speaker finds herself becoming a dumb part of the timeless landscape she is trying, as a poet, to name. She begins by humanizing nature, describing the vegetation of the cliffs as nature's needlework. Yet further on, walking among the mists, the speaker herself becomes written on by nature, just as the cliffs are embroidered, so the mists cover her face and release her "beaded with tears" (CP 169). Significantly, not only is the speaker written upon, but she also loses her own voice and power of naming, her mouth "stuffed" with cotton, muffled by the ancient mists of the place. This threat of immanence appears temporarily lessened by the focusing presence of the gigantic stone figure of Our Lady of the Shipwrecked, to whom both anachronistic "peasant" and stone sailor are praying. This colossal figure, however, refuses positioning as a solid center or focusing presence in the scene as she is looking away from humanity, and celebrating the very impinging formlessness of nature, the sea, which threatens speaker, sailor, and peasant (CP 170). And so, in a move similar to that which concludes "Wuthering Heights," the speaker retreats from such claustrophobic immanence in nature to the mundane and nourishing comforts of twentieth-century "civilisation" in the form of the postcard stalls, gift shops, and food.

Certainly there are also differences in Plath and Brontë's attitudes toward nature. Each poet comes out of a different literary tradition. As Annette Kolodny argues, the American pastoral, "probably America's oldest and most cherished fantasy: a daily reality of harmony between man and nature based on an experience of the land as essentially feminine," is different from European pastoral because it "holds at its very core the promise of fantasy as daily reality."[58] The pastoral is arguably a mode more centrally caught up in the American than in the European imagination; that, combined with the fact that American pastoral more closely links the pastoral fantasy and its fulfilment (harmony between man and nature) makes that literary tradition potentially more threatening to the subjectivity of the women, like Plath, who are its descendants. Also, each poet responds in different ways to their fear of nature. While Plath, in the landscape poems cited above, characteristically retreats to some version of a mundane civilization, Emily Brontë's poems tend to move toward transcendence, a "hyperbolic view of heaven [which] is not spontaneous, but conditioned by her view of nature."[59] (Plath's own problematic treatment of transcendence, explored in later chapters, may, however, share similar roots with Emily Brontë's use of it as a negative response to the impingements of the natural and external world). Such differences, however, merely highlight the central relation between Plath's and Emily Brontë's poetry: a relation based on their shared ambivalence toward nature itself, filtered through and indistinguishable from the Romantic attitude toward it. Although the level of Plath's familiarity with Brontë's landscape poetry is unclear,[60] her relation to it is unique among these case studies, as it involves, not so much either an adoption (as in the case of Blake) or an "anxiety of influence" (as in the cases of Lawrence and De Quincey), but is the result more of an "anxiety of authorship," placing Plath and Emily Brontë together in a specifically feminine post-Romantic tradition.

Thomas De Quincey: Literary Father

While it is helpful in many ways to examine Plath's dialogue with aspects of various Romantic traditions, such as those characterized in the work of Blake, Lawrence, and Brontë, it is with Thomas De Quincey's particular treatment of traditional Romantic concerns that Plath's work is in most strikingly consistent sympathy. The impact De Quincey's prose writings had on Plath's poetry extends, as I will demonstrate, through both a shared project and tone to a direct dialogue on specific themes.[61] Although her journals and letters are full of references to literary "masters" such as Lawrence and Yeats, Plath rarely acknowledges De Quincey's influence on her work, either publicly or in her private writings. Yet De Quincey is a more central literary father for Plath than is immediately apparent, not only because of his central concern, prominent in various strands of Romanticism, with the ideal relation between intellect and emotion in creative life, but because of his treatment of memory and history, his insistence on the importance of struggle for creativity, and his linked interest in dreams and extreme states of mind: themes which, as later chapters show, form the core of Plath's poetry.

Examination of the Plath archives both at Smith College and at the Lilly Library is unable to give any conclusive evidence about when and how Plath became interested in De Quincey's writing. Plath's undated copy of his *Selected Works* was published in 1949, and no essays or notes on him remain from either Plath's periods at Smith or at Cambridge. It is likely, however, that she studied his work at Cambridge, on her moralists course, when she wrote essays on questions about the relationship between intellect and experience.[62] (However, as with her copy of Blake's poems, her copy of De Quincey's works is also an American publication, so it is difficult to be certain when and where she acquired it—it was certainly in her possession by 1957.) As the introduction showed, Plath was often fascinated by the details of the lives of writers with whom she sympathized, delighting in finding similarities between their experience and her own. In her copy of De Quincey's *Selected Writings*, she marks several of Philip Van Doren Stern's editorial comments about De Quincey's life, such as the impact the death of his sister had on him as a child,[63] and his relative political conservatism in comparison with other radical Romantic contemporaries,[64] which showed parallels with Plath's own life (while not a conservative, her often divided desires to conform, the roots and results of which are explored in the next chapter, puts her in striking contrast to the more clearly radical contemporary literary movements such as the Beats). In addition to these biographical similarities, Plath also marks Van Doren Stern's comments about De Quincey's writing practice (that he "sounded every syllable in his ear" before he wrote the words down[65]), which must have seemed to be a welcome confirmation of, or perhaps inspiration for, the writing methods she adopted in her late work: in an interview accompanying a BBC radio reading of her poems in October 1962, Plath compares her early and late work, asserting that her *The Colossus* poems were not written to be spoken and that they bored her. In comparison she declared that the meaning and sense in her recent poems is bound up in her practice of writing them to be spoken.[66] Plath's perception of such biographical and professional similarities form the base of her wide-ranging and surprisingly close dialogue with De Quincey.

Intellect and Emotion: Privileging the Private and Extreme

As I have emphasized, Plath's interest in the relation between intellect and emotion, or objectivity and subjectivity, was intense. It is perhaps in the context of her Cambridge moralists course that she annotated parts of De Quincey's essay, "The Literature of Knowledge and the Literature of Power," in which he distinguishes between a literature that teaches and one that moves— "the first is a rudder; the second an oar or sail"[67]—and implicitly privileges the emotional rather than intellectual impact of art by describing the "great" writers as writing the literature of power. Indeed, in another essay (which Plath also annotated), "On the Knocking at the Gate in *Macbeth*," De Quincey is even more forthright, declaring the need for a person "never to pay any attention to his understanding when it stands in opposition to any other faculty of his mind."[68] De Quincey's attitude is a traditionally Romantic one (which Plath also probably noted in Blake), but his distinctive treatment of this traditional general privileging of emotion is interesting in Plath's case because of De Quincey's unique concentration on the details of individual psychology. Of all the early Romantics, it was De Quincey who, as Van Doren Stern notes (and Plath duly marks),

> went beyond Rousseau by leading the reader into the innermost recesses of his subconscious mind. . . . He wanted to go beyond the concrete phenomena of physical existence to the *shadowy domain of nonmenal substance.*[69] [Plath's emphasis]

As Van Doren Stern implies, De Quincey's interest in the "innermost recesses of his subconscious mind" and his subsequent exploration of the impact of childhood trauma and its expression in dreams explicitly prefigures the Freudian project, which was gaining steady popularity in American and Britain in the 1950s. Further, De Quincey's essay "On the Knocking at the Gate in *Macbeth*" foreshadows the kinds of psychological literary criticism that became prominent in 1950s America, and which so profoundly influenced Plath's poetry.[70] There are two aspects to De Quincey's particular treatment of the "inner life," and Plath is in great sym-

pathy with both: his emphasis on the personal, individual visionary experience (with the resulting exploration of memory and
dreams) and his subsequent privileging of the extreme and terrible in such individual experience.[71]

De Quincey's exploration of his own unconscious fears and desires seemed to take Romanticism to its logical extreme. Such an
exploration was, as Van Doren Stern notes, "novel and thrilling
to the romantic mind for *the romantic was an individualist who was
interested primarily in himself*" [Plath's emphasis].[72] De Quincey, like
Freud later, saw memory and its expression in dreams as central
to the exploration of the mind, comparing, in "The Palimpsest,"
the mind's store of hidden memories to the ancient parchment
whose surface text conceals previous, partly erased writings:

> the endless strata have covered up each other in forgetfulness. But by
> the hour of death, but by fever, but by the searchings of opium, all
> these can revive in strength.[73]

De Quincey's description of the ways to gain access to such hidden,
potentially visionary depths or dreams found its post–World War
II reflection in Aldous Huxley's *Heaven and Hell* (1956), which
Plath bought on publication in 1956 (J 130). In it, Huxley also
notes that while the two main ways to open up the hidden "antipo-
des of the mind" were through drugs (mescaline or LSD) or
hypnosis,[74]

> *Similar intrusions of biologically useless, but aesthetically and sometimes spir-
> itually valuable material may occur as the result of illness or fatigue; or they
> may occur by fasting, or a period of confinement in a place of darkness and
> complete silence.* [Plath's emphasis][75]

This mutual affirmation between past and present notions of the
ways in which access is gained to the "dream-work" throws light
on the importance Plath places, in poems such as "Fever 103'"
(1962), on physical ways to achieve new vision. Certainly, Huxley
takes his title from Blake's visionary poem sequence *The Marriage
of Heaven and Hell,* and indeed, such an interest in the visionary
experience was a common strand in Romantic thought. Yet it is the
unique importance the later De Quincey places on the individual,
biographically situated nature of the "dream"—its rootedness in
early trauma and the approbation he gives to pragmatically seek-
ing out such states of mind—which gives him a special place in
Plath's work.

From the ways in which De Quincey recommends the achievement of personal visionary experience, his interest in extreme experiences is easily deduced. His privileging of childhood memories contrasts strikingly with Wordsworth's celebration of infant innocence—due, perhaps, to his own childhood experiences, De Quincey concentrates on the way the sorrows and trauma of infancy can affect the adult mind. In his description in "The Palimpsest," cited above, of how dreams are the expression of hidden memories, De Quincey describes such memories as "the deep deep tragedies of infancy . . . these remain lurking below all, and these lurk to the last."[76] In Plath's work, too, depiction of childhood memories (in prose such as "Ocean 1212-W" [1962], and poems such as "The Beekeeper's Daughter" [1959], "Lament" [pre-1956], and "Daddy" [1962]) cluster around the traumatic experience of the death of a close relative—in her case, the death of her father (for De Quincey it was his sister). The roots of this psychological project lie, for both writers, in an ideology which combines a traditional Romantic conviction in the value of intensity for its own sake—Plath quotes Keats to form the epigraph to a Cambridge essay on Webster and Tourneur: "The excellence of every art is its intensity, capable of making all disagreeables evaporate from being in close relationship with beauty and truth"[77]—and a belief (most powerfully expressed by Nietzsche) that the knowledge of extreme trauma is necessary for the full experience of life. Van Doren Stern writes of De Quincey:

> He was interested in the way the mind works at moments of fearful stress—at the instant before death, or at that frightful pitch when it is ready to kill. His *preoccupation with murder* was no superficial thing . . . [resulting from] his own deeply introspective nature which was forever turning to the secret springs of human action that have their sources in the inexplicable mysteries of birth and death.[78] [Plath's emphasis]

Plath, in a similar vein, declares in a letter to her mother in October 1962 that she will not, as her mother suggested, write in the *Ladies Home Journal* style about what Aurelia apparently phrased as "cheerful stuff" (LH 473) and "decent courageous people," because she "believe(s) in going through and facing the worst, not hiding from it" (LH 477). Although much of Plath's bitterness in making these points is due to her separation from Hughes and perhaps her rationalizing of the good of such an experience, her previous rationally worked out philosophy at Smith and Cambridge is merely expressed more strongly, not changed by circumstances. She also, in her famous description of the importance of artistic control of personal experience, gives examples of those experiences as the extreme ones of "madness, being tortured."[79] Plath's own interest in such extremes and her concentration on the darker emotions and moments in life are often perceived either as expression of her psychological difficulties and evidence of her self-centeredness, or as characterizing a particularly twentieth-century malady, which culminated in the "confessional school" of extremist poets which also includes Robert Lowell, John Berryman, and Anne Sexton. Such definitions of the roots of Plath's poetry all have some merit, yet they are ultimately narrowing and ignore the literary and cultural history of such an interest in extremes.[80] While such a privileging is characteristic of Romanticism generally, Plath is particularly similar to De Quincey in the modes of intensity (murder, death, despair) she explores and expresses.

Beyond this broad background of shared assumptions and beliefs, Plath is also in direct dialogue with De Quincey on many themes and concerns that are central to her work. While with Lawrence, for example, she broadly reacts to his influence in terms of Bloom's first revisionary ratio, *clinamen* ("imply[ing] that the precursor . . . went accurately up to a certain point, but then should have swerved, precisely in the direction that the new poem moves"[81]), her relation to De Quincey is more subtle and more profound; effecting, again, to broadly use Bloom's terms, a *tessera* ("antithetically 'complet[ing]' his precursor, by so reading the parent-poem as to retain its terms but to mean them in another sense, as though the precursor had failed to go far enough"[82]).

Creativity and Struggle: "Levanna and Our Ladies of Sorrow" and "The Disquieting Muses"

Plath's belief in the value of extreme experience and states of mind is demonstrated in her own teaching. In the notes she made for the final freshman class she taught at Smith (in 1958), she explains that death is an important and frequently treated literary subject because "we must learn to live more keenly, if necessary more painfully, in order to fully live."[83] It is through De Quincey that Plath expresses her Nietzschean belief in the importance of struggle for life. Her only public reference to De Quincey occurs during a BBC reading of her poems in July 1961, when, introducing "The Disquieting Muses" (1957), she describes her De Chirico—inspired muses as suggesting a modern equivalent of female "sinister trios" such as the fates, Macbeth's witches, and "De Quincey's sisters of madness."[84] De Quincey's trio occur in his Oxford "dream-piece," "Levanna and Our Three Ladies of Sorrow," much of which Plath marked in her copy of the text. Levanna, De Quincey tells the reader, is the Roman goddess of childhood education—not academic learning, but the education of experience, the most powerful of which is grief. Her three "ministers" define three levels of grief, the most rare and dangerous being Our Lady of Darkness, who is the "seductress of suicides." De Quincey writes, and Plath marks, that their "commission, which from God we had" is "to plague the heart until we had unfolded the capacities of his spirit."[85]

In "The Disquieting Muses," while the figures' names and physical appearance are, as Plath states, derived from De Chirico's painting, their role (as teachers) and placement (from early childhood) more resemble the purposed commission of De Quincey's "sisters." Yet Plath goes beyond De Quincey in the significance she gives her figures. While De Quincey positions "our ladies of sorrow" as one of many other groups of female figures, such as Muses, Fates, and Graces, Plath, by describing her "ladies of sorrow" as muses and positioning them centrally as fairy-tale godmothers ("unasked to my christening"), emphasizes the primary importance of dark and extreme states of mind.

Time and Memory: "Savannah-La-Mar" and "Lyonesse"

As in "The Disquieting Muses," in "Lyonesse" (1962) Plath's treatment of the theme of memory (a theme which, as the following chapters make clear, is central to her work) appears to be glancing very firmly in the direction of one of De Quincey's Oxford dream-pieces. Plath's "Lyonesse" owes more than a passing debt to De Quincey's "Savannah-La-Mar," not only in terms of theme and background, but also because of its imagery. Both poem and prose piece are dreamlike meditations on the painfully ragged insubstantiality of the present in comparison to the quiet timelessness of a submerged civilization. Though Lyonesse is a mythical tract of land that once extended between Land's End and the Scilly Isles, fabled as the birthplace of King Arthur,[86] and Savannah-La-Mar was a real town—"a Jamaican port destroyed by a tidal wave during the West Indian hurricane of 1780,"[87] the image Plath creates of Lyonesse is strikingly similar to De Quincey's description of Savannah-La-Mar. De Quincey, in his

dream, describes examining the bells in the belfry towers. A similar image occurs in Plath's poem, as the speaker watches an air
bubble escaping from the bells. Neither civilization is destroyed;
rather they exist, in De Quincey's piece, "enshrine[d by God] . . .
in the crystal dome of my tropic seas," and in Plath's poem, possessing a green but otherwise "quite breathable atmosphere."
Even the quality of the light of both places is similar; De Quincey's
town is "set in azure light," in Lyonesse the light dazzles like water.
Similar also is the movement in both toward consideration of the
timeless God who allowed or directed the submergence and His
relation to the city's timelessness and the present.

In De Quincey's piece, consistent with his concern in "Levanna,"
the notion is that such destruction occurred for a reason: "Upon
the sorrows of an infant, he [God] raises often times from human
intellects glorious vintages that could not else have been." This
then leaves De Quincey free to explore the insubstantiality of the
finite moment (and its sorrows) in comparison to the infinite timelessness of a purposeful God. In "Lyonesse," however, there is no
comfortable reason for such destruction. God had no purpose,
but had merely "lazily closed one eye," and forgotten His creations
as they sunk both under the sea and beneath history (CP 233).
By removing any sense of God's purpose, seeing Him equally as
"caged" by the timelessness and anesthesia of his position as the
world is by disaster, Plath shifts the focus of her poem to emphasize the importance of memory (of recognizing the past as living
like the surviving Lyonessians) in such an insubstantial present.
This movement in emphasis away from De Quincey's "parent-
piece" is accentuated in Plath's companion poem, "Amnesiac,"
which not only echoes the starting phrase of "Lyonesse," but
which originally formed the second part of "Lyonesse."[88] In this
way, Plath expands De Quincey's theme of the insubstantiality of
the present moment to condemn as immoral the idea of trying
to achieve the peace of timelessness and ahistoricism, the danger
of trying to "make of the moment something permanent." Plath
writes of the potent attraction of Plato's paradise of timeless perfection that could rise above "the present quagmire of quarrelling
relativities," but sees this desire for immutability as "the greatest
threat to creative growth throughout life."[89] Plath also goes further than De Quincey with the idea of the necessity of life as
struggle. She uses De Quincey's scene and imagery, but by effectively removing any higher sense to life's difficulties and struggle
(in the form of a purposeful God), she makes the struggle to live

for the moment, and to live creatively at that, even more important.

Stasis and Movement: "The English Mail Coach," "Years," and "Ariel"

In "Lyonesse," Plath extends her focus from De Quincey's theme of the insubstantiality of the present in "Savannah-La-Mar" to concentrate on the importance of history, but she returns to his celebration of the infinite nature of the finite moment in the glorification of energy in poems such as "Ariel" and "Years," written one month later in November 1962. Indeed, a fitting epitaph to "Ariel" might be taken from "Savannah-La-Mar":

> All is finite in the present; and even that finite is infinite in its velocity of flight towards death.[90]

In her copy of his works, Plath marks many passages from one of De Quincey's more famous pieces, "The English Mail Coach," which celebrates explicitly what is intimated in "Savannah-La-Mar": the ambiguity of life as a series of infinitesimal moments. "The English Mail Coach" is notable for its powerful expression of the passion of movement generated by the coach's horses, and Plath's celebrations of equine movement in poems like "Years" and "Ariel" share both De Quincey's terms and attitudes. In her copy of his works, Plath marks many of the sections from his essay which deal explicitly with the exhilaratingly dangerous power of the horse. De Quincey, for instance, describes a near-collision on the night road:

> The actual scene ... transformed into *a dream, as tumultuous and changing as a musical fugue* ... this *duel between life and death narrowing itself to a point of such exquisite evanescence as the collision neared:* all these elements of the scene blended, under the law of association, with the mail itself; [Plath's emphasis][91]

Notable here is the visionary sense of velocity leading to harmony, a harmony to which De Quincey refers frequently, and which Plath equally frequently marks, such as the description of the post as

> a thousand instruments, all disregarding each other, and so in danger of discord, yet all obedient as slaves to the supreme baton of some great leader, terminate in a perfect harmony like that of heart, brain, and lungs in a healthy animal organization.[92]

This kind of celebration also characterizes Plath's own poems, such as "Ariel" and "Years," in their expression of the antithetical belief that transcendental vision is achieved through the dangerous energy of velocity. Indeed, "Ariel" perhaps can be seen more positively not just as a struggle with Lawrence, but as an expression of the earlier Romantic, De Quincey's vision of a balanced wholeness achieved only in the midst of passionate and dangerous headlong movement. In this, the ambivalence of the poem's ending (does it lead to death or rebirth?) reflects the ambiguity of its theme—the vision of a sudden death leading to fullest experience of life. In "Years," however, Plath again tries to move beyond De Quincey's project in "The English Mail Coach." In this case, her expansion relates not to De Quincey's idea of God, but to his typically Romantic attitude toward the modern world, in an attempt to step out of the conflict between old and new (between reactionary primitivism and revolution) she notes in Van Doren Stern's introduction as characterizing the Romantic tradition, which he describes as:

> the artistic expression of the mighty forces that were reshaping the world . . . [containing] a reactionary element—a nostalgic and backward looking gesture toward the glories of the feudal past . . . This spiritual dichotomy in the romantic movement was reflected in many of the writers themselves. [Plath's emphasis].[93]

De Quincey, in common with many early Romantics, was deeply mistrustful of the achievements of the industrial revolution. He exhibited this in "The English Mail Coach" by adversely comparing the mechanized rail-driven postal service to that of the equine mail coach,[94] a comparison between horse and machine which became a popular image for writers as diverse as Lawrence and Dickens through which to express anxieties about industrialization. Plath, too, frequently makes use of both horse and rail imagery. A cursory inspection of poems such as "Getting There" (1962) and "Totem" (1963) gives the impression that Plath, too, is mistrustful of the mechanized nature of the train. In "Getting There" the train is described as a brutal animal, connected to war and despair, with none of the majesty of the horse of "Ariel." In "Totem," too, the inexorable nature of the train's progress, of "progress" itself, is described in anxious tones, as the poem opens with a description of the engine eating the delicate silver track (CP 264). In both cases, the train is described in animal terms. This may be due to Plath's perception of the postindustrial eminence of mechanization over flesh and blood as she effects a similar inversion in the earlier "The Night Shift" (1957) between man and factory machine. Yet in other poems Plath places horse and train in such a way that it becomes impossible to distinguish between them. In "Sheep in Fog" (1963), for instance, the distinction between the train the speaker sees and the horse she may be riding is unclear (CP 262). In "Years," a celebration of energy similar in theme, though not content or development, to "Ariel," horse and engine are very clearly celebrated equally as the speaker states her love of the movement of both engine and horse (CP 255). Even the poem's climax is shared equally between mechanical and animal velocity:

> The hooves with not have it,
> In blue distance the pistons hiss.

> > (CP 256)

The "blood-hot and personal" world she affirms in "Totem" also includes the products of industrialization. Indeed Plath is trying to take De Quincey to his natural conclusion, not only stressing the importance of accepting life in its painful totality (exploring those elements of life, such as mechanization which are not apparently beautiful or life-affirming), but also linking the energy of *movement* with the *progress* of civilization, and affirming the dual nature of both.

Plath's relationship with Romanticism, then, is profound, affecting her attitude toward many of the themes her poetry approaches, such as unresolvable conflict, individualism, nature, and gender. Her relationship with this heritage, however, finds its focus in the father figure of De Quincey, with whom she shared the overriding concern to examine humanity through the intensities of individual subjective experience. It is this concern which leads to the apparently morbid dwelling on death, grief, and anxiety, and the almost oppressive nature of the ever-present "I" at the center of each writer's visions (different from the visions of the Romantics with whom Plath is more usually placed, such as Blake and Yeats). Yet beyond this, De Quincey also figures as Plath's Romantic father because the focus of his concerns—memory, struggle, and psychological enquiry—mirrors the central themes of her poetry, themes which, as the next chapter explores, are bound up in, and informed by, Plath's political concerns.

2

Politics—History—Myth

I'm rather a political person as well.
—Sylvia Plath, 1962

In a real way we all lead something of a "double life."
—Robert Jay Lifton and Eric Markussen, 1991

Plath's treatment of political issues in her poetry is frequently considered opportunistic and perceived only to appear in poems written at the very end of her career. This attitude (which usually stems from an uninformed reaction to the small number of late poems, such as "Daddy" [1962] and "Lady Lazarus" [1962], in which Plath treats controversial historical material) must be challenged by closer study of her poetry and background. Such a limiting view not only masks the complexity of the relationship between politics and subjectivity in her work, it also fails to examine the roots of the uncomfortable reaction generated by Plath's appropriation of historical events such as the Holocaust and Hiroshima. This chapter, then, divides its examination of the workings of politics, history, and myth in Plath's poetry into two parts. After showing the depth of Plath's interest in such traditional American and Romantic concerns as individualism and mechanization, the first section examines her attitude toward the relationship between politics and private experience to show that much of her poetry is caught in an unresolved ambivalence about the uses of poetry (as, broadly, either aesthetic or didactic utterance). This conflict is central to Plath's work and feeds into her often controversial positioning of historical material, with which the second part of this chapter deals. Addressing Plath's treatment of history and myth, I propose that the often emblematic nature of her historic imagery is not a fault but rather a response to the supra-personal nature of recent history and tied to a wider cultural

77

problem in "placing" the Holocaust. This exploration will show that Plath's treatment of political concerns and historical material focuses on the issue of cultural memory, and therefore, that her poems of transcendence and amnesia, while often read as a negation of her political interests, are an integral example of her struggle between desires for mythic transcendence of, or politically motivated remembrance of history.

POLITICS AND POETRY

"A political person"

Even the most cursory examination of Plath's life shows the depth of her intellectual and emotional engagement with political issues. From her youth, she considered herself a "political person"[1] and was strongly swayed by two teachers at Gamaliel Bradford High School in Wellesley, which she attended from the ages of fifteen to eighteen, between 1947 and 1950. Her English teacher, Wilbury Crockett, deeply committed to the American ideal of integrated liberal education, combined his teaching of literature with discussion of specific social and political issues. Wagner-Martin notes,

> if the class read Thomas Mann, he discussed current politics in Germany . . . he also arranged international pen pals, and from 1947 through 1952 Sylvia corresponded with . . . a German student. In these letters . . . she discussed the atomic bomb, the Korean war and its atrocities, the peace movement, and other events on the international scene.[2]

Besides this well-known influence, Ruth Inglis (who attended Wellesley High School several years before Plath, but who encountered the same staff) describes the more direct impact of Plath's history teacher, Raymond Chapman. She writes of her own, and by implication, Plath's probable experience of Chapman's class:

> weary of our affluent, teenaged complacency, [he] had photographic blow-ups made of the inmates of Bergen-Belsen and Buchenwald, Dachau and Auschwitz. These tragic, skeletal inmates looking out from their packed bunk beds in their ragged striped pyjamas stared down upon our crisply shampooed heads, giving us the shudders.[3]

Both Chapman's desire to shake his students' complacency and the strategies he used foreshadow Plath's similar treatment of such material in her late poetry.[4] Plath was further "politicized" shortly after this time by her correspondence with Eddie Cohen, a college student from Chicago, several years her senior, who wrote to her after reading her first published short story, "And Summer Will Not Come Again," in 1950 (it goes without saying, however, that had Plath not shared many of his views, the correspondence would not have taken the form it did). Linda Wagner-Martin writes of Cohen, "He was a rebel; he was a would-be writer. Politics continued to be a refrain in their correspondence,"[5] and describes Plath's powerful antiwar stance in their discussion of America's involvement in Korea.[6]

Wagner-Martin's biography of Plath is one of the few which acknowledges her political concerns. She insists, however, that Plath's interest in politics was motivated by purely personal factors:

> Much of this interest occurred when she was upset about her own life, as if she could legitimately show anger about international subjects when it was difficult for her to express anger about her more personal concerns—or too upsetting for her family.[7]

This is a limiting attitude toward Plath, which views her as ultimately apolitical. It sees her as only reacting to inescapable current events like the Korean War, and as emotional rather than political, for example, in her "proper" female stance against war. Wagner-Martin, then, implicitly concurs with the general view that Plath's treatment of political imagery and concerns in her poetry is the result of an appropriation for altogether selfish reasons. Yet Plath was intellectually interested in political issues, as well as being emotionally stirred by them, and felt the political as integrated not only with her emotional life, but also with literature. The dynamics of this integration make Plath's poetic treatment of the political more complex than many commentators on her work allow.

As early as 1950, when she was eighteen, Plath's intellectual interest in political issues is clear. In this year she published not only poems and short stories, but also a political piece, written with a high school classmate and friend, Perry Norton, titled "Youth's Plea for World Peace," which appeared in what was to become her early staple publisher, *The Christian Science Monitor.* The piece is a passionate, yet logically argued case against the arms race, extolling the aims of a Unitarian peace group, the World Federalists, to which Plath belonged.[8] After high school, as an undergraduate at Smith College (1950–1955), Plath elected to follow a politics course and studied other subjects, such as religion and history, whose relation to social and political concerns were emphasized by her professors.[9] Examination of her unedited letters to her mother show, not only, as Rose notes, that Plath wrote more often about political issues than the edition of *Letters Home* suggests, but also that her comments are considerably more detailed than the published extracts imply. They also frequently deal with social and political issues less obviously overwhelming than Suez, Korea, and the nuclear threat. For example, in a letter Plath wrote to her brother, Warren, in 1952, her comment on the results of the American presidential election appears in the published edition of *Letters Home* as a brief remark, squeezed between talk of dates and schoolwork,

> I am terribly disappointed that Stevenson lost the election. I don't remember knowing who you were for, except for Pogp or Krajewski. But poor mother was for Eisenhower (LH 96).

The unedited letter is much fuller: Plath continues, from the comment above:

> I don't think the need for a change in party justified the horrible combination of men that will take over the Eisenhower crusade—just think of Taft and foreign policy, Jenner and Rules and Civil rights, McCarthy and appropriations and all the rest of the witch-hunters and undemocratic guys. It isn't Eisenhower I'm against, but all the men in his Trojan horse. Stevenson certainly was the Abe Lincoln of our age, and I felt that it was my funeral when I got up the morning after his defeat.[10]

Plath also wrote a letter to her mother on the same day (6 November), no part of which appears in *Letters Home*. In this letter, Plath's usual calm and girlish humor of her early correspondence is replaced by anger and bitterness, both at the election result and at her mother's rejection, by voting for Eisenhower, of Plath's detailed reasoning in an earlier letter (25 October, also unpublished) for giving Stevenson her vote.[11] Although these letters were probably not included because of the amount of repetition between them, they provide one example of the misinterpretation the published edition allows of Plath's depth of interest in political affairs.

In England as well, as an undergraduate at Cambridge (1955–1957), Plath's intellectual involvement with politics continued, not through an elected academic course, such as the one she took at

Smith College, but as part of her everyday life. She mused on this change in an article she wrote on Cambridge life, observing that undergraduates in Britain pursued their interests in politics, music, and the theater independently rather than through their university courses.[12] On her arrival in England, Plath enjoyed the various political lectures given by MPs she attended with her fellow Fulbright scholars.[13] She wrote home shortly after this, on 9 October 1955, of her intention of joining the Labour Club "as I really want to become informed on politics and it seems to have an excellent program,"[14] and asks about the possibility of voting in America if she is resident in England. In the same letter, she also declares a desire to attend Socialist and Communist party meetings, although this comment was probably included, at least partly, to shock her Republican-voting mother. Evidence of Plath's political awareness appears consistently throughout her letters to Aurelia Plath. In 1960, for example, she asks her mother in February for a subscription to *The Nation* to "keep up with American liberal politics,"[15] in April, she exhorts her not to vote for Nixon, and in September argues why everyone should vote for Kennedy.[16] In addition to communicating her concerns with politics and government to her mother, many of the essays Plath wrote both at Smith and at Cambridge refer to broad political and cultural issues such as mechanization, individualism, and democracy. As well as writing a directly political essay, in her Smith history course, on Eric Fromm,[17] she returns to such issues in essays not required to address political questions. In an essay on Blake written at Cambridge, Plath explores Blake's concerns about "the external systems of authority—heavenly and earthy."[18] In an essay written around the same time on Plato and Popper, Plath refers both to Nazism and to Erich Fromm in her discussion of individual and collective good and problems surrounding the equality of all people.[19] In an essay on Dostoevsky, Plath again refers to Nazism when she discusses "the danger of the man-god theory."[20] While these references to Hitler and Nazism seem natural in response to the clear memory of the war in the minds of all her generation, Plath's own emphasis is clearly in terms of issues surrounding individualism and conformity. Examination of Plath's library also reinforces the consistency of her concerns about individualism and mechanization: in her copy of Sinclair Lewis's *Babbit*, she annotates "horrible glittering mechanization of everything including death"; in D. H. Lawrence's *Essays*, she heavily marks his essay, "Democracy;" and in her Smith College politics text on civil rights, she annotates references to McCarthyism.[21]

In relation to the sociopolitical context of her poetry, Plath's interest is evidenced in a cutting she kept from a lecture given in Northampton (the location of Smith College) on the social and political responsibility of the writer—a lecture she probably attended, although there is no date to indicate whether it was when she was a student or a teacher at Smith (1957–1958).[22] While Ted Hughes influenced much of Plath's thinking and thus her poetry during the years they spent together, the relation between poetry and politics was an issue which, it appears, held little interest for him, but about which Plath felt strongly enough to pursue independently. In autumn 1961, both poets responded to a request by the *London Magazine* to write about the context of their poetry. Plath wrote about the relationship between poetry and "the issues of our time which preoccupy me," declaring that such issues influence her writing "in a sidelong fashion" (JP 92). Hughes, in contrast, wrote in more generally aesthetic terms about the importance of the poet's sensitivity to his gift. Hughes *does* mention political and social issues, but only in relation to Romantic poets such as Wordsworth, Blake, and Coleridge, and then only to develop his point about the importance of the writer being true to his gift.[23] Plath's divergence with Hughes over the political context of literature finds further support in her criticism, in a letter to her mother, of an interpretation Hughes gave about his play, *The Harvesting:*

> Don't take his elaborate metaphysical explanations too seriously . . . I think [it] reads perfectly as a symbolic invasion of private lives and dreams by the mechanical war-law and inhumanity such as is behind the germ-warfare laboratory in Maryland. (LH 401–2)

Plath, then, was clearly more deeply and consistently interested in politics than most critics allow. In addition, her linking of personal experience and wider political concerns, found only in the late poetry (and perceived, therefore, as opportunistic), occurs throughout her other writing. In her letters and in her journals, Plath frequently writes of the political and the personal in the same breath, in her comments both on inescapable "events" and on more general political concerns. In response to the Suez Crisis in 1956, Plath declares to her mother, "Well, between my private crisis and the huge crisis aroused by Britain's incredible and insane bombing of Egypt the universe is in a state of chaos!" (LH 282). The self-directed irony does not lesson the importance of Plath's connection of the two "crises," rather it indicates her awareness of the connection she cannot avoid making. In her early journals, Plath's soul-searching on issues of feminism and materialism often directly results from her personal concerns about marriage. She writes in 1951 concerning her doubts about a friend, Dick Norton, as a suitable husband and moves from the specific to the general, to declare her mistrust of the "material attitude" of many men toward women (J 38). Plath also annotated her academic books with personalized comments. In a section of her copy of José Ortega y Gasset's *The Revolt of the Masses* which deals with how the "masses" or pseudo-intellectuals had invaded the intellectual sphere, Plath annotates "Eddie?," a reference to her correspondent Eddie Cohen. In Eric Fromm's *Escape from Freedom*, next to his comment that, "people are not sadistic or masochistic, but there is a constant oscillation between the active and the passive side of the symbiotic complex," Plath annotates, "explains the apparently contradictory 'mutually exclusive' urges I have to dominate and use the weak and to be directed and mastered by others at the same time."[24] As I emphasized in the introduction, however, it is wise to avoid making simple distinctions between Plath's intellectual and emotional attitude toward any text. While she approached such texts with more than an intellectual interest, she did not "use" them as mere explanations for her own personal states of mind. Her annotations to Fromm's book, for instance, also show her attention to the intellectual coherence of his argument: when Fromm declares that the way for societies to avoid becoming prey to authoritarian control is for all individuals to find meaning and purpose in their work, Plath annotates, "sounds great, but *how*? What of the endless routine of men in the huge machine factories etc.?"[25] Further, in an interview in 1962 for the BBC, when asked why she includes references to Dachau and Hiroshima in the poetry she was writing at the time, Plath indicates her awareness of the links she makes between political and private histories, links which I will show are integral to her poetry. She declares that she is interested both because her Austro-German roots make her concerns with the brutalities of Nazi Germany "uniquely intense" and also because she's "rather a political person as well."[26]

This invasion of the political (both as concerns about general issues such as conformism and mechanization, and with inescapable contemporary and recent events) into the emotional sphere of the individual affected many in Plath's generation. The 1950s in America are often viewed as a period of prosperity, conformity, and complacency after America's (economically as well as mili-

tarily) successful intervention in World War II. Yet the memory
of this war and the rapid escalation of the Cold War, with all its
overtones of potential nuclear holocaust, ran as a nightmarish
undercurrent to such apparent complacency, finding expression
in the scare tactics of McCarthyism. As Richard Gray writes,

> No consensus, however, is quite as complete as it seems . . . abundance
> breeds its own anxieties, not least the fear of losing the comforts one
> enjoys; in many ways, the calm society is the one most susceptible to
> sudden, radical fits of panic. This uneasiness that hovered beneath
> the bland surfaces of the times found its expression in many forms
> . . . in the political life of the period . . . perhaps the most significant
> expression of this fear of invasion, subversion, or even destruction by
> covert agencies was the phenomenon known as McCarthyism.

David Caute notes other postwar anxieties:

> Despite material progress, this was a time of universal shocks and
> traumas. The Celebration [of America's war success] remained
> haunted by the war itself, the loss of life; by the coming of air power
> shrinking the world; by the atomic bomb, an agent of mass destruc-
> tion; then by Korea—the return of the ghost at high noon. Though
> science, technology and centralization lent wings to material progress,
> these alien, remote powers and mysteries also frightened people into
> a state of largely incoherent resentment, generating a need for scape-
> goats—spies, treacherous scientists, pederastic State Department of-
> ficials with an allegiance elsewhere. In short—Communism![27]

Indeed, in the fear and disorientation it inspired, the nuclear
threat itself contributed to such social consensus: as Robert von
Hallberg notes,

> Nuclear War was the perfect political subject for an age of consensus.
> Everyone ought to be terrified of the prospect; the normal political
> divisions of the population . . . seem irrelevant in the fact of nuclear
> threat.[28]

Yet, as Robert Jay Lifton and Eric Markusen note, such apparent
consensus only partially masks anxiety or terror.

> A valuable study of the generation subjected to the "duck and cover"
> nuclear air-raid drills in American schools during the 1950s and
> 1960s brings out a characteristic psychological sequence: initial anxi-
> ety or even terror give way to long periods of suppression or numbing,
> punctuated in turn by outpourings of anxiety and nightmares evoked

by events inwardly associated with nuclear danger. In a real way we all lead something of a "double life."[29]

Although Plath was old enough to escape such school drills, this description of the terrifying, self-protective "doubling" has broad parallels throughout her poetry (most specifically in her conflicts between radicalism and conformity[30]) and shows that the emotional nature of Plath's involvement with political concerns reflected, and perhaps characterized the relationship of American society with such issues at the time.

American Concerns: Individualism and Conformism—"I Am An American"

Although a political content is generally identified only in Plath's later work, many early poems deal with the same themes of mechanization, conformity, and cultural amnesia evident in the late poetry. In "The Thin People" (1957), Plath explores the theme of dehumanization, characterized by the eponymous figures. The danger they represent (either as aggressors or as victims of dehumanization, the Jewish subjects of the Holocaust) is heightened due to man's comfortable ignorance, and cultural amnesia:

> . . . They
> Are unreal, we say:
> It was only in a movie, it was only
> In a war making evil headlines when we
> Were small.
>
> (CP 64)

Plath also links the dangers of dehumanization, conformism, and amnesia in the later "Daddy" (1962), explored below. In "Nightshift" (1957), Plath views humankind's slavery to the machine as resulting in his dehumanization—the factory is more lifelike than the sterile and automated men who circle, unceasingly tending its machines (CP 77). Two years later, in "Suicide Off Egg Rock" (1959), the despair of the suicidal figure is described in terms of the infectious dehumanization of the industrial landscape which surrounds it; indeed the landscape is implicated in the man's despair that he is "A machine to breathe and beat forever" (CP 115). Again, Plath links this theme of man's dehumanization by the machine to the added dangers of cultural amnesia in her late poem "Getting There" (1962), explored below.

These earlier works are probably ignored as examples of "political" poetry because they are not as emotionally charged as later poems such as "Daddy" or "Getting There." This is not to say that Plath was less preoccupied by these themes in her early poetry, but rather that in most of such work, she aimed to write in the distanced, dry, stoical style of the formalist poets (such as Auden) whom she admired at the time. As Plath declares in exasperation to her mother in 1956, "They [Cambridge magazine critics] abhor polished wit and neat forms, which, of course, is exactly what I purpose to write and when they criticize something for being 'quaintly artful' or 'merely amusing' it is all I can do not to shout 'That's all I meant it to be!'" (LH 214). An early (though undated) poem, while written in the same rigid forms that characterize her early work, shows an emotional involvement in social and political issues not found in the early poems mentioned above. It deals with individualism, conformity, and mechanization, and contrasts strongly with the "juvenilia" available in the *Collected Poems*. The first stanza of this four stanza poem gives a taste both of its strict form and of its powerful emotion:

I Am An American

We all know that we are created equal:
All conceived in the hot blood belly
Of the twentieth century turbine;
All born from the same sheet
Of purple three-cent postage stamps;
All spewed like bright green dollar bills
From the same government press;
All baptized with Chanel Number Five
In the name of the Bendix, the Buick,
    and the Batting Average.[31]

Although undated, "I Am An American" was probably written at school or at Smith College.[32] It expresses the traditionally Romantic concerns about mechanization, conformity, and individualism explored in chapter 1. Such concerns reached a peak in 1950s America, and were reflected in many of the texts Plath studied at Smith (on a variety of courses), such as *Babbitt* (1922), *Escape from Freedom* (1941), *The Lonely Crowd* (1950), and *The Revolt of the Masses* (1932), all of which are discussed below. "I Am An American" shows Plath's emotional and intellectual engagement with these issues. The poem is a quasi-religious parody of a hymn to America and democracy, responding to an America she saw as lacking individuality and warped by anti-communist feeling (itself a way of inducing conformity to some rigid idea of Americanness). The poem's title refers ironically to the Hearst-sponsored anti-communist "I Am An American" events held around the country in the early 1950s, which were another form of conformist influence on the American individual.[33] The "easy democracy of mind" to which the speaker declares, in the third stanza, all Americans are prey, appears as inimical to real democracy, which, for Plath, rests on individualism. Social standardization and the smug, easy conformity of a nation which believes it personifies God's ideal society appears to Plath as a hideous twisting of the democratic ideal. Her concerns in this poem mirror those of Sinclair Lewis in *Babbitt*, which Plath read at Smith. She refers to the population receiving their ideas in "ten easy lessons / With a money-back guarantee," recalling the anti-hero Babbitt's own approval of his son's interest in such commercial and automatized forms of "education." For Plath as for Lewis (and indeed many postindustrial writers), conformity appears partly as a result of such mechanization, and the glorification in mechanization is at the expense of man's individuality and soul. The machine or the inventor of the machine is God; humankind's spiritual barrenness is connoted in Plath's revision of Genesis, where it is Edison, not God, who says, "'Let there be light'." Plath views the "averaging" of the individual as a result of much of what America, as a modern society, is proudest: the mass transportation on the faceless "super highways" (which recur in the later "Private Ground" [1959] as more explicitly oppressive and antihuman) and the standardization of precooked, prepacked, even prebitten (in the form of "bite-sized") food. People are "spewed" "From that same government press" as sheets of stamps and dollar bills—they are identical "products" whose value in such a society is seen in purely monetary, materialistic terms. Even freedom of speech appears to Plath as suspect. While "we are all free to speak our piece from the ivory soapbox / And to letter our liberal opinions," such opinions are standardized, unthinkingly assimilated: "We all know that certain truths are self-evident: / That we believe in liberty and justice for all." Because of this standardization, Plath views such ideals as unworkable in practice—freedom of speech is only granted to those conformist enough not to use it; it is also, ironically, exclusive to American society, jealously guarded by a "Members Only" door standing beside the Statue of Liberty. The soapbox, then, is "ivory," not only as an ironic reference to the popular and heavily advertised Ivory soap, but because it is an ivory tower of American privilege. In this, Plath could well be responding to the more extreme results of McCarthyism whereby, depending how one used one's freedom of speech, an American citizen could be refused the right to travel and a foreign national could be deported from or refused entry to America.[34] As a writer and potential academic when Senator Joseph McCarthy's political witch hunts against the mistrusted intellectual professions were still causing anger and fear in the academic community, freedom of speech was a topic of great concern to Plath. Butscher notes that in Plath's second year at Smith, "the student newspaper announced that the House Committe on Un-American Activities had listed Smith as one of the colleges found to have three or more Communist members on its staff. An investigation was almost sure to follow,"[35] and in the back of her copy of Eric Fromm's *Escape from Freedom,* she notes several points about the needs and purposes of academic freedom. Several years after leaving America, her concerns with freedom of expression are undiminished, evidenced in the close interest she paid to the progress of the *Lady Chatterley* trial in London in 1960, taking detailed notes, many of which remain at Smith. Freedom of speech was not only a private concern—as a writer and a citizen (as well as constitutionally) she saw it as a central element of democracy, and her perception that most of American society, while proud of the right, failed to use it, makes the second stanza of "I Am An American" one of the more striking of this unusually emotive and venomous early (pre-1959) poem.

Plath did not confine these concerns, with the need to think for one's self and use the right to freedom of speech, to her poetry. She also expressed these interests in an undated (although pre-1961, the year of Kennedy's election), unpublished collage made out of magazine cuttings. The central dominating figure is that of President Eisenhower, holding a fan of playing cards, "playing" with America's future. Nixon (his vice president) appears in miniature at his side, perhaps whispering in Ike's ear. The theme of man's foolish playing with serious issues continues in an image of a satellite superimposed on a golfball (Eisenhower's hobby was golf), and a picture of two men playing with a "Scalectric" game which transforms into a jet fighter. Surrounding these pictures are various smaller images: the statement "sleep," a stein of beer, and a couple asleep under eye-shields, showing Plath's connection of the complacency of individual members of society with the self-satisfied irresponsibility of its politicians. Not only does the former encourage the latter, but the image of the couple asleep under eye-shields (sarcastically captioned "It's 'HIS and HER Time' all over America") implies that people are not only blind to political realities, they are also blind to each other. A life-size image of a packet of indigestion tablets placed on Eisenhower's desk removes any doubt about Plath's attitude toward such a society: it is, for her, unstomachable.[36]

Political anxieties about the conformity and mechanization of modern America are a traditional American intellectual interest, deeply embedded in the culture, and Plath's own carefully thoughtout personal philosophy clearly aligns itself with such concerns. She saw herself as a humanist, with a strong emphasis on a kind of Nietzschean individualism. In an essay written at Smith, "Religion As I See It," Plath's statement of her beliefs is precise and heartfelt: she describes her humanistic belief in the impossibility of perfection, or even the absolutes of "good" and "bad" in a manmade and therefore imperfect world, and denies any higher power than that of nature and "man's" intelligence, concluding that "His purpose is his own, and so is his destiny."[37] In a later essay written at the end of her religion course, she links her belief in individualism with a conviction about the importance of individual struggle, declaring that she can always adapt to new, even unpleasant experiences (such as premonitions of war) and is, further, "glad even of the pain and hurt which have heightened my sensibilities and awareness."[38] Plath's high estimation of the value of struggle is also reflected in her annotation of Ortega y Gasset's *The Revolt of the Masses.* He writes,

> All life is the struggle, the effort to be itself. The difficulties which I meet with in order to realize my existence are precisely what awakens and mobilizes my activities, my capabilities.

Plath responds:

> My *own* philosophy—out of struggle, conflict, hardship, comes a strong, vital, creative nature.[39]

For Plath life is, by definition, a series of changes, and the difficulties encountered are necessary for strengthening the individual on his or her way through it; it is this conviction which, as the last chapter showed, forms one of the bases of her (often critically derided) courting and privileging of extreme experience. This Nietzschean privileging of the "pain and hurt" of the struggles of life implies that Plath's interest in such situations in her late poetry was not merely due to some psychological imbalance, some morbid or neurotic desire to experience pain; such an attitude is grounded in Plath's consciously thoughtout personal philosophy.

The ideological commitment to individualism was fore-grounded for Plath, as for much of society in 1950s America, by the recent events of the Second World War and by contemporary fears of communism. While for many in Europe, Nietzsche's philosophy had become associated with the ideas of Aryan supremacy of the Nazis, in America at the time, a Nietzschean individualism stood in direct opposition to Nazism and all forms of authoritarianism. Many of Plath's Smith College texts, as well as popular books of the time, approach individualism in relation both to the conformity of American society in the first part of the century, and to the Nazi and Soviet totalitarian regimes. Plath's main text from her government class, *Elements of Democratic Government* (1951), considers the American tradition of individualism in comparison to the Nazi and Soviet regimes. A political study, it comments in detail, however, on psychological and sociological issues relating to individualism, declaring, for instance (which Plath highlights), that political freedom is not an end in itself but a "means to the liberation of personality, and justified only to the degree that it serves that purpose."[40] The cover blurb on Plath's copy of Eric Fromm's *Escape from Freedom* (a set text on her first year history course), also indicates the contemporary interest in psychological considerations relating to the political questions of individualism and democracy. It reads "Freedom is frightening—Why? A psychologist examines modern man's choice between flight to authoritarianism and achievement of democracy."[41] David Riesman's *The Lonely Crowd,* which Plath also studied at Smith, uses an anthropological and sociological method to do much the same thing, describing contemporary America as "outer-directed," group-orientated, and so very conformist. Plath approves of the author's censorious view of such conformity, writing "good" next to his conclusion that,

> Today . . . all little pigs go to market; none stay home; all have roast beef, if any do; and all say "we-we."[42]

Ortega y Gasset's essay, *The Revolt of the Masses,* also acquired by Plath at Smith, explores similar issues and is also heavily marked. But it is Eric Fromm's book which made the central, lasting impression on Plath—she underlined and annotated it throughout and continued to refer to his theories in essays written both at

Smith and later at Cambridge.[43] For Fromm, writing in the 1940s, but very relevant to the "reds under the bed" fears of the 1950s, the threat to American democracy lay not in the infiltration of external ideas (the fear which galvanised McCarthy's witch-hunts), but internally, both to the country's institutions and to its individuals. Fromm writes of

> The truth that has been so forcefully formulated by John Dewey that I express the thought in his words: "The serious threat to our democracy" he says, "is not the existence of foreign totalitarian states. It is the existence within our own institutions of conditions which have given a victory to external authority, discipline, uniformity and dependence upon The Leader in foreign countries. The battlefield is also accordingly here—within ourselves and our institutions."[44]

Plath underlined the last sentence and marks the whole section with an enthusiastic "yes!" in the margin. Fromm sees these conditions ("which have given a victory to external authority") as a result of man's fear of freedom. He describes the individual's response to this fear as taking one of two forms: conformity (as seen in contemporary America) and the more extreme version, authoritarianism (seen in Nazi Germany and the Soviet Union). Fromm declares that the modern freedom from older systems such as the Church creates a sense of aloneness that frightens the individual, who often becomes victim to sadistic and masochistic desires:

> The annihilation of the individual self and the attempts to overcome thereby the unbearable feeling of powerlessness are only one side of the masochistic striving. The other side is the attempt to become part of a bigger and more powerful whole outside of oneself, to submerge and participate in it. This power can be a person, an institution, God, the nation, conscience, or a psychic compulsion.[45]

This description may well represent the root of Plath's unresolvable ambivalence about Romanticism (an ambivalence inherent *in* Romanticism): a conflict between the desire to submerge one's self in nature, and the desire to transcend or remain apart from such a power, which informs, in political terms, the discussion in the preceding chapter of "Ariel" (1962) and D. H. Lawrence's short story, "The Woman Who Rode Away." Fromm sees the result of such conformism in dire terms:

> The person who gives up his individual self and becomes an automaton, identical with millions of other automatons around him, need

not feel alone and anxious any more. But the price he pays, however, is high: it is the loss of the self.[46]

Escape from Freedom was important for Plath in a number of ways. Essentially, Fromm uses his analysis of Nazism to define potentially universal problems. While accepting that Nazism's rise was "moulded by socio-economic factors," he saw it rooted in a "psychological problem"[47] that also affected (albeit in a lesser way) American society. His combination of psychology and history appears to have influenced Plath's own association of the two in her later poetry. Fromm's exploration of Nazism concentrates on how "the Nazi system expresses an extreme form of the character structure which we have called 'authoritarian,'"[48] and he examines, in detail, examples of neurotic symptoms that are exhibited, in an extreme form, in Nazism. In Plath's poem "Daddy," the controversial lines that begin "Every woman adores a Fascist" (CP 223) are trying to make a similar, though gendered, point. Throughout the poem, the speaker and "daddy," masochistic and sadistic figures, respectively, appear dependent upon each other. While this relates, to a certain extent, to Plath's exploration of the master-slave dialectic (as I will explore in the next chapter), both figures' connection to Nazism (as Jew and fascist) link their dependence on each other (lack of individuation) to Fromm's theorization. In the speaker's consciously disturbing overstatement that all women desire subjection to the physical and emotional violence of the fascist, Plath asserts that while the archetypal male figure appearing in the rest of the poem (as father and lover) connotes the escape from freedom through sadism, the female figure's adoration of the fascist is an extreme result of a more characteristically feminine escape from the feelings of aloneness associated with freedom through masochistic strivings. Freedom for the woman, in the context of "Daddy," is freedom from the authoritarian father figure. Political realities (in the form of Nazism) and psychological difficulties (in the form of neurosis) are inescapably linked both for Fromm and for Plath. Thus Plath's lines in "Daddy" are both psychological and political. They are psychological, not because "Daddy" is about Plath's relationship with her father, but in the sense that Plath uses the situation depicted in the poem to explore the dynamics of her attitude toward individualism. Her intellectual and moral approval of individualism contrasts with a consciously explored ambivalence in her desire for such freedom, an ambivalence which Plath notes in her copy of Fromm's book,[49] and which she sums up in the final line, so that in asserting to the father "I'm through" may mean either that the speaker is "through with daddy" or free from him, or that she is (in relation to the imagery of the black telephone in stanza 14) through *to* him, having made a final and inescapable connection with him, having, in short, given up her freedom.

Plath's academic studies of political issues such as individualism and mechanization, then, are not only reflected in the Audenesque political poetry she was writing while attending college, but heavily influenced much of her later, more directly personal work. The later "political" poems are not, however, more egotistical or less intellectually rigorous because of their lack of distance between subjective experience and political concerns. Rather, such late poems consciously work to emphasize the impossibility of drawing a boundary between politics and subjectivity.

Politics and Subjectivity—"Mary's Song"

"Mary's Song," written in 1962, deals with similar concerns of automatism and dehumanization expressed in the earlier "Night Shift" and "Suicide Off Egg Rock." The later poem, however, is able to explore these issues in a more complex way because it consciously foregrounds the dynamics of the relationship between intellectual concerns and personal emotional involvement. "Mary's Song" explores the ambiguous nature of technological achievement (as both good and evil), and examines humankind's position in such a world of equivocal "progress" (an interest Plath explored in relation to De Quincey, as chapter 1 shows, and a central concern to writers such as Lewis in *Babbitt* and Aldous Huxley in *Brave New World* [1932], a book Plath also owned). Yet these are not the primary concerns of the poem. Plath deals with the sociopolitical theme in a more complex and emotionally involved way than she achieved in the early poems precisely because the political is not the central impetus of "Mary's Song." In February 1959, at what was to become a turning point in her poetry, Plath wrote in her journal of her desire to turn away from her more clearly mythic subjects and write about

> The real world. Real situations, behind which the great gods play the drama of blood, lust and death. (J 296)

This conscious change of tactic is not a change in Plath's interests ("the drama of blood, lust and death," in her melodramatic terms), but a change in approach to them. In this period of her career, she was consciously moving away from abstraction and overt fantasy toward the concretely personal. "Mary's Song" is thus manifestly a personal account of a mother's fears for her child. Yet behind this "real situation" is the more universal "drama" of the poem's frame of reference: the political, religious, and historical concerns which are inseparable from the situation depicted. The subject of the poem, the child as "golden," is therefore inextricably associated with the "holy fire" of man's knowledge and achievement, of which it may become both part and victim; the "holy fire" itself is both good and evil, both knowledge and destruction, purity and persecution—it is "the same fire."[50]

The child is only referred to twice in "Mary's Song," in the title and the last line, surrounding the poem without being mentioned in its body. Plath further heightens this oblique approach by setting both references in a religious framework—the title is an ironic play on the traditional song of Mary, the Magnificat, a rejoicing in the renewal of the covenant between God and man, incarnated in Mary's child. The irony becomes clearer as the poem progresses away from such rejoicing and toward the two-edged fears of the speaker for her child as Christ-like sacrificial victim: "O golden child the world will kill and eat" (CP 257).[51] The body of the poem moves between these two statements about the child in a series of quickly transforming images, from religion, through history and politics, and back to religion. Religious purity, in the form of the "holy fire," is viewed as contaminated by religious persecution; such fire is also the fire of the auto-da-fé of the Inquisition and of the crematoria of the Nazi regime. Humankind's technological achievement appears in similarly ambivalent terms. Not only is humanity open to dehumanization by the machinery of its technological "progress" (in the earlier "Night Shift," people are perceived as less valuable than the machinery of the factory; here the astronaut is merely "emptied" into space by his shuttle), it may also be destroyed by it.[52] The space shuttle's rocket burners are described as ovens, reminiscent of the crematoria (instrumental in the persecution of the Jews), yet described in transcendental terms. In its conclusion, the poem returns to a more mystical stance, noting that, by its nature, humanity is implicated in destruction:

> It is a heart,
> This holocaust I walk in . . .

Whatever drives man after power, knowledge, and transcendental purity ("progress") necessarily also contains the seeds of destruction, of man's inhumanity to man. The word "holocaust" refers beyond the recent genocide of the Jews. The Greek root of the word (as "burnt whole") also links to Plath's divided view of the pain and necessity of creative life (explored in the last chapter), and implies that the situation described in "Mary's Song" is that explored by Greek tragedy, as old as mankind, and inescapable. These sweeping political and religious fears become centered in the last line on the child, as Christ-like victim, sacrificed to the world in being born, either in being killed by the world or in becoming part of the killing world.

The difficulty in establishing any clear boundary between the private and the public in "Mary's Song" can lead critics to view the poem as the expression of purely private anxieties. Robyn Marsack, for instance, declares that it "is less a case of Plath's thinking herself into another woman's mind than of using a particular woman and all she stands for, as a point of departure, a ground from which to explore the feelings of both mother and victim. Her readiness to see herself as victim is unnerving."[53] Yet Plath's letters clearly show that, for her, such a simple boundary between internal and external worlds did not exist. Political concerns and historical imagery are not simply used as enabling structures or metaphors through which to explore her own experience (as Wagner-Martin might argue), but are a framework of emotional and political history from which personal experience cannot escape. In December 1961, for instance, a year before "Mary's Song," Plath consciously connects her fears for her child with her political concerns, writing to her mother of the oppressing effect of reading in *The Nation* of the Cold War and its effects "I began to wonder if there was any point in trying to bring up children in such a mad, self-destructive world (LH 438). In an earlier letter, Plath shows more clearly her blurring of such boundaries (in this case, between her child and children in general), in her description of an Easter "ban the bomb" march she attended in Trafalgar Square in 1960, expressing her pride that her child's first real outing was in protest against the lack of future other children have because of nuclear fallout (LH 378). The way in which "Mary's Song" moves by ambiguous connections, between political and religious precepts, between the indivisible nature of good and evil, and between man's technological advances (as will be seen, Plath does appear to see mechanization as something produced specifically by men), which may be used both for productive and destructive purposes (such as space flight and genocide), reflects, and is a part of the blurred boundaries between emotional or personal and intellectual political concerns.

"Mary's Song" is thus more powerful in its treatment of political issues than the earlier "Night Shift" or "Suicide Off Egg Rock" because of its recognition of the indivisible nature of private experience and the political world. In common with critics such as Seamus Heaney, Marjorie Perloff defines Plath's effective poems as those in which the boundaries between public and private are blurred.[54] Perloff views the relation between private (or personal) and more general concerns in Plath's poetry in terms of "angst and animism." She sees Plath as a writer of "'oracular poetry' in the tradition of such later eighteenth-century poets as Smart, Cowper, Collins and Blake,"[55] and writes,

> The oracular poem, the poem of ecstasis, is, by definition, one that centres on the self, a poem in which "objectivity" is impossible because the seer, unable to detach himself sufficiently to describe the things outside himself, can give voice only to his own emotional responses. If Sylvia Plath's early poetry strikes the reader as being too "careful" and "seldom exciting" it is no doubt because prior to 1960, the date that she herself considered the diving line between Juvenilia and her real poetry, she did not yet understand that third-person description, narrative or ironic observation were alien to her poetic vision.[56]

Perloff states that

> In the poetry of angst and animism, not only the flower and animals but even an object may be endowed with human traits.[57]

This strong personal connection the "ecstatic" poet feels toward the objects of the world, which Perloff perceives as characterizing Plath's imagination, can also be extended beyond Perloff's theorization to connect the poet with abstract political issues. Because politics was a concern of emotional as well as intellectual importance to Plath in her early poems, where she tries to achieve a dry, distanced tone, the political concerns come across in a lifeless way. One of the problematic results, however, of Plath's connection between private, individual concerns and wider political ones is that the late poems may not immediately appear to contain both political and personal issues. Poems such as "Daddy," "Lady Lazarus," "Fever 103°," "Getting There," and "Mary's Song" (all written in 1962), through a combination of intimate-sounding title, emotive tone, and first-person narration, suggest that something autobiographically personal is being written. Yet, the moot point is, as Rose asserts, that for all human beings (not only "ecstatic poets"),

> The division between history and subjectivity, between external and internal reality, between the trials of the world and the trials of the mind, is a false one.[58]

For Plath, the injustices of history and her sweeping political anxieties about conformism and individualism did not simply reflect her emotional wounds and worries, they were as real and immediate to her as such individual hurts and personal anxieties, and she consciously explores such a situation in her poetry. In a BBC radio interview that accompanied a reading of many of her late poems, Peter Orr asked Plath whether her recent socially and historically aware poems came from her reading rather than her experience. Plath replied, famously, denying that they did:

> I think my poems immediately come out of the sensuous and emotional experiences I have, but I must say I cannot sympathize with these cries from the heart that are informed by nothing except a needle or a knife, or whatever it is . . . Personal experience . . . should be relevant, and relevant to the larger things, the bigger things, such as Hiroshima and Dachau and so on.[59]

Not only, Plath is saying, should the personal experience depicted in poetry be relevant to "larger things," but those larger things, in the form of history and political concerns, are part of these "sensuous and emotional" personal experiences; in her later poetry she consciously asserts and attempts to enact the impossibility of drawing a line between history or political concerns, and subjectivity.

The Uses of Poetry—"Getting There"

Plath's personalized treatment of political concerns and historical imagery is not, then, opportunistic in the late poems, as the blurred boundaries between the personal and the political in these poems express her perception of a link between the two which, as her other writing shows, she felt from her adolescence. Yet, accepting this, Plath's treatment of history and political issues remains problematic, caught up in her wider intellect-emotion dialectic, and characterized here in her conflict about the uses of poetry. Jacqueline Rose mistakenly shifts the focus away from this central dilemma in her assertion that the ambiguity in Plath's deployment of the political lies in a conflict in her political ideals, between democracy (which Plath fears leads to conformity) and individualism. Rose writes about Plath's annotations of *The Revolt of the Masses:*

> down the margins of Ortega Y Gassett's *The Revolt of the Masses,* generally considered to be one of the most reactionary texts on cultural politics of the 1950s, she voices her enthusiastic agreement with its critique of the "commonplace" in American culture, although she condemns the "aristocratic bias" of the book.[60]

Certainly, Plath felt a conflict between an individualistic critique of conformity and a desire to conform to the *Ladies Home Journal* image of the young woman. Nancy Hunter Steiner notes Plath's attitude toward the group of radicals who shared their dorm at Smith College: "she actively disliked the little band of rebels in the house. Their bare feet, rude manners, and coarse language offended her."[61] In an essay Plath wrote entitled "America! America!," published in 1963, she, on the one hand, celebrates the egalitarian nature of American schooling, yet on the other, condemns it for its suppression of individuality and genius (JP 34–38). In her early poem discussed above, "I Am An American," a similar ambivalence toward the competing claims of democracy and individualism that was felt by many of the educated members of Plath's generation is evident. In this, Plath is perhaps subject to an "anxiety of influence" in cultural rather than purely literary terms. Yet the specifically political conflict Rose sees, between individualism's critique of the power of the commonplace and leftist ideals of democracy, did not exist for Plath in these terms. Rose bases her argument on Plath's approving annotations to *The Revolt of the Masses,* which she describes as a reactionary book, imposing on its American left-wing readership British left-wing ideals of collectivism. Yet Ortega y Gassett's concerns with individualism and democracy, were, as I showed above, shared in America by left and right alike. Plath's conflict between her ideals of individualism and democracy are an interesting feature of her work, but they are more usefully explored, as shown in chapter 1, in poetic terms; in the Romantic conflict between the poet as a "man of the people" (in Romantic, gender-biased terms), or as some isolated oracle, speaking from a position of greater knowledge to the people.

Plath's "political" poetry, rather, is caught in an unresolved conflict between the prominence of private experience and wider

political concerns. While "Mary's Song" uses the political primarily in terms of (albeit inescapable) framework and imagery, in
"Getting There," written in the same part of 1962, this is not the
case; indeed, due to the expectation that Plath will use the political
as image or frame of reference (as opposed to theme), the poem
has often suffered serious misreading. If, as in "Mary's Song,"
the private experience of the speaker were the central theme of
the poem, Judith Kroll's reading of "Getting There" (cited below)
as a simple progression toward personal transcendence would fit,
and other critics' assertions about Plath's selfish misuse of horrific
historical facts would be justified. Perloff, who *does* see the poem
as political, says it fails, however:

> The less successful poems in *Ariel* are, to my mind, those like "The
> Swarm" and "Getting There" that try to make a comment on the
> horrors of war or the viciousness of the Nazi ethos. In an interview
> of 1962 Sylvia Plath insisted that, although she was naturally con-
> cerned about such issues as the "genetic effects of fallout," these con-
> temporary problems were not the mainspring of the poetry . . .
> "surely the great use of poetry is pleasure" . . . didacticism is essen-
> tially alien to the "ecstatic" poet.[62]

Perloff bases her argument on a selective reading of Plath's own
words, influenced by her desire to situate Plath unproblematically
in a literary tradition. The statement Perloff uses is (actually)
taken from "Context" (1962), an essay Plath wrote in response to
the questionnaire from the *London Magazine* mentioned earlier.
The published article, in which twenty-six poets are featured, is
prefaced by information about the questions put to each poet
which they were asked "to answer individually or to use as a basis
for a general statement about the writing of poetry today." Of
the seven questions, the first two have a directly political content:
"Would poetry be more effective, i.e., interest more people more
profoundly, if it were concerned with the issues of our time?" and
"Do you feel your views on politics or religion influence the kind
of poetry you write? Alternatively, do you think poetry has uses
as well as pleasure?" The next five questions cover more formalist
areas such as poetic diction, the lyrical form, contemporary literary influences, and whether the period is a good or bad one in
which to write poetry. Plath's response centered on the first two
questions, on the direct relationship between the sociopolitical
context of her poetry.[63] Plath writes, as Perloff notes, of her anxieties about nuclear fallout and the marriage of big business and
the military in America, and carefully situates her poems as "de-

flections" of these concerns rather than an "escape," because "the real issues of our time are the real issues of every time" (JP 92). Yet Plath's clarity here conceals a contradiction in her ideas about the purposes of poetry. She does declare, as Perloff notes, that, "that unicorn-thing—a real poem" has its value as an autonomous object rather than as a vehicle of communication, showing, in this reification of the poem, the still strongly persisting influence of New Critical theories of literature:

> Surely the great use of poetry is its pleasure—not its influence as religious or political propaganda. Certain poems and lines of poetry seem as solid and miraculous to me as church altars or the coronation of queens must seem to people who revere quite different images. I am not worried that poems reach relatively few people. (JP 93)

Yet Plath *also* perceives the poem as a vehicle of some kind of message: as communicating something good, teaching, or healing, by comparing its "distance" as reaching, "farther than the words of a classroom teacher or the prescriptions of a doctor."

Plath's belief in the importance of poetry as communication is backed up earlier in her life when, in 1955, she writes to her mother about her desire to teach in Africa for a year as a way to combine her "creative urges with a kind of service to the world," in her efforts to "counteract McCarthy and much adverse opinion about the US" (LH 163). In the period in which Plath wrote, of Cold War fear and McCarthy's witch-hunts against artists and intellectuals with inappropriate ideologies, such a connection between art and politics was often unavoidable. Plath also writes in 1956 (a year before the overtly political "Night Shift" and "The Thin People"), in more direct relation to her poetry, about developing "a 'new line'":

> bringing the larger social world of other people into my poems. I have been terribly limited hitherto . . . Now I am making a shift. The world and its problems of an individual in this particular civilization are going to be forged into my discipline. (LH 222)

Plath's conflict, between ideas of poetry as either a timeless mythic object or as a political and/or personal communication, characterizes the period in which she wrote, a time of shift from poetry as mythology, dream, and archetype toward the poetry of autobiography and occasion. Richard Gray, in his panoramic study of twentieth-century poetry in America, describes this first phase of the postwar period, quoting W. H. Auden, Plath's sometime poetic "god":

> Writing in 1952 . . . he observed [that most poems] fall into one of two categories: those in which "the historic occasion is . . . on the outside and the general significance on the inside" and those in which the reverse is the case. Auden called these, respectively, "occasional" and "mythological poetry," then added, "it is impossible not to recognise . . . the increase of interest shown today, both by poets and critics, in myth, and a corresponding turning away, on the part of poets at least, from occasional subjects, whether political or private."[64]

Gray sums up this attitude using the words of Richard Wilbur, another strong early influence on Plath's work:

> "Poems are not addressed to anybody in particular," Wilbur declared, "The poem . . . is a conflict with disorder, not a message from one person to another."[65]

Gray contrasts Wilbur's attitude with that of other poets such as John Berryman, Robert Lowell, and Adrienne Rich (who all started out as formalists before writing in a more directly personal way) who represent the movement back toward the personal, recovering, in Gray's terms, "one of the major impulses, probably the major one, in American tradition,"[66] and who strongly influenced Plath's later poetry. Plath's conflict between these two uses of poetry characterizes both the nature of the period and the shifts in direction of her most powerful contemporary influences.

Plath's culturally situated struggle between her ideas of poetry as "mythological" or "occasional," or (though not strictly parallel) as object or communication, informs her different uses of the political in "Mary's Song" and "Getting There" and throws light on critics' misreadings of the latter poem. In trying to locate a stable attitude in Plath toward poetry as purely personal myth, Perloff views the political as failing, and Kroll fails to see any political content at all. Kroll (in common with many critics) misreads "Getting There" as a stage in a mythic progression toward personal transcendence:

> This image [deathcar/cradle] represents a transfiguration and transcending of history—of the war, the train, the death-camps and the "old bandages, boredoms, old faces" . . . the narrative of the poem should be understood as the enactment of a willingly undertaken purgatorial ritual, in which the true self, purified by the Lethe of all

false encumbrances finally emerges . . . discarding the "old bandages"
. . . is a symbolic resurrection.[67]

"Getting There," which Plath wrote on 6 November 1962, is
similar in many ways to "Mary's Song," written two weeks later. It
incorporates (at its conclusion) a birth of sorts and treats many
of the same concerns as the other poem. It has the same immedi-
acy of named places and events as "Mary's Song," and many of
its images express Plath's more general anxieties about the dehumanization of people and the frightening animation of the machine. Yet in this poem, the personal (the description of the
speaker's journey through the Bosch-like battlefields of history)
is the pretext for a more central, political theme. Plath appears
to deny this broader perspective by opening the poem with direct
and insistent interrogation, focusing interest on the individual
experience of the speaker (CP 247). Yet, as the poem progresses,
the speaker becomes, in common with her fellow travelers, depersonalized and dehumanized. She is "dragging my body," as if it
were not a part of her, and describes herself as "a letter in this
slot" (CP 248), posted to a destination itself formed of dehumanized parts, merely a name and eyes. The soldiers are merely broken arrows, primitive and ineffectual means of destruction in
comparison to the mechanical efficiency of the engine. Their lives
and their journey are seen as one, pumped ahead both by blood
and pistons, into life and distance, but unable to control either
life or journey. The situation of the poem, while described in a
personal, conversational tone, is a universal and indistinct one—
"some war or other"—emphasized by references to Napoleon, the
First and Second World Wars, and Joan of Arc. The speaker and
her companions' individuality is further diminished in comparison to the humanization of the mechanical engine, a theme to
which Plath returned throughout her career (in "Night Shift"
[1957],"Suicide Off Egg Rock" [1959], and "Totem" [1962]).

Just as the speaker's personality is less important than indicated
initially, so the ending of "Getting There" is not the simple positive
transformation it first appears. Plath's attitude toward transcendence in many of her poems is typically fraught with ambiguities,
and the instability of the transcendental ending of "Getting
There" works in a way similar to that of other "apotheosis" poems,
such as "Lady Lazarus," by destabilizing the security of previously
constructed meanings. In "Getting There," the ending reflects
back over the experiences of the poem to make them less personal
than critics such as Kroll assume. The destination of the poem,

"A minute, a dewdrop" is, in comparison to the journey, a small, pure and safe place. Yet its appeal is qualified by the earlier statement, "All the gods know is destinations": it is this godlike drive for destinations, rather than the emphasis on the journey itself, which results in the reification of the speaker and the men as they exist merely as machines to pump forward to such a destination. Plath's concerns here reflect a classic theme of political ethics, the morality of ends and means, as well as relating to her anxiety about mechanization and conformism. In her copy of *Babbitt*, Plath marked a statement by Seneca Doane, a radical intellectual, describing Babbitt's city, a monument to American ideals of "progress":

> I hate your city. It has standardized all the beauty out of life. It is one big railroad station—with all the people taking tickets for the best cemeteries.[68]

Similarly, in "Getting There," the image of the train inexorably transporting people toward death symbolizes the mechanized society, involvement in which may lead to loss of personal will, as the passenger is carried along, a mere observer, toward both physical and spiritual death. Plath is even more specific about this potential connection between mechanization and death in her references to war. War relies on technology and its necessary dehumanization of man. In an earlier draft of "Getting There," whose final version describes the wheels of the train as proceeding from the brains of the Krupp family (armaments manufacturers), Plath makes the age-old nature of the connection between war and mechanization more explicit, describing the wheels of the train as "Mechanical heirlooms."[69] Thus, when the speaker declares that the earth out of which she rises in such pain is "Adam's side" there is a double sense—she is asserting her mythic and "natural" origins, in opposition to the mechanization of everything around her, but also man (as opposed to humankind), as Adam, is perceived as the root of mechanization. Freudian symbolism reinforces this image: not only are the soldiers characterized as "broken arrows" (a conventional phallic symbol), but in a draft of the poem, the train also becomes "an arrow." To reach the destination, the goal toward which "progress" (the arrow and the train) is headed, the speaker denies any fellow feeling both for her companions and for the past. She declares that she will count, but bury the dead, leaving their souls to agonize. Only then, by actively dehumanizing herself (an activity seen throughout the poem as horrific and distasteful) can the speaker remove herself from the history of the poem, reach her destination, and disembark from the train of forgetfulness as pure as a baby. Given the powerful horror of what has gone before, oblivion, or the Lethe, does not represent an adequate response or antithesis, and the "purity" of the baby is defiled. As Margaret Dickie Uroff notes,

> the train that drags itself through the battlefields of history ultimately becomes the "black car of Lethe," a symbol of the forgetfulness of the past. It becomes a cradle, nurturing a new generation of killers: the pure baby who steps from it will perpetuate murder because she has forgotten the world's past history of murderousness."[70]

Because the ending of "Getting There" does not constitute an unambiguous positive transformation, the poem is not so much a personal account of the journey through life to rebirth, but is concerned with making a wider political and moral point about the importance of cultural memory. This theme is the focus of Plath's political concerns about mechanization and individualism, which she also explores in a similarly apparently personal way in "Daddy" (to gain freedom from the authoritarian father-figure, the speaker needs to name the past that has been mechanically "Scraped flat by the roller / Of wars").[71] If, in its inexorable drive for destinations and "progress" a culture forgets its past terrors and atrocities, then it loses both its collective humanity and its individual identity. As a result these terrors can continue, and life itself becomes merely "some war or other."

An awareness of Plath's treatment of and struggles with the interrelation of personal and political, then, allows such traditionally controversial poems as "Getting There" and "Mary's Song" to be read in terms of the complexities with which they deal. Such an awareness also clears the ground and enables the perception that Plath's interest in using historical material was not primarily because of its inescapable links (for her as for everyone) with emotional concerns, but because of its relation to the central theme of her poetry, memory.

History and Myth

Just as Plath's treatment of political concerns is often viewed as inappropriate and selfish, so her deployment of historical imagery is generally considered irresponsible. This section will show that

Plath used such imagery because of her politically motivated interest in the theme of cultural memory, and that her treatment of this material is ultimately informed by the same conflict which affects her treatment of political themes: between the aesthetic and didactic uses of poetry, between her use of such a shocking combination of history and personal experience either as a reflection of her own subjectivity or as an attempt to shock the reader into remembering. I will approach the two main problems in Plath's deployment of historical material: its appearance over only a short period of time, and the contrast between its emblematic appearance and the resonance of her treatment of myth, a contrast which forms the root of her ambivalent treatment of transcendence.

Amnesia, Conformism, and Rhetoric

Many of the writers Plath respected viewed cultural memory as inescapably linked to their concerns about mechanization and conformism outlined above. Ortega y Gassett, in *The Revolt of the Masses*, makes the connection explicit; ignorance of the past, for him, characterizes the nature of the conformist "masses":

> the new generations are getting ready to take over command of the world as if the world were a paradise without trace of former footsteps, without traditional and highly complex problems.[72]

In a similar way, Aldous Huxley, with whose work Plath was familiar, as I showed in the introduction, was equally concerned with the myth of "progress" and resulting dehumanization of mankind: Plath notes with irony in her journals that the "progress" achieved in Huxley's *Brave New World* results in a world where comfort and peace is attained at the expense of creativity (J 139). A feature of Huxley's dystopia of mechanized conformity, *Brave New World*, is the rejection of the past—"history is bunk"—which Huxley viewed as crucial for the continuing success of the soulless society.

Plath, too, always linked the issues of cultural memory and conformism. This pairing of concerns appears as early as 1957 in "The Thin People" and in drafts of other poems, such as "Finisterre" and "Wuthering Heights" (explored in the conclusion). Indeed, for Plath, the trope of amnesia focuses these concerns, around which cluster the related themes of mechanization, individualism, and conformity. While Huxley and Ortega y Gassett explore the link between cultural memory (or amnesia) and such staple American anxieties, Plath treats the theme of amnesia more widely and frequently than she deals with the themes of mechanization and individualism. She explores the dangers and attractions of individual amnesia in poems such as "Suicide Off Egg Rock" (1959), "Who" (1959), "Tulips" (1961), "The Jailor" (1962), and "Amnesiac" (1962), and cultural amnesia (and its resulting automatizing of perception) is at the center of her treatment of the Holocaust and Hiroshima in late poems such as "Daddy," "Lady Lazarus," and "Fever 103." Plath's concern about this issue is evident in her journal entry about the American reaction to the execution of the Rosenbergs (convicted of selling nuclear secrets to the Soviet Union). She writes bitterly, on 19 June 1953, the date of their execution, about the hypocrisy of American society, which kills to prevent others from obtaining their expertise in killing (J 81), and blames such hyprocrisy on America's cultural apathy and amnesia: "The largest emotional reaction over the United States will be a rather large, democratic, infinitely bored and casual and complacent yawn" (J 81). She is disgusted at the self-righteous prurience of the American public, declaring ironically, "too bad . . . it could not be televised . . . so much more realistic and beneficial than the run-of-the-mill crime program," yet behind this lies a hope that if the event were televised, the reality of execution would shock the nation out of its apathy. The heavy sarcasm in the text, however, undercuts this hope. And yet this desire to shock the "public" out of its perceived apathy informs Plath's own shocking use of historical material in her late poems.[73]

While Plath may have used such an often scandalizing, combination of private experience and public, historical knowledge in her late poems in order to characterize the way the two combined in her mind, clearly she also felt a desire to associate events such as the Holocaust with an intimate tone and subject matter in order to shock, remind, and bring such history closer to home. Plath's commitment to this project was a response to the political situation of her period. In the fifties and sixties, although still recovering from World War II and the war in Korea, America was engaged in a Cold War whose depersonalized rhetoric Plath found terrifying because of its necessary mythologizing and thus amnesia of the horrors of war. The widely publicized trial of Nazi war criminal Adolf Eichmann (1961–62) showed the importance of such a use of rhetoric (and its resulting distortion of reality) in the smooth running of the Nazi genocide machinery in the Second World War. Hannah Arendt notes, in her famous report of the trial:

> all correspondence referring to the matter ["final solution"] was subject to rigid "language rules" . . . the prescribed code names for killing were "final solution," "evacuation" . . . and "special treatment" . . . for whatever other reasons the language rules have been devised, they proved of enormous help in the maintenance of order and sanity in the various widely diversified services whose co-operation was essential in this matter.[74]

As a student at Smith, Plath marked Fromm's comments on the misuse of rhetoric, in *Escape from Freedom*, with a determined "yes!"

> Never have words been more misused in order to conceal the truth today. Betrayal of allies is called appeasement, *military aggression is camouflaged as defense against attack.* [Plath's emphasis].[75]

Several years later, she writes both in her letters to her mother and in "Context" about her fear of such an abstracting and dangerous use of language. In *Letters Home* in December 1961, she declares how disturbed she was by

> all the warlike talk in the papers, such as Kennedy saying Kruschev would "have no place to hide" and the armed forces manual indoctrinating soldiers about the "inevitable" war with our "implacable foe." (LH 437–38)

In "Context," written in the same period, Plath returns to this question of rhetoric when she writes of her belief in,

> the conservation of life of all people in all places, the jeopardizing of which no abstract doubletalk of "peace" and "implacable foes" can excuse. (JP 92)

Plath demonstrated her poetic interest in the power of language in her textual annotation of Freud and Frazer's explorations of the power of names and naming,[76] and shared her fear of the grave misuse of the power of language with other, broadly contemporary writers, such as George Orwell. In his dystopian classic, *1984* (1948), Orwell depicts language as an effective instrument of social and thought control (similar to the control of cultural memory in the form of history Huxley approaches in *Brave New World*).

It is only recently, however, that critics have explored in depth the formation and workings of the particularly nuclear rhetoric of the Cold War. Such language is, as Christopher Norris and Ian Whitehouse note,

> a language of entirely suasive, rhetorical or—in speech-act terms—performative character which achieves its purpose by evading the requirements of rational discourse.[77]

This irrationality works, as Paul Chilton describes, through its appeal to myth:

> in spite of the scientific background, in spite of the technical theorizing, most talk about nuclear war and weapons reflects irrational, not to say, superstitious, processes of thought. Myths, metaphors, paradoxes and contradictions abound. . . . We have traditional ways of talking, myths, symbols, metaphors, which provide safe pigeon-holes for what is "unnatural" or "other-worldly." This is a dangerous tendency in human culture, one which perhaps helps to explain the spell-bound ambivalence of our attitudes towards the bomb.[78]

In America, as Norris and Whitehouse assert, such a rhetoric becomes more potent through a powerful construction of specifically American mythic history. The authors write about the components of this American myth, specifically in relation to the Reagan administration, but with application to all modern American governments:

> The notion of identity, the right of territorial expansion, the absolute conviction of a divine mandate licensing that expansion, the ineluctable will of the individual empowered by that divine mandate—these are the remarkable durable stuff of which the myth is made. To confront American nuclear rhetoric is to confront that mythic psyche in all its religious fervour. . . . To illustrate further this tie between the rhetorical strategy and a mythologised history, one need only review the nomenclature of the American weapons system . . . "Hawkeye," "Honest John," "Minuteman" and "Pershing"—all heroes of one or another American campaign—mix easily with godlike heroes such as "Atlas," "Hercules" and "Thor."[79]

To be an "American," then, means to unthinkingly share the discourse and the myths and mythic history behind it.

Plath showed her general awareness of the danger of this mythic construction of Americanness in her early poem, "I Am An American," where the unthinking assimilation of such nostalgia is perceived as leading to conformity. In relation to the pseudological rhetoric of war, and more specifically, nuclear war, Plath found the power of such a rhetoric, and its resulting cultural consensus (due to a comfortable amnesia about actual war) terrifying. Her relationship with the idea of "Americanness" *can* be seen as a cultural version of Bloom's "anxiety of influence"—combining a desire to accept the myths of Americanness (as loyal, democratic, individualistic) with a paradoxical motivation to assert this American individuality by breaking out of such comfortable myths. Yet Plath's fear of mindless conformity, in terms of nuclear rhetoric, is also more immediately based on her very real perception of the potential destructive consequences of the abstracting, mythic discourse of the nation's leaders, which uses such apparently logical terms to talk of potential world annihilation. As Norris and Whitehouse assert, however, questioning this discourse is not simple.[80] One of the ways Plath attempts to do this is through her discomforting use of the "language of atrocity" in her late poems. One of the reasons this often appears to fail in such poems is the very complexity of the relationship, for Plath, between history and myth. Yet before directly approaching this, the final question relating to Plath's motives in using historical material, her deployment of such imagery only at the very end of her career needs to be addressed.

Timing—Poetry of October and November 1962

While Plath was clearly deeply interested in politics and treated political issues (more and less successfully) throughout her poetry' until October 1962 they never appeared in the form of the explicit historical references which have made "Lady Lazarus," "Daddy," and "Fever 103°" so (in)famous. When asked by Peter Orr in October 1962 about her "sudden" interest in such historical "facts," Plath describes her burgeoning interest in Napoleonic and modern military history, declaring

> I think that as I age, I am becoming more and more historical. I certainly wasn't at all in my early twenties.[81]

One might argue that Plath's newly found historical perspective, her perception of the repetition of wars and battles, gave depth to her own knowledge of such things and made the "naming of names" increasingly important, due to her fear of cultural amnesia. Yet Plath was clearly intellectually interested in and emotionally moved by political and historical issues from adolescence, so a less obvious reason for Plath's sudden "naming" of historical events must be sought. This other reason rests on the abrupt appearance of such a concentrated use of historical imagery. The first most evident and sustained appearance is in "The Swarm" on 7 October 1962, a part of the "bee-sequence" of poems, which critics generally view as Plath's assertion both of poetic and personal independence. It was at this time that Plath and Hughes's separation was declared final. Pamela Annas, exploring the impact of Plath's gender on her poetry, claims that Plath felt no relation to recent social history and relied instead, in her poetry, on myth, because as a woman she had little part in shaping history. Annas's argument is a fanciful and, in the terms in which it is framed, unproductive generalization: she writes:

> social history (World War Two etc.) seems to stop for Plath where her own life starts, and it is replaced at that point by a mythic timeless past, populated by creatures from folk tale and classical mythology. This is not surprising, since as a woman this poet had little part in shaping history. Why should she feel any relation to it?[82]

Yet Plath was alive during World War II and writes of Dachau and Hiroshima, events that were still emblazoned on the minds of the public in the fifties and early sixties, and if, as a woman, she felt she had little part in shaping history, there is nothing to suggest she would feel more in command of historic events from before her birth, or even mythology. Annas's general point about women's involvement with, but difficulty in shaping history is, however, useful. Until the time of her late poems, Plath's personal writing shows a certain separation, not from the events themselves, but from influence on such events. In her journals for the winter of 1958 (when Plath and Hughes lived in Boston, and Plath pursued a course of therapy with her psychiatrist, Dr. Ruth Beuscher), Plath describes the completeness of her relationship with Hughes and her dependence on him as barring her from a full social existence:

> Between us there are no barriers . . . I must be myself—make myself and not let myself be made by him. (J 245)

Her sense of personal lack resulting from the closeness of her relationship with Hughes becomes a refrain in her journals of this time, as she later writes of the difficulties in becoming more independent (by keeping things from Hughes) because of their constant companionship and her lack of an "outer life" (J 277). Ted Hughes, it appears, has also written about the "completeness" of their poetic relationship. Hayman quotes him as saying, "You begin to write out of one brain . . . We were like two feet, each one using everything the other did."[83] (Although against this must be placed Eileen Aird's memory of Plath's statement that "We do criticize each other's work, but we write poems that are as distinct and different as our fingerprints themselves must be."[84]) Plath connects her lack of independence with her writing difficulties, as in her journals in December 1958 she notes that she will only be able to start writing successfully when, "I'm sure I'm myself and not him" (J 282). Certainly, Hughes's influence on Plath's writing was not wholly repressive. What *is* clear is the strength of his influence; the many lists of poem subjects he drew up to help Plath start writing and which bear close resemblance to her finished poems are one example that attests to this.[85] While Hughes's lists were probably generated as a result of discussion between him and Plath, the very number of poems that Plath wrote from the starting point of Hughes's suggestions is surprising. Such help and influence was not confined to poetry. On Christmas Eve 1960, Plath writes to her mother of making up plots for stories with Hughes and how they are dividing the research. She concludes, however, by noting that the great thing about them is that "I can do them by perspiration, not inspiration," implying that these "joint projects" are in fact short stories Plath was working on, with a large amount of help from Hughes.[86] Perhaps more surprising is that in a interview and reading of her poetry in 1958, Plath is asked to name the poets she reads for pleasure. She lists a few names (Hughes and Yeats the most prominent), falters, then asks Hughes, who is sitting in on the recording, who else she reads for pleasure.[87]

Plath herself felt a certain amount of conflict between her desire for independence, necessary for her writing, and a need to conform to the prevailing ideal of conjugal "togetherness." A few weeks after her journal entries bewailing her dependence on Hughes, she writes, in January 1959, of visiting a friend who had recently become a mother, and describes her own feelings of contentment in a purely female world and her lack of interest in men, declaring that "It is as if Ted were my representative in the world of men" (J 293). In its context, this is less a statement of female solidarity than an abnegation of public responsibility and personal wholeness, responding to the traditional ideal of "completeness and togetherness" to which Plath felt, at times, that her relationship with Hughes should conform. This ideal was pervasive in the 1950s and critically explored shortly afterwards by Betty Friedan in *The Feminine Mystique* (1963), who summarizes:

> The end of the road is togetherness, where the woman has no independent self to hide even in guilt; she exists only for and through her husband and children. Coined by the publishers of *McCall's* in 1954, the concept 'togetherness' was seized upon avidly as movement of spiritual significance by advertisers, ministers, newspaper editors. For a time, it was elevated into virtually a national purpose.[88]

Yet Plath's apparent approbation of "togetherness" contrasts strikingly with an earlier, pre-Hughes journal entry in which she asserts that, as an artist, she is "part man," and writes of her ability to perceive the female body through men's eyes, privileging a certain Woolfian poetic androgyny (J 23). Plath thought of this self-contained completeness as necessary for the artist in her youth, yet it is missing from the specifically gendered conception of herself as a "female" poet after her marriage and motherhood. While Hughes undeniably exerted a positive influence on aspects of her poetic development, not only did his lack of interest in the political context of poetry affect her, but also, in conforming to social expectations in her marriage with him, Plath denied herself certain aspects of a full relationship to the world. The appeals of such conformism in marriage were hard to resist and extended to many areas of life. In terms of the political, Friedan describes the pressures of social expectations from the highest quarter, summarizing Adlai Stevenson's (Plath's Democratic hero) commencement address at Smith College in 1955 (the year Plath graduated), a speech in which he

> dismissed the desire of educated women to play their own political part in "the crises of the age." Modern woman's participation in politics is through her role as wife and mother, said the spokesman of democratic liberalism . . . the only problem is woman's failure to appreciate that her true part in the political crisis is as wife and mother.[89]

Al Alvarez shows the domestic and literary results of this cultural norm, to which Plath appeared to conform when she was with Hughes: he notes that when he first met Hughes and Plath in London, Plath as a poet seemed effaced by Hughes and by her role as housewife. It was only after Plath had mentioned his choice of "Nightshift" to print in *The Observer* that he realized Hughes's wife was Sylvia Plath the poet.[90] After Hughes's departure, the manuscripts of *Letters Home* show, more clearly than the published edition, Plath's feelings toward her husband. On a number of occasions she writes explicitly about her intellectual and poetic resentment of Hughes and her joy at her newfound writerly freedom.[91] Much of such evidence, written at a time of great upheaval, may be the projection back of the resentment from an unhappy present to an actually quite contented past. Yet, if Plath's characteristic feelings of rivalry toward contemporary poets are taken into account, her previously happy marriage might well have blocked her natural feelings of rivalry and resentment toward Hughes (both as husband and as poet), as someone who inhibited her poetry and her achievement of a full relationship with the world.

When Plath became both independent and solely responsible for two children in October 1962, this may have released not only (as has been widely acknowledged) a more powerful poetic voice, but also a new sense of possessing history, of being in a position to name it. Perhaps this appropriation went too far, or perhaps the critics who are discomfited by it say more about their own attitude to female usurping of such male preserves than about Plath. Yet Plath's appropriation of such material was a political act in two senses—she was concerned to shock her readership into remembering, and she declared her social and poetic power by her very use of such facts. In this sense, then, the poetry is both broadly "committed" (in terms of Sartre's definition), and committed to communicating a sociopolitical meaning.

In many of the finished poems, however, there appears a gap between intention and execution. Plath's handling of historical references often appears one-dimensional, seemingly untransformed by poetic craft. In "Daddy," for instance, the mention of Dachau seems wanton. In setting up a victim-persecutor relationship in such extreme and yet stereotypical terms, the reader is forced into becoming one of the "peanut-crunching crowd," a voyeur of both the personal and historical situations of the poem. Unlike in "Lady Lazarus" where, as I show below, Plath more forcefully confronts the reader with the voyeurism implicit in the reading of all lyrical poetry, in "Daddy" the poem appears less clearly to lead the reader to any distinct enlightenment about the voyeuristic attitude it expresses toward the concentration camps— the poet appears merely to confront the reader with the camps and with an imposed attitude toward them. What needs to be addressed is not whether Plath's intentions behind the inclusion of historical material were admirable (they were), but why the effect of such material in her poetry is so disturbing. Fully to explore the difficulties in Plath's treatment of historical material in her poetry, her use of myth and the contrast between the appearance of both in her poetry must be examined.

Emblematic History, Resonant Myth

Plath felt a similar sense of involvement with mythic subjects as she did with political and historical concerns. Yet many of her most famous late poems, such as "Fever 103°," "Lady Lazarus," and "Daddy," combine history and myth in an uneasy partnership. In "Daddy," it is not so much the style of "light verse" and the connection of the very personal to the very extreme horrors of (in Heaney's terms) "the history of other people's sorrows" that cause unease. Myth and history combine (Electra, vampirism and voodoo rub shoulders with the Holocaust), but in such a way that the mythic and psychoanalytic aspects of "Daddy" are more immediate than the real history of Nazi persecution of the Jews. "Fever 103°" shows this uneasy combination of history and myth more clearly. In this poem, the speaker's journey toward some sort of cathartic transformation works through mythic references to Cerberus, and a myth-making account of the death of Isadora Duncan (a figure both mythic and political) to a historic-political image of the effects of atomic destruction and Hiroshima. Images of "smokes," used to describe both Isadora's fatal scarves and a nuclear holocaust, act as the transition between the mythic and the historical imagery. This transitional imagery of fire and smoke is strongly reminiscent of the central motif of the more successful "Mary's Song," written one month later, where again fire is transformed into "thick palls" of smoke which connect Christian myth and twentieth-century cruelty. In "Fever 103°," however, the link between myth and history is more tenuous.

The mythic material frames the poem: it begins with a reference to Cerberus guarding the gates to a fiery hell and ends, even taking into account its destabilizing ironic overtones, in a move toward mythic transcendence (CP 231–32). In contrast to these sustained and vivid tropes, the historical-political image-transitions in the center of "Fever 103°" appear violently swift and lack the resonance of the mythic imagery. Plath expresses concerns about modern science by transforming the "Hothouse baby" into first hothouse flora (orchid) and then fauna (leopard), which, the reader is told (in relation to the drawbacks of such scientific wonders) is swiftly bleached and destroyed by radiation. These startlingly swift metaphoric transitions, while working in complete contrast to the more sustained progression of the mythic frame of the poem, nevertheless appear to cohere, both together, and to the rest of the poem. The lurching transition from these metaphors to those in the next lines is not as well sustained, however. (In "Mary's Song," the transition from smoke to ash is also a lurch, but is better supported by the more integrated nature of the mythic framework.) The connections between radiation, Hiroshima, grease, ash, and human relations (in the form of "adulterers") in this section of "Fever 103°" are too many, too contrived, and ultimately too weak to support the transition from the extended image-play of scientific advances and drawbacks to the return to "the sin, the sin" of the mythic opening. Such arbitrary swiftness may arguably represent the illogical, almost surreal thought processes of the fevered subject; yet this interpretation leaves unexplained the very specific unsettling contrast Plath sets up between a resonant myth and an emblematic history.

Hughes, like Perloff, views Plath's sensitivity toward the external world as central to her poetic power and originality and provides a possible explanation of the contrast between her uses of history and myth. He writes:

> Her openness to the ambiguous populations of the "living ether" took its toll. Her reactions to hurts in other people and animals, and even tiny desecrations of plant-life were extremely violent.[92]

In contrast to Perloff, he sees this sensitivity, not as evidence of Plath's connection to a tradition of "oracular" poets, but directly resulting from her sense of immediate personal participation in myth, "the ambiguous populations of the 'living ether'," who, he believes, "were deeply involved in her affairs."[93] Plath's nonpoetic writing supports this, as it is often equally as full as her poems of mythic references. For example, in the letter to her mother in 1956 in which Plath describes the incident which formed the basis for "The Eye-Mote," her account is shot with literary and mythic references to Oedipus, *King Lear*, and Eden (LH 229). Hughes's argument that Plath's openness to myth not only characterizes but forms the basis of her wider closeness to the world about her is compelling, and would make her treatment of myth "naturally" more resonant than her deployment of history.

While such a personalized appropriation of myth could constitute a sign of self-aggrandizement or the "literariness" that

Hughes denies, Plath's relationship with this material is not idio-syncratic. The twentieth century has seen, in the advent of Freud-ian and Jungian psychoanalysis, a blurring of boundaries between the mythic and the personal: Freud's use of myths such as those of Electra and Oedipus to explain his theories of personality de-velopment and Jung's exploration of archetypes have both been culturally powerful. Plath was poetically and personally interested in Jung and Freud's theories,[94] and her poetry effects a compa-rable blurring of boundaries between myth and personality as that practiced by these figures. Introducing her reading of "Daddy" for BBC radio in 1962, for instance, she describes the speaker in conventional psychoanalytic terms as a girl with an Electra complex (CP 293). "Electra on Azalea Path" (written three years before "Daddy" in 1959) addresses the same psychoanalyti-cally resonant theme as "Daddy"—the coming to terms with the powerful absence of a dead father—and similarly positions the eponymous speaker in a mythic-psychoanalytic framework. Yet in the body of "Electra on Azalea Path" (CP 117), Plath makes the mythic connection explicit by including, in the form of a quota-tion, the classical myth of the sacrifice of Electra's sister, Iphigenia, by their father, Agamemnon, and his subsequent murder by his wife, Clytemnestra[95] (which leads to Electra's revenge and Freud's appropriation of the myth for his theorizing of the infant girl's feelings of hate toward the mother). In the three lines which form her italicized "quotation," Plath combines two myths (with a possi-ble reference to The Odyssey's famous description of the "wine dark sea") to explore her perception that the structural relationships of the speaker's family reflect those of the mythic family, whose relationship is formed through links of blood, signifying both kinship and mutual guilt and murder. Plath also more directly explores metapoetic concerns about the use of myth. Immediately after the "quotation" cited, the speaker stands back from personal involvement in the mythic aspect to note her appropriation of "the stilts" of this ancient tragedy, and later in the poem to comment on the actions of the actors in this mythic play. Plath's conscious treatment of the poetic and personal uses of myth emphasizes the immediate importance it held for her: she needs to explore the relationship between myth and personal, lyrical utterance as she does in "Electra on Azalea Path" precisely because, as Hughes notes, she feels these mythic personalities to be "deeply involved in her affairs." This kind of clear reflexivity is not as apparent in her utilization of historical material and leads many readers to perceive such deployment as unmediated or irresponsible. This does not, however, mean that Plath was unaware of the problems surrounding her use of history. Rather, because of the differences between her perceptions of history and myth, such a clear self-consciousness was less appropriate.

Although Plath's sense of personal identification with both history and myth is similar, the parallels stop there. Seamus Heaney attempts to make a further connection between the two in Plath's narrowness and selfishness in her use of both. He writes of "Daddy" that it "rampages . . . permissively in the history of other people's sorrows" and, in relation to Plath's use of myth in "Lady Lazarus," "the cultural resonance of the original story is harnessed to a vehemently self-justifying purpose, so that the suprapersonal dimensions of knowledge—to which myth typically gives access—are slighted in favor of the intense personal need of the poet,"[96] although he does qualify his general view about Plath's use of myth, saying that:

> [while] her use of myth . . . tends to confine the widest suggestions of the original to particular applications within her own life. This is obviously truer at the beginning of her career, and does not apply to such first-hand "mythic" experiences as "Elm."[97]

It is indeed true that in some earlier poems, such as "Virgin in a Tree" (1958), Plath's use of myth is one-dimensional and narrowing, just as her later experiments with history as both image and theme appear limited and limiting. Yet, finally, Heaney's (albeit qualified) generalization about the similarity between Plath's limiting use of history and myth is inadequate. Examination of the appearance of myth throughout her poetry shows that her appropriation of such material significantly differs from, and varies more than her use of the historic emblem. While historic imagery appears emblematically and in only a small number of Plath's (late) poems, she uses myth more frequently and more diversely. She works with many different types of myth, from classical allusions to Oedipus and Electra (studied during her Tragedy course at Cambridge), to the Northern European myths of Lyonesse and the Lorelei (stemming from her interest, shared with and encouraged by Hughes, in Frazer's *The Golden Bough* [1922] and Robert Graves's *The White Goddess* [1948],[98] two popular and influential books of the time). In addition to the variety of myths Plath uses, she works with them in diverse ways. They appear both as overt and less obvious references throughout her career. In 1956 Plath refers to Persephone; in 1957 and 1958, respectively, Dryads and Lorelei appear. In 1962, overt references can be found to Medusa and less overt references to Clytemnestra and Agamemnon in "Purdah." She also appropriated and struggled with archetypal myths in building her own ambiguous, mythic system; again, Plath explored this function of myth from quite early poems, such as "The Thin People" (1957) through to "The Munich Mannequins" (1963).[99]

The contrast between the resonance and diversity of Plath's use of myth and the single-dimension of her use of history does not, however, simply result from Plath's greater experience and confidence in handling myth, or her more "natural" affinity with it. Graves, in *The White Goddess,* separates history and myth in their relation to poetry. He writes of "the tendency of history to taint the purity of myth" and disdains "originality" in the poet who "takes his themes from anywhere he please[s]," by which Graves appears to mean "occasional" rather than "mythic" themes.[100] While Plath agrees with Graves about the importance of a deep personal feeling for myths, gained through "a severe Classical education [which] can impress them on a child's mind strongly enough to give them emotional relevance,"[101] she did not feel such an attitude towards myth need preclude a similar connection with history. Yet, as Rose notes, quoting Graves's comment on the appearance of the "dark satanic mills" in William Blake's poetry:

> Reading Graves, it is clear that his mythic conception of poetry is set quite explicitly against politics and history: "The White Goddess's Starry Wheel here multiplied into the twelve wheeling signs of the Zodiac . . . are misread as dark mechanistic images of capitalistic oppression."[102]

Rose argues that Plath's commitment to Graves's theories in *The White Goddess,* and specifically to the poetic importance of myth over politics and history, was not wholehearted. Plath's dissension, however, runs deeper, as she not only disagrees with Graves's view of the poetic dominance of myth, but extends his exhortation about the importance of a personal feeling for, and connection to myth, to reverse the dichotomy he sets up between myth as pure, history as impure. In her poetry, it is myth which Plath appropriates (more and less successfully) for more idiosyncratic and personal ends (connecting, for instance, myth with psychoanalytic themes). Notwithstanding her sense of involvement with political and historical themes, it is history which stands as somehow unchanging and "pure," emblematic, and suprapersonal in her poetry. This impersonal "purity" of emblem, seen in "Fever 103°" and "Daddy," is that which, when applied to such real horrors of the twentieth century as Hiroshima and the Holocaust, makes their inclusion in Plath's poetry so shocking.

Problems of Mythic History—"Dachau and Hiroshima"

Plath's reversal of Graves's history-myth dichotomy directly results from the nature of the historical events on which she draws—primarily, the Holocaust: and the resulting difficulties besetting her emblematic treatment of this material relate to wider issues around the "placing" of the Holocaust. Jon Harris notes that in the decade following World War II, very little poetry was written in Britain about the Holocaust.[103] (In America as well, with a few notable exceptions, the Holocaust tended to be approached in other media, such as fiction, autobiography, and film.[104]) He sees two reasons for this. First, "The horrors were so extreme that they seem to belong to another world entirely."[105] In other words, the Holocaust assumed a mythic dimension in response to its extremity, and the difficulty of understanding it in human terms (because of the mechanical efficiency with which it was carried out, and its inconceivably large number of victims). Second, myth, through which, Harris asserts, poetry works, was unable to enclose or make sense of the subject. Plath's reversal, then, of Graves's dichotomy, between pure myth and impure history, results not primarily from a more personal attitude to myth but as a reaction to recent history—such atrocity, although historically factual, takes on the suprapersonal dimensions usually held by myth. Indeed, when Plath declares, in her BBC interview in 1962, that even the most personal poetry must be relevant to "the larger things," she details these not as general "truths" or mythic archetypes, but as "Hiroshima and Dachau and so on."[106]

Plath's fascination with the Holocaust was not unique. As Harris asserts, though very little poetry was written in Britain about the Holocaust in this period, the late 1950s and early 1960s were marked by a great cultural interest in, and many attempts at approaching the event both in England and in America. Its impact on education has been noted in terms of Plath's experience of Raymond Chapman's high school history class and in college texts such as Fromm's *Escape from Freedom*. In terms of popular culture, the impact of the Holocaust was equally powerful at this time, partly due to the wide publicity of the Eichmann trial and the increasing power of the American Zionist lobby, which mobilized after the war to fight for a Jewish homeland in Palestine. Fictional and nonfictional literature about or relating to the Holocaust, such as Anne Frank's autobiographical *The Diary of a Young Girl* (1952), Katherine Anne Porter's *Ship of Fools* (1945),[107] and Leon Uris's *Exodus* (1959) became best-sellers. At this time, Hollywood produced a number of popular and star-studded films, often from successful books, plays, or TV presentations, such as *Judgement at Nuremberg* (1961) starring Spencer Tracey, *Exodus* (1960) starring Paul Newman and Sal Mineo, and *The Diary of Anne Frank* (1959). In addition to the general cultural power of the Holocaust in these years, Plath, in this period of her greater poetic freedom, was influenced more directly by her friendship with a South African Jewish couple, Gerry and Jillian Becker. It was during the time in which Plath was writing such poems, autumn 1962 (after her separation from Hughes and her removal from Devon to London), that she became close friends with the Beckers, to the extent of sharing their meal on Christmas day. Both Jillian and Gerry were keenly interested in the events of the Second World War and the Holocaust (Jillian later wrote a study of terrorism, *Hitler's Children,* and Gerry had read much about, and visited a number of the concentration camps). Ronald Hayman writes of this friendship:

> Sylvia, who was interested but ill-informed, learnt a lot . . . [from Becker about the Holocaust], and on his way home from work he'd been calling in at her flat two or three times a week for a chat.[108]

So, although little poetry that dealt with the Holocaust was written in Britain at this time, Plath was strongly influenced in her fascination with such events by intellectual, cultural, and personal factors.

Plath's interest in the Holocaust was also a response to her general political fears. With the Cold War at its height in the late 1950s, the potential for a different, nuclear genocide made concerns about the Holocaust immediately relevant. The literary critic (who was also a friend of Plath) Al Alvarez, notes that he

> suggested, (in a piece for the *Atlantic Monthly* in 1962) that one of the reasons why the camps continue to keep such a tight hold on our imaginations is that we see in them a small-scale trial run for a nuclear war. . . . Then there are those other curious, upside-down similarities: the use of modern industrial processes for the mass production of corpses, with all the attendant paraphernalia of efficiency, meticulous paperwork, and bureaucratic organization; the deliberate annihilation

not merely of lives but of identities, as in some paranoid vision of mass culture.[109]

Plath's connection of recent history, in the form of the Holocaust, with her current political fears about the Cold War may seem merely an instance of her "rampaging" in history for her own personal ends, reducing the Holocaust to a simple symbol of atrocity. Yet, respected writers in the 1950s such as Eric Fromm felt it important to use the Nazi regime as an example of the social and psychological extremes to which all societies, for various reasons, were vulnerable. Otto Preminger, in his film version of Leon Uris's *Exodus*, makes a direct comparison between the anti-Semitism of the Nazis and the Arabs[110] and Elie Wiesel, a respected, Nobel Prize–winning commentator on, and survivor of, the Holocaust, writing in the 1980s, specifically connects the genocide carried out by the Nazis with the universal potential genocide of nuclear war:

> Once upon a time it happened to my people, and now it happens to all people. And suddenly I said to myself, maybe the whole world, strangely, turned Jewish. Everybody lives now facing the unknown. We are all, in a way, helpless.[111]

Robert Jay Lifton and Eric Markusen define the problems of making such a connection, which forms the framework of their study, *The Genocidal Mentality: Nazi Holocaust and Nuclear Threat:*

> It is neither easy nor pleasant to invoke the Nazis for comparison with groups within our own democratic society . . . we are much more comfortable viewing them as a separate tribe of demons.[112]

They see, however, direct similarities between the way the Nazi system and the nuclear narrative works,

> Both Nazi and nuclear narratives are crucially sustained by certain psychological mechanisms that protect individual people from inwardly experiencing the harmful effects . . . of their actions on others. [The authors use the specific example of Nazi doctors in the concentration camps to make their point.] Various bureaucratic procedures, by divesting the individual of a sense of responsibility for destructive collective behaviour, would greatly enhance numbing and doubling as well as brutalization. In the nuclear case, the domination of technology makes the numbing all the easier.[113]

Plath's fears concerning the mind-numbing nature of American mythology about the Cold War must have suggested strong parallels with the numbing procedures which allowed a nation, Germany, to practice the inhumanities of the "Final Solution." For Germany under the Third Reich, the myth was of the Aryan, for America in the Cold War it was Americanness (with all its overtones of international responsibility for democracy and anti-Communism). Her treatment of the Holocaust attempts to confront this mythologizing of the past and its resulting assimilation in the present.

Plath's disquieting use of historical material is founded in a conflict between desires to confront such attitudes by writing about the Holocaust in a personal way and the viewing of such history in suprapersonal terms. The difficulties which Plath's poems enact characterize the problems surrounding the relationship between literature and the Holocaust. Aharon Applefield writes:

> By its very nature, when it comes to describing reality, art always demands a certain intensification, for many and various reasons. However, that is not the case with the Holocaust. Everything in it already seems so thoroughly unreal, as if it no longer belongs to the experience of our generation, but to mythology. Thence comes the need to bring it down to the human realm. This is not a mechanical problem, but an essential one . . . I do not mean to simplify, to attenuate, or to sweeten the horror, but to attempt to make the events speak through the individual and in his language.[114]

Many critics who explore the "literature of atrocity" recognize this conflict between the "naturally" mythic nature of the event and the problematic need to remove the events from such an easily assimilated mythology. Irving Howe, for instance, writes in similar terms to those of Lifton and Markussen:

> It is a grave error to make, or "elevate" the Holocaust into an occurrence outside of history, a sort of diabolic visitation, for then we tacitly absolve its human agents of their responsibility.[115]

Yet, as Jon Harris recognizes, there are equal dangers in trying to "de-elevate" the Holocaust,

> The problem, in fact, is twofold; first we must accept that the horrors were so extreme that they seem to belong to another world entirely, not the one we regularly write poetry about. . . . Secondly, in claiming that we can conceive of the horror of the Holocaust, we lay ourselves open to the accusation that by imposing a critical form and structure

on it we are *ipso facto* justifying it: by attributing a rationale of any sort
to it, we admit that the Holocaust could be seen as a rational act.[116]

This problem, which Plath's treatment of the Holocaust both enacts and attempts to approach, is also exhibited in the Hollywood
films produced at the time (as well as, with the notable exception
of *Shoah* [1983], many similar "popularizing" cinematic treatments from then on). Annette Insdorf describes the difficulties
inherent in cinematic treatments of the Holocaust; she writes,
"Whether on a small or silver screen, there is perhaps nothing
inherently wrong in an entertaining film set against the backdrop
of World War II. . . . But as we move further in time from the
realities of Nazism and closer to comforting myths, many people
shrug off the complexity of history to embrace the simplifications
offered by films,"[117] and cites John J. O'Connor (a *New York Times*
TV critic) who writes,

> *The Diary of Anne Frank* and *Judgement at Nuremberg* . . . depend on a
> confined theatrical setting, superfluous dialogue, star turns, classical
> editing (mainly with close-ups), and musical scores whose violins swell
> at dramatic moments. These studio productions essentially fit the bris-
> tling raw material of the Holocaust into an old narrative form, thus
> allowing the viewer to leave the theater feeling complacent instead of
> concerned or disturbed.[118]

The act of trying to bring such horrific events to a popular audi-
ence involves rationalizing and conventionalizing the material,
which ultimately runs the risk of trivializing the very events it is
trying to commemorate. In Plath's case, the "old narrative form"
is that of a lyrical expression through personalized myth-making,
within which the Holocaust fits uncomfortably and which Plath
attempts to highlight.

Edward Alexander defines the roots of this discomfort over
fitting the Holocaust into something other than itself (be it a conventional form or a current political argument) as a problem relating to the resulting metaphoricalization of the Holocaust. While,
as James E. Young notes, in extension to Rose's point about the
impossibility of dividing history and subjectivity, that no one has
control over which subjects become metaphors,[119] Alexander expresses a common concern when he declares his unease about
the sorts of connections made, not only by Plath (between her
current fears and Jewish suffering, or between, in Young's terms,
their shared "era of victimhood, victimized by modern life at large
as the Jews and Japanese had been victimized by specific events

in modern life"[120]), but also by the other writers mentioned above (who connect the Holocaust with a potential nuclear holocaust):

> Stealing the Holocaust . . . [is the process of] reduc[ing] Jews from the status of human beings to that of metaphors for other people's suffering . . . we must keep steadily before our mind's eye the truth that, as Cynthia Ozick once wrote, "Jews are not metaphors—not for poets, not for novelists, not for theologians, not for murderers, and never for anti-Semites."[121]

The fear Alexander expresses is that once the Holocaust and its Jewish victims become mythic metaphors for suffering, it is easy to extend the metaphoric treatment into the very anti-Semitic stereotyping that resulted in the Holocaust itself. Specifically in terms of poetry, the symbolic approach which characterizes poetic utterance appears as more directly tainted by the Nazi regime's abuse of metaphor, in the "language rules," cited above. Lawrence Langer quotes Ortega y Gasset about the symbolic approach (using metaphor) to naming that which is too awful to name—"name it "vicariously and surreptitiously." He writes,

> The rulers of the Third Reich, especially the framers of the "final solution" put this principle to viciously cynical use (explaining in part, why critics like George Steiner felt so strongly that language had been corrupted for an artistic expression of the theme.)[122]

These problems, surrounding the depiction, treatment, and metaphoricalization of the Holocaust, not only inform Plath's late poems, but are difficulties which such poems enact. Langer's tentative conclusion about the way out of the impasse (between the necessary and actual impact of the Holocaust, and the ethical problems associated with its depiction) is through a creativity which works to collapse the distinction between history and the present, metaphor, and subject. He writes of an episode in Kosinski's *The Painted Bird:*

> Episodes like the gouging out of the eyes seek to induce a sense of complicity with the extremity of cruelty and suffering in modern experience from which history (with its customary distinctions between "then" and "now") conspiring with the readers' reluctance to acknowledge such possibilities, unconsciously insulates us. The art of atrocity is the incarnation of such possibilities through language and metaphor.[123]

Plath's late poems try to work in a similar way, "inducing a sense of complicity" by combining the events with such an intimate tone and material. Yet instead of trying directly to present the cruelty of the Holocaust itself, the feeling Plath's poems generate is one of complicity in the easy assimilation of such past cruelties. Her poems try to avoid the anonymity and amnesia contingent on the "us and them" and "then and now" distinctions that characterize the perception of history by highlighting her use of the Holocaust as metaphor. In such poems, the reader is *meant* to feel uncomfortable with the suprapersonal mythical depiction of Jewish suffering, and further, feels somehow implicated (because of his or her traditional identification with the lyrical persona) in the voyeurism such an assimilation of the Holocaust implies. This feeling of implication Plath's poems generate may be viewed in broad terms as their success. While there is not the familiarity with the subject (due to its mythic dimensions), which allows Plath to mobilize the kinds of overt reflexivity seen in her treatment of myth in, for example, "Electra on Azalea Path," her poems which deal with the Holocaust also work to comment on metapoetic concerns. In "Lady Lazarus," Plath collapses the "them and us" distinction by confronting readers with their voyeurism in looking at the subject of the poem. To apply Theresa De Laurentis's theorizing of the cinematic position of women to Plath's poem, in "Lady Lazarus," the speaker's awareness of her performance for the reader (who is implicitly part of the "peanut-crunching crowd") works to reverse the gaze of the reader, relayed through the gaze of "Herr Doktor," so that the speaker becomes "overlooked in the act of overlooking."[124] In extension, by her parodic overstatement (Lady Lazarus as archetypal victim, archetypal object of the gaze), Plath highlights the performative (that is, constructed rather than essential) nature of the speaker's positioning as object of the gaze and, to extend Judith Butler's terms, the speaker enacts a performance that attempts to "compel a reconsideration of the place and stability" of her positioning and "enact and reveal the performativity" of her representation. This sense of performativity and the reversal of gaze also extends, in "Lady Lazarus," to compel reconsideration, not only of the conventional positioning of the woman as object and of the voyeurism implicit in all lyric poetry, but also of the historical metaphors as objects of gaze. Readers feel implicated in their easy assignment of the metaphoricalization of the speaker in her role as object and performer, and contingently are made to feel uncomfortable about their similar easy assimilation of the imagery of suffering of the Jews the speaker uses.[125]

In "Daddy," a similar, if more complicated relationship between reader, speaker, and metaphor is at work. Like "Lady Lazarus," "Daddy" does not attempt to depict the suffering directly for our view (an impossible task, for the reasons given above) but works by confronting the reader with, and compounding the problematic distinctions and connections between the private and the historical (*our* lives and *their* suffering). In other words, the reader's reactions of unease, discomfort, and outrage are necessarily a response to the surface, the poem itself, rather than the events the poem uses as metaphors for its subject (be it about individualism, freedom, memory, or a combination of these), because the events themselves are not graspable. The poem is effective because it leaves the reader in no clear or easy position in relation to the voyeuristic "gazes" operating within it (of reader at speaker, reader at poet, poet at speaker, and all at the events which are metaphoricalized), and able to take no clear stance regarding the metaphoricalizations involved.

Ultimately, then, George Steiner's divided attitude toward Plath's treatment of such material (in 1965 he applauded "Daddy" as "The 'Guernica' of modern poetry," and in 1969, declared his unease with its nature, asking, "Does any writer, does any human being other than the actual survivor, have the right to put on this death-rig?"[126]) most adequately and accurately represents the effect and effectiveness of Plath's project, a project meant to highlight the mythic constructedness of such pasts, intending to confront the reader with their implication in the viewing and metaphoricalization of other's lives and suffering, and aimed at foregrounding the complexity of the boundaries between myth and reality which form the root of the problematic placement of the Holocaust in our society.

Transcending History?—"Lady Lazarus"

The conflict Plath both expresses and struggles with in her poetry, about the mythic and personal dimensions of recent historic events (and their connection to contemporary concerns) is reflected in her treatment of transcendence. Contrary to the perceptions of many commentators on her work, Plath is ultimately ambivalent toward transcendence, and her ambivalence is bound up in her conflict between desires to write mythic or occasional poetry, to write poetry that moves toward a transcendence of life, or poetry that is "criticism of life," working to name, remember, and comment upon it.

Heaney, noting the difficulties surrounding Plath's use of history and much myth, argues that her poetry embodies the "problematic relation between artistic excellence and truth, between poetry as impulse and poetry as criticism of life." Plath was keenly aware of this problem, and her poetry not only demonstrates this "problematic relation," but also consciously explores it. Hughes, in his assertion that "little of her poetry is 'occasional' . . . the poems are chapters in a mythology," sidesteps this central issue about the relationship between the mythic and the occasional in her poetry.[127] Judith Kroll, in her work *Chapters in a Mythology*, whose title is taken from Hughes's statement, sums up the agenda behind such "archetypal criticism," arguing that Plath's poetry

> is not primarily literal or confessional. It is, rather, the articulation of a mythic system which integrates all aspects of her work, and into which autobiographical or confessional details are shaped and absorbed.[128]

Laudable enough as a reaction to those who view Plath's work as unable to escape from unmediated autobiography, this attitude, in ignoring the social and political content of her poetry, results in the one-dimensional view that

> in Plath's poetry, there is one overriding concern; the problem of rebirth or transcendence; and nearly everything in her poetry contributes either to the statement or to the envisioned resolution of the problem.[129]

However sincere her motives, Kroll's project radically underestimates the many textual and thematic ambiguities and complexities in Plath's poetry, so that while she explores Plath's struggles with transcendence—"The need to transcend personal history in a way more radical than that expressed by her poetry as mythic rebirth had long been implicit in her work"[130]—she fails to see Plath's difficulties with the idea of transcendence as a goal, difficulties which are crucial to note for any balanced perception of her treatment of political and historical subjects.

As a student at Smith, Plath linked her Nietzschean belief in the importance of individualistic struggle with a negative attitude toward bodily and earthly transcendence. In a first-year essay on her religious beliefs, she writes that, notwithstanding her reservations about Nietzsche's position on the alignment of power with goodness, she wholeheartedly supports his objections to the attitude of Christianity toward transcendence, quoting enthusiastically from his *Thus Spake Zarathustra,*

> Weariness which seeketh to get to the ultimate with one leap, with a death-leap: a poor ignorant weariness unwilling even to will any longer . . . the sick and perishing—it was they who despised the body and the earth, and invented the heavenly world, and the redeeming blood-drops! . . . But to what did they owe their convulsion and rapture in their transport? To their body and this earth.[131]

Several years later at Cambridge, Plath's misgivings about the goal of transcendence are unchanged. For her, there is no one state of perfection at which to aim—life is individual, willed struggle; the single leap to perfection or transcendence of the earthly struggle is therefore uncreative as it denies the very diversity and change which is creative life. She writes in an essay on Plato of the threat to creative growth of "man's" desire for perfection: "When man is seized with a vision of perfection, his first wish is to keep it, to preserve it beyond change," but sees its corollary as "death by stasis" and recognizes this conflict as an eternal one and central to Yeats and Keats's poetry.[132] Yet while viewing transcendence of life's struggles as an unrealistic and uncreative goal, Plath is attracted toward such an end and recognizes the roots of her conflict (between imperfect life and perfect transcendence of life through death) in a long-standing, Romantic literary tradition. She demonstrates her ambivalence in many of her "transcendental" poems, most notably, "Lady Lazarus."

"Lady Lazarus" is generally viewed in straightforward terms. Not only are Plath's metapoetic concerns often ignored, but the poem is usually read as a simple celebration of transcendence and apotheosis. In the poem, so the reasoning goes, the speaker, after experiencing two unsatisfying deaths and rebirths, finally, through an awareness of her objectification by her oppressors, is able to die for a third time and be reborn, phoenix-like, in some radically different and fulfilling way. On one level this reading fits. Plath's figure retains traces of D. H. Lawrence's poem, "Phoenix," which she underlined in her copy of his *Selected Poetry:* Lawrence's speaker tells the reader that unless she or he is willing to be completely destroyed, "you will never change," because the phoenix is only reborn "when she is burnt, burnt alive, burnt down / to hot and flocculent ash."[133] Indeed, in the drafts of "Lady Lazarus," two versions of the ending are more explicit in their phoenix-imagery, as Plath describes the reborn speaker as having either feathers, or feiry and feathery hair.

Yet recourse to Plath's reading also generates an alternative reading of the poem's concluding apotheosis. In an essay written on her Russian literature course at Smith, she writes with sympathy of the late nineteenth-century prose writer and dramatist, Leonid Andreyev's short story, "Lazarus," which deals with the tragedy of the biblical figure after he came back from the dead, but did not return with any tales of some joyous life after death.[134] Andreyev's Lazarus shares similarities with Plath's figure. Both initially retain marks of the grave, which the reader is told by Lady Lazarus will shortly disappear, as indeed most of them do in Lazarus's case. More significantly, the apparently transformed woman at the end of Plath's poem also recalls Andreyev's figure: his gaze makes hope and life wither in all who look into his eyes, and Plath's witchlike[135] Lady Lazarus is equally destructive, ascending, in the climax of the poem, from the ashes to destroy her oppressors (CP 247). Andreyev's Lazarus is a tormented figure; the same could be said, finally, of Plath's figure—that Lady Lazarus' triumphant breaking of the cycle of death and rebirth by a different type of rebirth does not happen. In "Phoenix," Lawrence's approval of the necessity of a total abnegation of the self required for rebirth and change conflicts with Plath's ambivalence toward the whole notion of rebirth. If there is nothing after death, to be reborn from death is a nightmare experience, and transcendence, resulting from some sort of "death-leap" (which Plath, with Nietzsche, rejects as an easy option), denies the creativity of stoical struggle. Plath sums up this conflict in a characteristic ambiguity of the poem's final line. "And I eat men like air" might connote the power and danger of the reborn witchlike figure, yet its very nihilism seems negative. By "eating" men the speaker signifies her continued attachment to the men seen as persecutors throughout the rest of the poem: as either lovers or victims, they are not transcended, but are still vital to the phoenix-woman's existence.[136]

Plath's attitude toward transcendence is not, then, as straightforward as Hughes and Kroll assume, and her "occasional" or political poems cannot be viewed merely either as single aberrations (Perloff) or as a more general treatment of personal struggles with transcendence (Kroll and Hughes), but are an aspect of Plath's conflict between the use of poetry as communication or as a purely aesthetic object, part of the mythic "system" Hughes and Kroll apprehend. Plath's emblematic use of names such as Hiroshima and Dachau in later poems not only denies the single-mindedness of the mythic progression asserted by Kroll and Hughes, they form a distinct attempt to deal with immediate cultural issues. The conflict between the uses of history and myth which Plath's poetry addresses and struggles with is, then, a conflict between a mythic or aesthetic desire to transcend history and a historic, didactic urge to remember and name it.

The striking nature both of the theme of transcendence and of the imagery of the Holocaust diverts attention from the less immediately powerful theme of memory and amnesia to which Plath more frequently returns in her late poems (in "Paralytic," "Amnesiac," "Lyonesse," "The Night Dances," and "Winter Trees" as well as the other poems already noted). This theme chronologically outlasts both the poems of apotheosis and Plath's use of historical imagery (both of which occur only in the poems of October and November 1963), and signals the focus of Plath's concerns about history and transcendence; amnesia appears to be the prerequisite for transcendence or transformation, and yet Plath's fear of cultural amnesia forms the root of many of the political poems discussed earlier. "Amnesiac," for example, deals with the theme of abnegation of self, responsibility, and memory. Like the earlier "Tulips" (1961), it is set in a hospital and views such abnegation as a negative resolution of the difficulties of life. In "Amnesiac," this negative withdrawal from humanity is achieved through discarding or peeling off the past. Yet the imagery of peeling used with so much censure in "Amnesiac" is reproduced in "Ariel," written six days later, on 27 October, to describe the speaker's apparently positive, ecstatic movement toward the "red eye" of transcendent self-hood, familiar in the apparent conclusions to "Stings" and "Lady Lazarus," also written in this period. In "Ariel" even the familial connection, seen as crucial in "Tulips" and "Amnesiac," is broken. Yet, as I demonstrated in the previous chapter, the movement toward transcendence in "Ariel" is not unequivocal. In "The Jailor" (17 October), amnesia is seen more directly negatively as entrapment, which the jailer uses against his victim (CP 227). Amnesia leads to the participation of the victim in her victimization, so that the speaker asks rhetorically, reminiscent in both theme and tone of "Daddy," what the jailor would do without her to victimize. Indeed, in "Daddy," after confronting the shock factor of the Holocaust imagery, the poem appears as clearly about the necessity of remembrance for individual freedom. An understanding of the difficulties surrounding Plath's treatments of the Holocaust and transcendence shows that these difficulties stem from more deep-rooted creative conflicts which pervade Plath's entire corpus of work: namely, her conflict about the uses of poetry and her ambivalence about memory and amnesia (which relates to her Bloomian anxiety about the power of the past). Indeed, the theme of memory and amnesia relates not only to her treatment of history and politics and to her relationship with literary precursors such as De Quincey, explored in this and the previous chapters, respectively, but also, perhaps most crucially, it relates to her utilization of psychoanalysis, which, next to her treatment of the Holocaust, has seen the most unbalanced critical assessment in her work.

3

The Psychoanalyzing of Sylvia

> our chief problem here is not to diagnose mental maladies,
> imposing order from outside. Rather, we shall stress the intrin-
> sic technique . . .
> —Sylvia Plath, "The Magic Mirror: A Study of the Double in
> Two of Dostoevsky's Novels"

Since the posthumous publication of *Ariel*, Plath's poetry has
elicited many and various forms of psychoanalytic interpretations.[1] There are three central reasons for this. The first, the most
obvious and also most problematic, relates to Plath's own life. Not
only her death by suicide at the age of thirty, but also her widely
publicized previous breakdown at the age of nineteen leads critics
to stress a perceived pathological connection between Plath's poetry, especially in terms of its frequent treatment of themes of
death and mental extremity, and the extremes in her own life.
Alicia Ostriker describes how the negative reviews of *Ariel* concentrated on antagonism toward the type of personality expressed in
the work and how, as one critic put it, the volume should be "best
viewed as a case study."[2] From then on, comments such as those
from Elizabeth Harkwick appear often: "In Sylvia Plath's work
and in her life the elements of pathology are . . . deeply rooted
and . . . little resisted . . . Her fate and her themes are hardly
separated and both are singularly terrible."[3] In these cases the
poetry is often treated symptomatically in a misguided and fruitless attempt to psychoanalyze the woman.

The second reason arises from the complexity and ambiguity
of much of Plath's late work. This has recently encouraged the
use of poststructuralist psychoanalysis, because the interest of
poststructuralist theories in the difficulties inherent in symbolization (and their acceptance, even privileging, of the resulting slip-
periness of language) allows the study of linguistic complexity

132

without demanding any final closure of meaning. Felman identifies "the quintessential service that Lacan has rendered to our culture: to have derived from Freud a way of reading whose unprecedented thrust and achievement is to keep an entire system of signification open, rather than foreclose it, so that the small, unnoticeable messages can grow by virtue of the fact that the big ones are kept still, open and suspended."[4] It is the desire for closure which tends to lead critics to simplistic judgments of, and equations between, Plath's life and work, and which poststructuralist psychoanalysis avoids. The third reason relates more directly to the content of Plath's poetry itself. The recurrence in it of psychoanalytic terminology and symbolism reflects Plath's thematic interest in dealing with the various workings of what Freud termed the "family romance." The frequency with which such images and themes recur makes a psychoanalytic approach attractive to even those critics who do not generally have recourse to psychoanalytic theory.[5] Of these three reasons, a biographical interest is perhaps understandable, but often misguided. The use of Lacanian psychoanalysis for textual elucidation is attractive, but must be treated with care to avoid undue abstraction. Plath's own use of psychoanalytic theory is an interesting and productive reason for psychoanalytic study of her poetry that so far has received little serious critical attention. The problem inherent in all psychoanalytic theory is that no part of it is provable—as Felman asserts, "In practice . . . one can use theories . . . only as enabling metaphorical devices, not as extrapolated, preconceived items of knowledge . . . The practice of psychoanalysis . . . is a process, not a set of doctrines"[6]—yet in relation to Plath's poetry, such theories are a useful, if not essential tool because of her own interest in and treatment of this body of knowledge in her work.

Most psychoanalytic approaches to Plath's poetry fall broadly into two categories, each with a different agenda. The first approach uses object-relations theory, the second, Lacanian theory. Object-relations theory is primarily interested in the relation between the mother and infant in the first year of life. It is generally seen to derive from Melanie Klein's theories, which attempted to transform the classic Freudian account of the Oedipal drama by making the mother (rather than the father) its central figure. Chief among object-relations theorists used by Plath's critics are D. W. Winnicott and the feminist critic, Nancy Chodorow. While David Holbrook's account of Plath's poetry, *Sylvia Plath: Poetry and Existence* (1976), relies on R. D. Laing[7] and Winnicott, most later object-relations approaches to Plath draw on Chodorow's theories.

In terms of literary criticism, this approach usually works to examine the "family romance" in material terms, examining the subject's response to the "real" mother and father. It tends to lead critics into discussion of the biographical and material bases of Plath's poetry, somehow to "discover" the woman behind the work. Lynda Bundtzen, for example, utilizes object-relations theory because she perceives Plath's mother as a more "unmanageable influence than Otto Plath on her poetry,"[8] and this kind of theory desires to transform the Oedipal conflict into a mother-, rather than father-centered conflict. Bundtzen concentrates on Plath's biography in her analysis of the poetry, viewing it as "more significant than literary history for understanding Plath's poetic development," not out of any professed interest in Plath's psychological troubles, but because of her feminist desire to see Plath "turning away from received literary tradition as a significant context for defining [herself] as creator, and a turning inward and backward, to the personal past and [her] psychological development."[9] However laudable the reasons behind this strategy, Plath's own keen interest in her literary past and her writerly desire to situate herself in literary tradition casts doubt on both the accuracy and the value of Bundtzen's argument.

Stephen Gould Axelrod, while using a combination of object-relations and poststructuralist psychoanalytic theory, also wants to situate Plath's poetry very firmly in the actual or conjectured psychic disturbances of her past. He writes, for instance, of Plath's late interest in poetry as an oral, rather than a scripted medium:

> Plath's compulsive orality appears throughout her discourse in the linked figures of *mouthing* and *eating*. These metaphors suggest that her need to voice poems was connected to disturbances in her earliest experience of parental nurturance. The style of that experience may have conditioned her enduring sense of hunger, suffocation, and deprivation as well as her need to keep proving oral prowess, envisioned not as the source of discrete products but as a continuous, life-sustaining process.[10]

Axelrod's statement, like much of the psychoanalytic material relating to Plath's poetry, amounts to crude speculation, which does little to help understand or appreciate her work. His criticism suffers from the assumption that appears to lie behind most object-relations approaches to Plath's poetry: that psychoanalytic theory is primarily used to understand *abnormal* psychological states. The clearest example of this is found in David Holbrook's study of Plath, which aims at analyzing her poetry to identify and examine the "schizoid" nature of Plath's personality. Holbrook states, for instance, that "it will become evident that we need more than literary critical disciplines to fully understand her."[11] The conflation of Plath's personality with her poetry is obvious. Such an agenda results in pointless speculation about Plath's infancy and ridiculous statements about her poetry. In writing about "Poem for a Birthday" (1959), for instance, Holbrook states that "I have little doubt the poem is about the poet's own experience of mental breakdown and treatment of which a fictionalized account is also given in the novel *The Bell Jar*,"[12] and bases his analysis on the supposition that

> Sylvia Plath . . . seems to have experienced the mother's handling in infancy, for whatever reason, as something meaningless and bewildering, largely composed of "impingement," a kind of (male) "doing," substituted for (female) "being." Instead of a female "being for," what she experienced was "doing," scraps of maleness.[13]

He uses the second section of the poem "Dark House" to "argue . . . that Sylvia Plath had within her identity a split-off male element built on hate—and this is *all* she has. She doesn't have any female core. A fragment of maleness is the basis of her identity."[14] Axelrod and Holbrook's approaches are usefully categorized in relation to the two different forms of traditional psychoanalytic criticism identified by Shoshana Felman in her Lacanian approach to "The Case of Poe." Holbrook's attitude toward Plath's work resembles Edward Wood Krutch's 1926 appreciation of Poe's art as "only meaningful as the expression of morbidity," bearing "no conceivable relation . . . to the life of any people."[15] Axelrod's approach parallels that of Marie Bonaparte, which Felman sums up: "the pathological tendencies to which Poe's text gives expression are an exaggerated version of drives and instincts universally human, which normal people have simply repressed more successfully in their childhood."[16] And while Holbrook's approach, like Krutch's, is the cruder of the two, both these critics of Plath represent what Felman perceives as "the distinctive professional crudity of what has come to be the classical psychoanalytic treatment of literary texts . . . this blind nondifferentiation or confusion of the poetic and the psychotic."[17] Object-relations criticism, then, with its interest in the "real," tends to suffer from the same fault as traditional Freudian criticism, assuming that the text merely mirrors the unconscious obsessions or neuroses of the writer (or of the character within the text) and, as Roger Poole claims, that "in order to establish the nature of these obsessions, [critics] could interpret basic Freudian symbols as if these had an exact and unchanging denotative value."[18]

The Lacanian-based approach and its feminist offspring (which often applies the work of theorists such as Julia Kristeva and Luce Irigaray) avoid the pitfall of assuming that all psychoanalytic study must, by its nature, be interested in abnormal psychology or even in the actual psychology of the writer studied. In its most excessive form, Lacanian theory moves to the other end of the "real-symbolic" continuum, postulating that the language out of which the text is constructed is autonomous of its "scriptor" and thus has its own unconscious. The relation of this to the usual biographical interest in Plath is clear. At its extreme, by seeing the poem as a set of free-floating "signifiers" for which no "signifieds" can be established, the critic is freed from trying to establish, in any significant sense, an originating consciousness or presence in the text. This approach is also interested in the "family romance," but in a symbolic sense. It is not at all concerned with the relationships of real families, but concentrates instead on the difficulties of symbolization—of entry into the "symbolic order" of the Father, represented by language, from the pre-Oedipal "imaginary" of the Mother—and the instability of this movement, exhibited in the ever-present slippage or playfulness of language.

Both Lacanian and object-relations criticism have their uses. They both, however, often fall into the trap that besets most Plath criticism, that is, moving toward an extreme of either abstraction or biographicalizing. As Alicia Ostriker notes, many critics of Plath's poetry, by trying to avoid the prurience or sentimentality that characterizes the texts of writers such as Holbrook and Lynne Salop,[19] respectively, fall into the other extreme:

> No failure to distinguish art from life ... is quite so stupid as pretending that poetry is some kind of sterile, swabbed tissue of language unaffected by the poet's life and incapable of infecting the reader's life.[20]

Although Ostriker reserves the brunt of her censure for critics such as those who use Lacanian theory, both the extremes of this art-life continuum are equally limiting. Felman notes similar critical extremes in "The Case of Poe":

> The protestations [against "confusion of the poetic and the psychotic"] however, most often fall into the same ideological trap as the

psychoanalytic studies they oppose: taking for granted the polarity of sickness versus health, of normality versus abnormality, they simply trace Poe's art (in opposition, so they think, to the psychoanalytical claim) to normality as opposed to abnormality, to sanity as opposed to insanity, to the history of ideas rather than that of sexual drives, to a conscious project as opposed to an unconscious one.[21]

However, notwithstanding Felman's assertions about the dangers of critical polarities, her own, Lacanian analysis of Poe falls into the extreme of abstract generalization. Critical extremes like these characterize much Plath criticism, resulting in often simplified distinctions between Plath's early (read intellectual or abstracting) and late (read emotional or psychologically disturbed) poetry, and partisan attitudes which view the woman as either a feminist saint or a self-obsessed "bitch goddess."[22] The main reason for these extremities of Plath criticism is, as I explained in the introduction, that its authors generally fail to recognize the importance of the relationship between Plath's intellectual, academic background and her emotional and creative life; or, in Felman's terms, between her conscious and her unconscious projects.[23] Therefore, they fail to see the impossibility of any final separation of intellect and emotion (poetry as craft and expression) and the fruitlessness of any discussion inhabiting such extremes. In terms of psychoanalytic approaches to Plath, this failure, which leads to the extremes of biographicalizing and abstraction outlined above, exists in a critical blindness to her own lifelong interest (intellectually and professionally, as well as biographically motivated) in the theories of Freud and Jung.

ABJECTION AND THE MOTHER: "POEM FOR A BIRTHDAY"

Various critical approaches to "Poem for a Birthday" provide a useful example of this problem of the extremes into which both types of psychoanalytic criticism fall. On the one hand, Jacqueline Rose sees "Poem for a Birthday" in almost purely abstract terms, as about "the tension between division and unity."[24] At the other extreme, Stephen Axelrod, like Holbrook, reduces the poem to an account of the poet's biography:

"Poem for a Birthday" is a sequence about a woman's relationship to her parents . . . [Plath] especially liked its final segment, "The Stones" which alludes to her suicide attempt and recovery.[25]

The excesses of these approaches conceals the fact that psycho-analytic theory can be used profitably to help explore the poem sequence.

Plath wrote "Poem for a Birthday" in September 1959, shortly before her twenty-seventh birthday, while staying at the artists' colony, Yaddo, at Saratoga Springs in New York State. It is a highly complex poem, consisting of eight seemingly unrelated sections. Plath wrote it very quickly, a departure from her usual laborious way of writing, but a method which characterizes all her later poetry. Indeed, "Poem for a Birthday" is often viewed as a turning point between her early apprenticeship work and the later poetry on which her reputation rests. Plath first mentions the sequence in her journal on 22 October, five days before her birthday. She describes it as an ambitious venture, about a madhouse and nature, "vivid, disjointed. An adventure. Never over. Developing. Rebirth. Despair. Old women" (J 322). In addition to the obvious connection of the poem's title with her own birthday, Plath was four months pregnant with her first child, a fact with which she is preoccupied in many of her journal entries of this time. In the same entry, on 22 October, she writes of a dream about herself and her mother bearing a child at the same time and the confusions of family relations stemming from this (J 322). These struggles with identity and motherhood, both in terms of her own and her mother's, inform not only the dream but also the last enigmatic part of her description of the subjects of "Poem for a Birthday" cited above: "Developing. Rebirth. Despair. Old women."

In many ways, both as poet and as woman, Plath saw her pregnancy in a positive light, as some kind of affirmation of her femininity and creativity. She wrote earlier in her journal of her belief that motherhood would release in her a strong poetic power (J 166).[26] Several months before she did conceive, she writes of her fears of infertility, situating mothering as an experience above both "any orgasm or intellectual rapport":

> A woman has nine months of becoming something other than herself, of separating from this otherness, of feeding it and being a source of milk and honey to it. To be deprived of this is a death indeed. (J 308)

The extremity of her feeling about this becomes morbid, when several pages later in her journal Plath returns to the subject, declaring that a friend with multiple sclerosis is effectively healthier than she, because of her ability to bear children (J 310).

Hughes sees this period at Yaddo, both Plath's pregnancy and

"Poem for a Birthday," as the beginning of a new phase in her poetry, as indeed Plath hoped, writing on 10 October, "When will I break into a new line of poetry" (J 319). Hughes links "the new poetic world she had glimpsed" in "The Stones" to her pregnancy, declaring that "she took childbearing in a deeply symbolic way. Maybe it is truer to say that she accepted the symbolic consequences of an event."[27] Plath's positive attitude toward childbearing was noted not only by Hughes but, among others, by Al Alvarez, who writes, "The *real* poems began in 1960, after the birth of her daughter, Frieda. It is as though the child were a proof of her identity, as though it liberated her into her real self. I think this guess is borne out by the fact that her most creative period followed the birth of her son, two years later."[28] Yet such straightforward affirmation contrasts with Plath's description of the seeds of the poem: her feelings toward pregnancy and childbirth were as deeply ambivalent as her feelings toward her own mother. In 1956 she writes of her fears of carrying a deformed baby, viewing it as an expression of "that old corruption" inside herself she was always terrified would surface (J 101). In 1958, her fears are unchanged as she speculates in her journals that her "gross fears at having a baby" stem from her vivid memory of observing a woman giving birth at the Boston Lying-in Hospital and the raw physicality and pain involved in the process (J 219). Plath writes of another dream of childbearing at the time of "Poem for a Birthday," 3 October 1959:

> My mother furious at my pregnancy, mockingly bringing out a huge wraparound skirt to illustrate my grossness. (J 317)

The ambivalence of these feelings toward the "otherness" of maternity, as both potentially liberating and primitively gross, and toward being and having a mother, is reflected in "Poem for a Birthday."

Plath's awareness of the psychoanalytic ramifications of her attitude toward the mother is apparent in her treatment of a short story about the "mother" she was writing at the same time as "Poem for a Birthday." She notes in her journal on 29 September that her story would express the "horror of primal feelings" in a "diatribe against the Dark Mother, The Mummy, Mother of shadows. An analysis of the Electra complex" (J 316). Then on 4 October she writes of finishing the story, "really a simple account of symbolic and horrid fantasies," and her excitement at then reading a case history of Jung's in which she found "confirmation of

certain images in my story." She describes in detail these images
(such as those relating to a child's dreams of her affectionate
mother as a witch or a ravenous beast and the mother subse-
quently going mad and behaving in a beastlike manner) and concludes with satisfaction that it all "relates in a most meaningful
way my instinctive images with perfectly valid psychological analysis" (J 317). Plath was clearly concerned about the psychological
validity of these "instinctive" images (it is, however, important to
note she is not saying they are *her* real fantasies). This point is a
crucial one to bear in mind, because many of the images that
appear to have been in her "mummy story" (which is now lost)
are repeated in "Poem for a Birthday," most notably the eating
mother and the images of animalism. On 19 October, in fact,
Plath writes of "Medallion," "The Colossus," and "The Manor
Garden" (written immediately before "Poem for a Birthday") as
a "heartening" advance on the work she was doing the day before,
which was "too linked to the prose vision of the garden in my
Mummy story" (J 321), which implies that before she wrote "Poem
for a Birthday," Plath was trying to write poetry on similar lines
to those of the "Mummy story" with all its awareness of "valid"
psychological states. Indeed, not only does Plath refer to Jung in
her journals, she also kept extensive notes on his theories, much
of which find strong echoes in "Poem for a Birthday." She notes,
for instance, a number of points Jung makes about marriage as
a state which, in its perfect union of two people returns those
involved to childhood, and, in their new desire for creativity, robs
them of their rationality and individuality, as they are "made in-
struments of the life urge." These notes clearly show Plath's *conscious* inclusion of psychoanalytic themes and imagery in "Poem
for a Birthday," here in terms of the ambiguous nature of the
states of child- and parenthood.[29]

"Poem for a Birthday," as one of Plath's most densely metaphoric and semantically elusive poems, elicits widely differing
critical appraisals of both its content and its value. Many critics
see the poem as ineffective because of its fragmentary nature, its
lack of logical progression, and the instability of the speaker's
voice. Bundtzen, in her desire for stability and closure, sees the
fragmentary nature of "Poem for a Birthday" as the weakness of
an otherwise strong poem, declaring, in exasperation, of its shifting persona, "Throughout these poems she is so unformed, we
cannot tell whether she is animal, vegetable or mineral." Kroll is
more explicit in her criticism, stating that, "The shifts from one
image to another . . . give the effect of being fragmentary or

undisciplined ... by distributing the first person voice among so many different personae, its power as an organizing device is undermined."[30] While highlighting this instability as a central aspect of Plath's sequence, these critics fail to see beyond its resulting complexity to question whether this very complexity is a conscious reflection of the sequence's concern with identity. Most critics who see the poem as at all successful tend to see it as connected not only with identity, but, specifically, with maternity. Bundtzen writes, for instance, that it is "in many ways a celebration of passivity ... utterances from the womb ... the tone throughout is cheerfully childlike, filled with wonder," although her own cheerful generalizations are themselves in question.[31] Robyn Marsack describes the poem as "a defiant, sometimes frantic rejection of the mother, the unstoppable journey toward motherhood."[32] Yet these and other critics, writing without a well-defined psychoanalytic framework (that is, using psychoanalytic theory only opportunistically), struggle when they attempt to say anything more about the figuring of maternity in "Poem for a Birthday."

Writers who attempt more than a few lines of analysis of the sequence tend to be critics such as Rose and Holbrook who use a more consistent psychoanalytic framework (Lacanian-based and Laingian object-relations, respectively). This is not only due to the poem's central concern with identity (of the speaker of the poem and of the poem itself), but also because of its dreamlike, often surreal forms of expression and the lack of any discernible logical progression through the sections. Indeed, Plath writes in her journals about its composition that while she is perturbed by the lack of "a tightly reasoned and rhythmed logic," she also feels freed by it (J 324). Her initial resistance to such "freedom" reflects that of many of her less consistent psychoanalytic critics. An example of such critical inconsistency is found in the work of recent object-relations critics such as Bundtzen and Axelrod. Both their book-length studies contain frequent references to the theories of Nancy Chodorow to explain, for instance, Plath's ambivalence toward the mother. Indeed, Bundtzen sees this ambivalence as "nearly a governing principle in her poetry."[33] Chodorow, then, appears to provide theories which help to understand the ambivalence of feeling toward the mother (both "real" and symbolic) expressed in "Poem for a Birthday." Chodorow writes of the female's strong connection to the mother, noting the comparative instability of the developmental separation from the mother that female children experience:

The female's self is less separate and involves a less fixed "me-not-me" distinction, creating . . . difficulties with a sense of separateness and autonomy.[34]

She states, further, that this sense of connection to the mother, partially lost as the child develops, is emphasized when the daughter becomes pregnant herself. Yet when Bundtzen writes about "Poem for a Birthday," she does not utilize the psychoanalytic theories she uses elsewhere. Axelrod, too, while looking specifically at Plath's "family romance" in other parts of his book, does not attempt to apply Chodorow's theories to "Poem for a Birthday." This reflects not only the opportunism of such critics' deployment of psychoanalysis but also, perhaps, a central flaw in object-relations theory—oversimplification—an example of which is described by Lynne Segal. Writing about the theory in general, Segal asserts,

> There is . . . an idealization of "maternal" and "feminine" ways of behaving. For instance, as Jane Flax argues, in criticism of Sara Ruddick's now very popular concept of "maternal thinking," the mother's sexuality, aggression and the need and desire for an autonomous life are all ignored: "Important things like rage, frustration, aggression, sexuality, irrational intense love and hate, re-experiencing of one's own childhood, blurring of body boundaries, conflict between the demands of a child, one's mate, other children and other work are missing."[35]

In relation to the use of such theories as a literary tool, this idealization and oversimplification of the maternal does little to help illuminate a text as complex as "Poem for a Birthday." Lacan's theories of the subject, with their emphasis on fantasy, symbolism, and language, can be utilized more profitably.

The Lacanian theorist, Julia Kristeva, is as concerned as Chodorow to theorize mothering. Kristeva's concentration on symbolic events (rather than on concrete experiences of "real" mothers) makes her theories more available for use in textual analysis (by writers such as Rose) to elucidate the thematic and imagic complexities of "Poem for a Birthday." Rose uses Kristeva's theory of "abjection" to explore the complexities of the sequence in its figuring of "the permeability of boundaries . . . which allow objects to pass back and forth across inner and outer space."[36] Kristeva's theory of abjection, however, suggests more than Rose's application, which tends toward abstraction, implies. The theoretization of abjection is able to encompass not only the quite abstract topic of the difficulties of the subject's relation to the physical world, which Rose explores, but also the more material area of the ambivalence of feeling toward the mother, which object-relations critics such as Holbrook, Bundtzen, and Axelrod limitedly try to explore. Kristeva writes, with obvious debts both to Freud's *Totem and Taboo* (1913) and to Mary Douglas's anthropological study, *Purity and Danger* (1966),

> The abject confronts us, on the one hand, with those fragile states where man strays on the territories of *animal*. Thus, by way of abjection, primitive societies have marked out a precise area of their culture in order to remove it from the threatening world of animals or animalism, which were imagined as representative of sex and murder. The abject confronts us, on the other hand, and this time within our personal archaeology, with our earliest attempts to release the hold of *maternal* entity even before ex–isting outside of her, thanks to the autonomy of language. It is a violent, clumsy breaking away, with the constant risk of falling back under the sway of a power as securing as it is stifling.[37] [my emphasis]

This dual description of the abject, as figuring both the animalistic world and the infant world, gives coherence to the two linked movements of Plath's poem—the struggle with the mother and the struggle with the corporeal. In "Poem for a Birthday," however, the persona (or personae) is seen not merely as struggling to free herself from the mother, but as both child and mother. In this sense, Elizabeth Grosz's point about Kristeva's dual interest in abjection and maternity is relevant, "Like the abject, pregnancy is a borderline state in which there is an indistinction between subject and object."[38] Kristeva's theories then, while sharing common ground with Chodorovian ideas of the daughter's connection to and difficulty in differentiating herself from the mother, deals with this area in a broader way, enabling her theories to be used to elucidate textual difficulties rather than purely biographical motivations.

Due to the fragmentary nature of "Poem for a Birthday," a too unitary examination of its themes and concerns would not only destroy its vitality; it would not help to give the poem sequence coherence, as its meaning lies in the constant slippage of both image and theme. In an effort to be relatively logical, however, four central aspects of the poem sequence will be separated out, all of which relate more or less directly to the search, both in and of the poem, for identity. First, the lack of boundaries the speaker feels between herself and the world will be examined, and more specifically, the boundaries between the speaker and the mother/ infant. Second, the poem's horror of corporeality will be studied; specifically, the sense the speaker has of being bound by the abject (and occasionally of being the abject). Third, the problems relating to the relationship between abjection and transcendence will be examined, how the self is defined by what it casts out, in a continual process of moulting, rather than any single transcendence of the flesh. Finally, Time and Language will be explored in terms of their recognition as emblems of the Symbolic, toward which the speaker moves as she moves away from the mother, but also in relation to the ambiguity of their positioning, which denies any simple progression in the poem sequence from abject to subject. Such an examination will show that psychoanalytic theory *can* be used without falling into the extremes of either pathologizing Plath or abstracting the specificity of her poetry out of existence.

Boundaries

The title of the first section, "Who," preempts the reader's question in response to the title of the sequence—who is the subject of the birthday? In denying any stable knowledge of the subject of the birthday (the lack of a question mark leads the reader away from any reassurance that this question is going to be answered, indeed, that "who" is a question as much as a name), the poem denies that it is going to be a celebration of a day of birth. The openness of the title "Who," which does not say whether it means "who am I" or "who is it," also prepares the reader for the poem's instability of both identity and location. This instability relates directly to the mother. In the first stanza the speaker states that she is "all mouth," and as the devourer and storer of the October fruit, the mother's stomach described further on could well be the speaker's. Later in the poem, however, the speaker becomes less than a mouth, desiring merely to be a tongue to the mother's mouth or to be devoured by the mother's mouth (CP 132). The instability of identity and location, of the speaker figuring both mother and child, is approached more explicitly in the next poem of the sequence, "Dark House." The speaker describes her own burgeoning pregnancy in animal terms and notes the stirrings in her belly (CP 132). Yet she also declares that she finds comfort inside such a belly, "the bowel of the root" (where again, similarly to the "mummy's stomach," pregnancy and digestion are conflated[39]). In addition, the title "Dark House" refers to the paper house the speaker builds herself, like a wasp, the place in which the eggs are laid. Yet the speaker is also burrowing *within* a house, describing its numerous cellars. This shift of location (and so identity) gains pace so that in the last stanza, when the developing fetus is described, it is unclear whether the speaker is referring to herself or to something inside herself. The final line, declaring the arrival of the mother, emphasizes the shifting nature of the poem, because there is no clue whether the mother is the speaker or the speaker's mother. This instability of location and identity results from the difficulty in establishing boundaries between the self and the other, most notably in "Poem for a Birthday," between the self and the mother or infant.

The dreams Plath reported at the time of writing "Poem for a Birthday" are concerned not only with the grossness of birth, but exhibit a strong connection to her own mother. Several months before Plath and Hughes arrived at Yaddo, Plath underwent psychoanalysis in Boston in sessions which appear to have centered around Plath's effort to break the strong bond she felt with her mother, a bond Aurelia Plath describes in terms of "psychic osmosis" (LH 32). This maternal bond not only affected Plath's life, but also influenced her writing. Although Aurelia Plath's statements about her daughter's life, like those of any mother, must be treated with caution, in her introduction to *Letters Home* she states that "throughout her prose and poetry, Sylvia fused parts of my life with hers from time to time" (LH 3). Plath herself, at the time of her Boston psychoanalysis sessions, writes of the complexity and closeness of the relationship between writing, maternity, and her own mother:

> To spite your mother, you don't write because you feel you have to give the stories to her, or that she will appropriate them. (As I was afraid of having her around to appropriate my baby, because I didn't want it to be hers). So I can't write. (J 279)

The sense of a lack of boundaries between the self and the mother-other seen above is what makes "Poem for a Birthday" so fragmentary, so that the speaker is not so much seen as mother and then child, but as somehow inhabiting both states. This effect, of both describing and then crossing boundaries, is explicit in "Dark House," where the speaker states that she needs to make maps. Maps draw and define boundaries, in this case, the boundaries of the cellars of the "Dark House." Yet in the next line, the cellars are transformed into tunnels through which the speaker burrows. The maps then become maps of the tunnels the speaker makes, tunnels which transgress boundaries. Kristeva sees in this process of boundary-negotiation the figuring of the abject: "We may call it a border, abject is above all ambiguity."[40]

Both Chodorow and Kristeva view pregnancy as returning the (pregnant) daughter to a position of oneness with the mother, to the pre-Oedipal state of comfort and terror where the boundary between infant and mother is ambiguous. Pregnancy raises the problem of the abject directly, which, as feminist philosopher Elizabeth Grosz describes, "signals the precarious grasp the subject has over its *identity* and *bodily boundaries* . . . [and the] ever present possibility of sliding back into the abyss of corporeality" [my emphasis].[41] It is in this "abyss of corporeality" (of being merely a body, as yet undifferentiated from the mother/infant as subject) in which the speaker of "Poem for a Birthday" is situated, inhabiting the garden shed in "Who," the bowel-like "Dark House" of the second section, and the kitchen in "Witch Burning."

Plath connects her unconscious horror (articulated in her dreams at the time of writing "Poem for a Birthday") of bearing a deformed child with both her own mother and with the suffocation of the lack of some boundary between the mother and the child. She describes a dream she had at Yaddo, of giving birth to an underdeveloped and deformed child, and wonders of its significance

> Symbolic of smother in the womb? Image of mother dead with the Eye Bank having cut her eyes out. (J 313)

In "Poem for a Birthday," this dream is reflected not only in the poem's sense of claustrophobia in the lack of boundary between self and mother, and self and world, but also in an often surreal representation of the purely corporeal. In Plath's dream, the mother's eyes have been cut out by the Eye Bank. In "The Stones," the last section of the sequence, the speaker is in a city of human spare parts where the dead pass on their organs (specifically their eyes) to others. The body, dismembered for its parts, loses its humanity, becomes merely matter. As a poet, Plath makes repeated, conscious use of both such themes and their related imagery in "Poem for a Birthday," and as such the theory of abjection gives not only a certain amount of coherence to the instabilities of shifting images, but also a depth and resonance to these images and themes. To return to the image of the devouring mother in "Who," for example, an awareness of "abjection" gives coherence to the imagery of the speaker as a waste product, "an owl pellet" who asks the mother, the "wastebasket gaper," to "Eat me" or engulf the waste. The speaker, who describes her addressee as "Mother of otherness" (that is, something separate from herself), is then, by declaring herself abject (a waste product) and demanding engulfment by the mother, fighting against individuation from her.

Corporeality

The instability of boundary between self and other is not only represented in terms of infant and mother, but also in terms of self and material world. Abjection is, Kristeva declares (implicitly accepting the Cartesian mind-body dualism), a method of establishing the self as somehow other than merely material. Because of the flimsiness of the boundary between self and the merely material, the subject's attitude toward the corporeal is, Kristeva asserts, one of fascinated horror:

> Loathing an item of food, a piece of filth, waste or dung. The spasms and vomiting that protect me. The repugnance, the retching that thrusts me to the side and turns me away from defilement, sewage and muck. The shame of compromise, of being in the middle of treachery. The fascinated start that leads me toward and separates from them.[42]

In "Poem for a Birthday" the speaker appears both horrified yet fascinated by the foulness of corporeality that surrounds her. In "Who," the decaying cabbages are described in grossly sensuous terms. In "Maenad," the speaker, as a Maenad, is not only a crazed woman (connected to the madhouse described in "Who"), but a follower of Bacchus, god of fertility, vegetation, wine, and decay. The ambiguity of the corporeal, of life leading to death, is described explicitly: "The dead ripen in the grapeleaves." Even in "Flute-notes from a Reedy Pond," the most lyrical poem of the sequence, the pastoral scene is represented in terms of material decay, as all life is described sinking in "a soft caul of forgetfulness" (CP 135). The unpleasant yet seductive image of the "caul" is emphasized by the sibilance of "sink" through to "soft caul." The multiple meanings of "caul" are significant in their relation to abjection. The word describes both the inner membrane enclosing a fetus and a fold of membrane which connects the stomach with, and separates it from, the other abdominal organs. The conflation of pregnancy and digestion reflects that hinted at by the mother's stomach in "Who" and "the bowel of the root" in "Dark House" and works to somehow soil the fetus, so it is seen as abject or tainted. The deceptively simple image has connotations of the abject as boundary, separating fetus and mother, fetus and stomach, as well as describing an amnesia which is caught up in the purely corporeal (against which abjection is a defense). The folkloric connotations of the caul as a lucky charm against death by drowning work further to increase the sense of shift and ambiguity. The irony of sinking or dying (as amnesia implies) into a mythic charm against such a death is self-evident.

Yet throughout "Poem for a Birthday," notwithstanding the speaker's fascinated horror of the abject, because she lacks any stable identity she sees herself as not only surrounded by, but also frequently *being* the abject. Throughout the eight poems of the sequence, its personae are frequently inanimate and animalistic. The speaker describes herself variously as a root, a stone, a pebble, an owl pellet, a rice grain, an owl, and a wasp. More unusually (as many of Plath's other poems figure the speaker as inanimate object), in both "Dark House" and "The Beast," the speaker is situated in the bowel, the wastepipe of which its object, excreta, is that most abject of bodies. In a slightly different form, in "The Stones," the speaker describes how she is embraced by "food tubes." Here again, the speaker appears as abject waste, enclosed by the bowel, a tube of expulsion, or more likely, just a body merely taking in and expelling food. The speaker, due to the indistinction of boundary between herself and the purely corporeal, in seeing it as abject, sees herself necessarily as abject as well. Kristeva writes of this situation, in regard to the skin on milk, as part of the ambiguity of the process of gaining separate subjectivity:

> nausea makes me balk at that milk cream, separates me from the mother and father who proffer it. "I" want none of that element, sign of their desire: "I" do not want to listen, "I" do not assimilate it, "I" expel it. But since the food is not an "other" for "me" who am only in their desire, I expel *myself*, I spit *myself* out, I abject *myself* with the same motion through which I claim to establish *myself*.[43]

Abjection and Transcendence

The horror of the corporeal that abjection represents may be nothing more than the old romantic horror of the mortal—that which is alive must someday die and rot. Plath was conversant with this traditionally romantic horror, writing, as I noted in the previous chapter, in "Plato and Popper," of Keats and Yeats's treatment of the conflicting desires for deathly perfection and mutable life. As Grosz suggests, the roots of abjection are found in this dilemma:

> The subject recoils from its materiality, being unable to accept its bodily origins and hence its immanent death.[44]

Yet the horror of decay in "Poem for a Birthday" goes beyond romantic concern with mortality as a necessary fact of life. It is a fear of being *merely* corporeal—of "sliding back into the abyss of corporeality,"[45] which leads to the process of abjection. Yet this process is both ambiguous and doomed to failure. Mary Douglas, in *Purity and Danger*, writes,

> It is part of our condition that the purity for which we strive and sacrifice so much turns out to be hard and dead as a stone when we get it.[46]

Kristeva, although agreeing that the lifelong process of abjection can never end satisfactorily, disputes Douglas's view that in death we gain any measure of purity, however hard and cold. For Kristeva, the process of abjection ends in becoming, as a corpse, abject. She writes of this paradox:

> as in true theater, without makeup or masks, refuse and corpses *show me* what I permanently thrust aside in order to live. These body fluids, this defilement, this shit are what life withstands, hardly and with difficulty on the part of death. There, I am at the border of my condition as a living being. My body extracts itself, as being alive, from that border. Such wastes drop so that I might live, until, from loss to loss, nothing remains in me and my entire body falls beyond the limit—. . . cadaver.[47]

This sense in which the process of abjection (of defining the self by the material wastes one expels[48]) is necessarily continuous and unsuccessful informs the difficulties with images of apotheosis and transcendence of life which many of Plath's poems contain. The two penultimate poems in the sequence, "Flute Notes from a Reedy Pond" and "Witch Burning," both end in moves toward transcendence and transformation. In "Flute Notes," the transformation takes the form of a seasonal moulting. In its mention of

Golgotha and the description of the caddis fly emerging from the moults as "a god flimsy as a baby's finger," the metaphor extends to encompass a standard Christian image of Christ's ascension. Yet the moults, who by their action of releasing the fly, release the tongue to sing of this mythic event of emergence, are now tongueless, unable to perpetuate the myth. This loss of the myth is directly referred to in the line before: "The wingy myths won't tug at us any more." The statement is connected to the last stanza both by the repetition of "m" and "t" sounds, between "myth," "tug," and "more," and "molts" and "tongueless," and by a colon, which implies that what follows is either illustration or expansion of the statement. The elegiac tone throughout, of autumnal sleep and death, is not, therefore, transformed by the mythic movement of the final stanza, which takes the form of a drowsy memory or lost dream. The transformation is seen as leading toward, rather than through death—the caddis fly is short-lived. The transformation is also, perhaps more significantly, somehow merely part of the cycle of the seasons, immersed in nature and the corporeal, not transcending it. So "Flute Notes," through its concluding ambiguities, questions the possibilities of transcendence of the subject's relation with the material world. "Witch Burning" questions this aim of transcendence of the mother-infant relation.

In "Witch Burning," the ending of conflagration also appears positive, due to its connection with light in comparison to the positioning of the speaker throughout "Poem for a Birthday" where, as abject, she exists in various forms of darkness: in the bowel, in the shed, in the "dark house," and in stone's shadow of the line before. Yet there is a sense, left over from the previous lines when the speaker demands the return of her "shape," that this is not the triumphant transformation the reader is led to believe. The separation of the infant from the mother can only occur when the former becomes "another," sees itself to have a human shape separate from that of the mother, and becomes too developed to return to the womb. The speaker of "Witch Burning" asks the mother to "unclench your hand" so she can be released into her own shape. Yet she loses this shape in the final conflagration (as, if the lines are seen to have Christian overtones, the self becomes lost in Christ). Even earlier in "Witch Burning," the speaker describes her movement toward this apparently transcendental moment in terms of the purely corporeal, as a moth flying through (rather than into) a candle flame. In this statement, both the image of the self as moth and the description of the candle as a mouth return the speaker to the positions she inhabits throughout "Poem for a Birthday," as small, vulnerable, and abject.

Neither Rose nor Marsack, in their different approaches, are able to elucidate fully these problematic endings. Marsack sees the conclusion of "Witch Burning" in purely material terms, as moving toward the pain and fulfillment of childbirth: "The speaker herself, swelling with pregnancy, is forbidden to be inert as the heat is turned up and the lick of the flame renders the pain of giving birth. The 'mouth of a door' the 'mouth of a flame': devouring dark or devouring light, inescapable one way or another."[49] At the other extreme, Rose characteristically abstracts, declaring, in general terms, of all the mutations throughout "Poem for a Birthday," "Transformation is always liable to go back on itself. Bodies go forward and wind back into the origins of themselves."[50] Yet the ambiguity of the endings of "Flute Notes" and "Witch Burning" reflects the ambiguity of life as a process of abjection. The abject, as Kristeva notes, must be expelled "to establish the clean and proper body of Oedipalization, yet can never be expelled."[51] While there are moments in "Poem for a Birthday" of the gaining of subjectivity in the form of Time and Language discussed below, the casting off and drawing of boundaries involved in abjection have no sense of linear progression, not even the running and retreating pattern Rose perceives. If transformation, as either death or (re)birth is just a moulting ("Flute Notes") or a disintegration ("Witch Burning") (that is, a return to the pre-Oedipal, as either purely corporeal or as a disembodied nonsubject), then the only form of renewal available to the subject is a materialistic reconstruction of the body. And it is with this less romanticized, imperfect renewal that "The Stones," the last section of the sequence, ends (CP 137).[52]

Time, Language, and Orality

Time is mentioned regularly throughout "Poem for a Birthday." Kristeva, in line with most recent psychoanalytic theorists, directly connects the sense of Time with the symbolic order. Kristeva writes:

The symbolic order—the order of verbal communication, the paternal order of genealogy—is a temporal order. For the speaking animal, it is the clock of objective time: it provides the reference point, and, consequently, all possibilities of measurement, by distinguishing between a before, a now and an after. If *I* don't exist except in the speech I address to another, *I* am only *present* in the moment of that communication. In relation to this present of my being, there is that which precedes and that which follows.[53]

From an anthropological viewpoint, Douglas also sees the connection between "purifying" (or "abjecting") and creating order, and views Time as a sophisticated form of this organisation of the environment.[54] Subjectivity (separation from either the mother or the infant) demands its incorporation, as the speaker recognizes in "Maenad," when she declares that she must swallow the glittering line of Time as it unwinds from the sun. Yet the devouring image of "swallow," reminiscent of the devouring mother and of the speaker as "all mouth," sullies the purity of the process of individuation, and reminds the reader of the final ambiguity and impossibility of achieving "pure" subjectivity. The textual ambiguity of Time recurs throughout "Poem for a Birthday." In "The Beast," for instance, the speaker declares "I housekeep in Time's gut-end," combining the subjectivity of Time with the corporeality of the gut-end. Many of the poem's openings are situated squarely in temporality: in "Who" describing the end of summer, in "Witch Burning" describing autumn, in "Maenad" describing what the self was once like, in "The Beast" describing what the beast was once like. "Flute Notes" also starts with a placement in time, more specifically, in autumn (like "Who" and "Witch Burning"), but is more extended in its description of the change in season from a fertile and protected summer to a lyrical, but unKeatsian autumn. The poem sequence's placement in temporality is not, however, only in *comparison* to the descriptions of the speaker as purely corporeal, but also figures explicitly *within* the corporeal world, so the frequent references to time cannot be seen as any positive movement toward a stable subjectivity. For Kristeva, this constant alternation between "time" and corporeality is the ultimate female aim: an "impossible dialectic of two terms, a permanent alternation,"[55] to avoid the danger and powerlessness associated, for women, with either total identification with the Symbolic *or* the Imaginary, respectively.[56] In "Poem for a Birthday," however, such ambiguity leads to a fragmentation which, while appearing to be stoically accepted in "The Stones" as unable to be transcended, never appears as revolutionary or empowering because of the final victimization of the subject by her subject-position.

This unstable positioning of Time extends to the treatment of the theme of memory throughout "Poem for a Birthday," a theme that is not only the basis of all Freudian psychoanalysis (recalling repressed memories gives freedom from their expression in neurotic behavior), and, as the last chapter showed, central to Plath's work, but also of great interest to the major twentieth-century writers whom Plath admired (such as Eliot and Joyce). In Plath's poem sequence, the recognition of Time is bound up in the ability to use memory, which is seen as central to the speaker's subjectivity. In "Who" she declares, "I said: I must remember this, being small," which, through the double meaning (the importance of remembering being small, and the importance of memory if one is small), affirms the crucial nature of memory to one who is in other ways very vulnerable. By the past tense of "said," the statement is, in itself, an instance of remembrance, of self-exhortation to remember. At the end of "Who" as well, memory and its lack are seen as the result of being treated as an inanimate object (with naturalistic overtones of electric shock treatment in the madhouse) as the speaker describes the lack of memory stemming from being subjected to such "inhuman" treatment. The ambiguity (that verges on irony here) is that the speaker, in declaring herself without memory, describes her abject position within a timescale (it is for weeks that she is amnesiac), in other words, from within a position of temporality and subjectivity. The immanence of memory, even within an apparently purely corporeal state (which would deny memory as a quality of subjectivity) emphasizes the ambiguous position of Time throughout "Poem for a Birthday." For Plath, this project of recognizing Time, and thus memory, was not only important in terms of its individual psychological import (as that by which one exists as a human individual), but also (in relation to the previous chapter) in macrocosm, crucial for the morally sound organization of society. Psychoanalytic theory is thus able to show and explore direct connections between Plath's "personal" poetry (such as "Poem for a Birthday") and her more socially engaged writing (such as "Getting There" [1962]) in their shared themes of time and memory. By implication, "Daddy" (1962), therefore, does not have to be about either the personal or the social—its concern with memory includes both micro and macrocosm.

In "Poem for a Birthday," Language appears in a similarly ambivalent form due to its status, like Time, as a device by which one exists as a subject. Kriseva writes of the connection between Time and Language in relation to the symbolic order, "There is no time without speech. Therefore, there is no time without the father. That, incidentally, is what the Father is: sign and time."[57]

As Kristeva notes in relation to the process of differentiation from the body of the mother, "we ex-ist . . . outside of her thanks to the autonomy of language."[58] The similarities to the eye in English, of "month" (as time, yet also the monthly cycle of menstruation, an abject) and "mouth" (as language, yet also the devourer, the "rim" which defines the abject) add to the thematic links between the two. The mouth is both devourer and speaker. It is not only involved in, but also articulates abjection: as Grosz notes, of verbal articulation in its most refined form:

> poetry . . . [is a] more or less successful attempt to sublimate the abject . . . by naming or speaking it . . . [we are able to] hold the stable speaking position.[59]

Thus the images of orality throughout "Poem for a Birthday" do more than situate the speaker in the pre-Oedipal oral stage: they are the pivot around which the ambivalence of the poem moves.[60] The tongue is viewed as a privileged object, something that sets the mouth apart from merely devouring—so the empty carcass of the chrysalis in "Flute Notes" is described as a mouth without a tongue. In "Witch Burning," the scarlet tongues who are teachers of truth refer both to the fire (with overtones of the Inquisition) and back to "Maenad," when "A red tongue is among us." This image is threatening, but also the liberating catalyst which enables the speaker to assert her separate identity. The daughter demands that the mother leave her barnyard, her arena of basic animal noises or echolalia, the meaningless noise before speech in which the infant delights, so that she can become another— either to become a subject separate from the mother or to transform her subject-position by becoming a mother herself.[61] The second interpretation is backed up by the closeness of rhyme between the first and last words, "mother" and "another"—with one small consonant change, this becomes "I am becoming a mother." The dual meanings of this line relate directly to Plath's thoughts on maternity, which, as I noted above, she views as a development into something other, and then separating from the otherness (J 308). At the end of the poem, the speaker asks a "Lady" to "tell me my name." This demand for the verbalizing of an identity potentially achieved (significantly it is "tell me" not "give me") is directed to a female "other" crucially different from the "mother." The "lady" can be either the mother in her new role as independent woman, some other female, or the speaker in her new identity.[62]

The Pitfall of Abstraction

As shown in the preceding sections (treating boundaries, corporeality, transcendence, time, and language), the use of Kristeva's form of Lacanian psychoanalytic criticism helps give coherence, without necessarily imposing form, both to the images and the themes of "Poem for a Birthday." In its broad concerns with unstable subjectivity and symbolization as well as with fantasy, Lacanian psychoanalysis can be used with fewer of the pitfalls of using a theory of personality formation (which is what psychoanalysis is) on a poem, into which object-relations critics fall. (The most obvious of these pitfalls is of equating the "mother" of the poem exclusively with Plath or her mother.) Yet, for example, Rose's otherwise intelligent and productive use of these psychoanalytic tools to analyze Plath's work tends often to fall into the opposite trap. Rose frequently ignores the corporeal and the personal in Plath in a determined effort to apply psychoanalysis in a way as different as possible from that of critics such as Holbrook. She reads "Poem for a Birthday" as being purely about symbolization:

> If Plath is laying out the conditions of symbolisation, then it becomes
> as impossible to pathologize her as it is to insist that everything nega-
> tive in her writing is the fault of others.[63]

Rose is determined to answer other Plath critics—both those who denigrate and those who sacralize her writing.[64] She sees these extremes of criticism arising from a too biographical interest in Plath, which, due to the circumstances of the poet's life, tends to center on the question of blame. Rose's concern with the inadequacy of theories of blame appears recurrently in her chapter on "Poem for a Birthday" and tends to warp her own reading of the poem, leading to statements such as "One of the meanings of the poem's transformations is therefore that blame belongs to no-one and to everyone, because it is something which is passed around: 'It is easy to blame the dark'."[65] Throughout the chapter Rose's argument is weakened by an unnecessary defensiveness about her unbiographical use of psychoanalysis, as when, for instance, she writes: "to read the poem in terms of abjection does not involve some personalized accusation against the mother (there is absolutely no point in trying to decide whether Plath's mother or husband is at fault),"[66] which leads her to perceive the whole of Plath's life as irrelevant. Her use of Plath's journals to elucidate "Poem for a Birthday" centers on the odd tangential academic reference Plath makes, for instance, to Oesterrich and Defoe (to illustrate her perception of Plath's concern with the "relation between inner and outer worlds"[67]). There is a conspicuous absence of reference to the wealth of material in the journals where Plath writes of her own feelings of undifferentiation from her husband or mother and of her fascinated attraction to and repulsion from her own corporeality, the most striking example of which is early in the journals when Plath writes of "the illicit sensuous delight I get from picking my nose," and goes on to fill a page with gloriously extended descriptions of the "many subtle variations of sensation," declaring the activity to be "a sexual satisfaction!" (J 69). This is surprising because in her criticism of the editing of the Plath archive, Rose declares that

> The editors of the *Journals* and of the *Letters Home* take out much of Plath's body in this further sense: "nasty bits" meaning not what might be judged ethically distasteful . . . but the body at its most abject in the more familiar sense—in Plath's case the sinusitis which runs through her writing.[68]

In fact, Rose's continual denial of the importance of Plath's life beyond her writing life has the opposite effect of *emphasizing* the biography. In trying to avoid classifying Plath as mentally ill, trying to use psychoanalysis, not to diagnose illness but to illuminate universalities, Rose ignores the very earthy and corporeal element in "Poem for a Birthday" to see it as a poem about representation, writing of "The Stones": "Less personally, more pertinently, what is it that Plath at the level of poetic representation and language is being asked to relinquish?"[69] This results in the loss of potentially crucial points in an abstraction that does not reflect the impact or content of the poem. In relation to my earlier discussion of the problem of transcendence in "Poem for a Birthday," Rose writes, for instance:

> the encounter between Plath and Hughes takes place in this territory over the function and purpose of poetic language, over the poetic and fully gendered distinction between abjection and transcendence, or, more precisely, between the different and antagonistic images of femininity we can attach to each.[70]

By trying to make "Poem for a Birthday" solely about poetry, Rose fails to explore how the poem sequence figures these "antagonist images of femininity" in relation to maternity. Rose ignores the various "antagonistic" treatments of childbirth (as the "sign" of woman—a problematic in Kristeva's equation of femininity with maternity), which appears as transcendent, in "Witch Burning" and, conversely, as abjectly corporeal in "Dark House" and "Maenad." It could be that Rose ignores the relationship between abjection and maternity because of Kristeva's problematic treatment of the relationship between femininity and maternity. On the one hand, Kristeva denies any relationship between feminine identity and the maternal. Grosz points out that she

> gives women no special link to the maternal body—either in infancy . . . or in her position as mother. The female is both *too close* and *too distant* from the maternal (too close because she never really resolves her Oedipal relation to establish a relation with the mother; and too far because, when she does acquire a distance between herself and the maternal body, she does so as a pale or inadequate reflection of the male, who, by this fact, is more able to represent the complexities of the infant-maternal relation)."[71]

Yet on the other hand, as Grosz notes, Kristeva theorizes maternity as a betrayal of identity:

> Woman, the woman-mother, does not find her femininity or identity as a woman affirmed in maternity, but, rather, her corporeality, her animality, her position on the threshold between nature and culture. Her "identity" as a subject is betrayed by pregnancy . . . "She" does not exist as such.[72]

The principle reason, however, behind both Rose's abstraction and Bundtzen's biographicalizing of "Poem for a Birthday" is that they ignore Plath's use of her own psychoanalytic readings. Rose sees the two influences behind "Poem for a Birthday" as Paul Radin's collection of folk stories and Theodore Roethke's "greenhouse poems" but ignores Jung, an important influence, not only on "Poem for a Birthday," but also on Plath's story, "Johnny Panic and the Bible of Dreams," which Rose mistakenly asserts Plath wrote at the same time.[73] In fact, Plath wrote the story a year earlier, mentioning it in a journal entry for 16 December 1958 (J 275). The similarities Rose notes between this story and "Poem for a Birthday" are not, therefore, thematic similarities of one moment in time, but are concerns, the tools of which are the psychoanalysis of Freud and Jung, to which Plath repeatedly returns.[74] Granted, Kristeva's theories of abjection were not in existence at the time Plath was writing, but, as Grosz notes, "Abjection . . . is not a new insight but a variation of Freud's position in *Totem and Taboo*,"[75] a work with which she was clearly familiar.

Plath's Knowledge of Psychoanalytic Theory

It is possible to move away from both these extremes of the "art-life" continuum by recognizing Plath's own intellectual interest in psychoanalysis. An awareness of this interest helps avoid the critical prurience of trying to psychoanalyze the woman (by accepting that Plath's treatment of psychoanalytic themes and imagery was conscious) but still avoids abstraction by giving credence to the very material basis on which Plath, from the watershed of "Poem for a Birthday," tried to write her poetry (by accepting that Plath used psychoanalysis as a tool for writing about "real things").

It might be argued, and has been on a number of occasions, that Plath's interest in psychoanalysis was purely a result of her own experience of psychiatric hospitals and psychological extremes. Butscher writes of the psychological content in Plath's honors thesis: "the entire subject obviously meant a great deal to her as it reflected her continued intellectual awareness of her own schizophrenic nature."[76] This is very likely a contributory reason for its appeal to her, but only one among others. Psychology interested Plath in more ways than just as a method of inspecting her own psyche. Even before her first breakdown and psychiatric experiences in the summer of 1953, she applied to Harvard summer school, not only to enroll on the famous O'Connor writing class (rejection from which is often said to have been the catalyst for her breakdown), but also to take a psychology course.[77] Her correspondence with Eddie Cohen between 1950 and 1955 is littered with psychoanalytic jargon—Cohen professed an interest in psychiatry, though not the commitment to qualify in medicine. In 1951 Cohen writes of a friend with a castration complex involved with a woman who was neurotic, and several years later, in 1953, the inclusion of Freudian terminology in Cohen's chatty style continues when he writes of Plath "projecting" when he responds to her query about his inability to take marriage seriously.[78] Class notes and essays Plath wrote at both Smith and at Cambridge show the intellectual appeal psychoanalysis held, not only for her, but also for the contemporary academy.[79] Her Smith College honors thesis, "The Magic Mirror—A Study of the Double in Two of Dostoevsky's Novels," demonstrates the importance Plath placed on a specific connection between literature and psychoanalysis. Throughout the thesis, Plath discusses the figuring of the Double in *The Brothers Karamazov* (Ivan Karamazov) and *The Double* (Golyadkin) in specific relation to psychoanalytic theories of schizophrenia, supporting her arguments with an extensive bibliography of psychoanalytic articles.[80] Indeed, partly due to the powerful influence of R. D. Laing's *The Divided Self* (1960), theories of schizophrenia became of great interest to Plath's generation, evident in the number of psychoanalytic studies of Plath in the 1960s which use and/or abuse his theories.[81] It is important, however, to note Plath's attitude toward her use of psychoanalytic theory. She writes that while "it would be both precarious and presumptuous for a novice in psychology to attempt a clinical analysis of the Double," theories of schizophrenia provide a useful background to her literary study, and is emphatic that

> our chief problem here is not to diagnose mental maladies, imposing order from outside. Rather, we shall stress the intrinsic technique of the stories themselves, and seek to find in the concrete expression of divided character the abstract conflicts which are the polarities of Dostoevsky's universe.[82]

In this preface to her study, Plath is clear about her desire to avoid using psychoanalytic theory either to diagnose illness or to impose some sort of simplistic order on a work of art. Many of her later critics would benefit from such advice.

Plath's interest in psychology and psychoanalytic approaches to literature reflected the increasing cultural interest such matters held for much of American society in the late 1950s and early 1960s. A psychoanalytic, if unsophisticated approach to discussing literature was gaining in popularity in America and Britain at the time.[83] Plath owned a copy of Ernest Jones's well-known Freudian account of *Hamlet and Oedipus* (ca.1949) and heavily marked Jones's chapter on how the Oedipus complex can be seen as an archetype in Western literature, reappearing in many different guises in both literature and myth. Such interest in psychoanalytic approaches to literature is also found in the production as well as the interpretation of texts. Plath noted in a BBC broadcast in 1963, reviewing Donald Hall's influential anthology *Contemporary American Poetry*, that "There is a new spirit at work in American poetry," which she describes as

> an inwardness of . . . images, [a] plummeting subjectivity . . . the uncanny faculty of melting through the leaves of the wallpaper through the dark looking glass into a world one can only call surrealistic and irrational. The analyst's couch has played its role here, I think—that important and purgatorial bit of American literary furniture.[84]

This literary interest was not confined to poetry, as a book Plath owned, *The World Within—Fiction Illuminating The Neuroses of Our Times* (1947), shows. It is an odd collection of short stories from authors as diverse as Dostoevsky and Truman Capote: each story is followed by a psychological analysis of its characters by a psychiatrist. From the knowledge of Plath as a market-orientated, competitive writer, part of the introduction to this book is illuminating. The editor declares,

> That writers today are inordinately interested in the more complex, more intense character of the neurotic personality is undeniable . . . *one password to popularity is psychiatry.*[85] [my emphasis]

Plath marks sections from many of the stories in this collection, and many of the often standard images contained in them re-emerge in her later poetry. For example, Plath underlines a description by Capote in his story "The Headless Hawk": "Her mind was like a mirror reflecting blue space in a barren room."[86] This finds strong echoes in Plath's poem "Mirror" (1961), where the speaker, as mirror, describes herself as having "no preconceptions" and simply reflecting the opposite wall of a room (CP 173).

Plath mentions her intellectual interest in psychology and psychoanalysis frequently in her journals, especially in the spring of 1959, when she was in Boston. This is partly a result of her admiration for her analyst, whom Plath visited weekly at the time, but also as a result of her firsthand knowledge of other people's psychological extremities through her work as a records clerk in the psychiatric clinic of the Boston Hospital (winter 1958–59). Many of the notes Plath made from the patients' case histories find their way into "Poem for a Birthday," written later in 1959 (such as the reflection in "Who" of one woman who felt she was pregnant with a horse, or the treatment, specifically in "The Beast," as well as throughout the sequence, of another woman's fear of the dark and horror of motherhood).[87] At the time she was writing "Poem for a Birthday," Plath also made several pages of notes on Jung, noted earlier. These notes *do* cover areas that applied to her own life, such as marriage, and the daughter's relationship with her mother, but she also took notes on Jung's more general psychoanalytic principals and theories, noting, for instance his belief that in modern life, "man" has developed from being at the mercy of the external elements to being at the mercy of his psyche.[88]

Plath's attitude toward psychoanalytic theory is, then, complex.

On a simple level, she, like many writers of her generation, was keen to use psychoanalysis in her poetry due to its popularity and the mythic power of its archetypal symbolism. She was also interested in it on an individual level, because of her own experience of psychiatry and mental extremity. Sometimes these motives conflict. On one hand, she sees psychoanalysis as a powerful tool to "confirm" her "instinctive" imagery (J 318), in an effort to make it universal, or, as she puts it, to "get philosophy in" (J 295). She was fascinated by the potency of psychoanalysis, writing in her journals,

> is our desire to investigate psychology a desire to get Dr B's power and handle it ourselves? It is an exciting and helpful power. (J 280)

She sees the power of psychology as similar in many ways to that of art, writing of a particularly useful session of analysis that it was as if she had experienced the cartharsis of watching or taking part in a Greek play (J 284). Elsewhere in her journals for this period, she compares the potential creative benefits of a career as a literature teacher and a psychoanalyst. Teaching comes off worse, as it appears too abstract, while psychoanalysis "supplies more reality situations" in terms of the concerns of the people with whom the psychoanalyst, as opposed to the teacher, deals (J 281). It was at this time in 1959, after a year of successful but unstimulating teaching at Smith College, that she was thinking about careers that would inspire rather than stifle her writing. This move toward conscious psychological, rather than poetic influences marks a stage at which Plath, in comparing herself to Adrienne Rich (as she did throughout her career), felt a conscious need to get more of her own world into her poetry. In February 1959 (at the same time of her Boston psychoanalysis sessions and notes on the value of psychology) she writes of successfully rewriting a "ghastly" formal poem, which originally had lacked emotion but had, in its rewriting, achieved the "graphic description of the world." She concluded:

> My main thing now is to start with real things . . . and leave out the baby gods, the old men of the sea, the thin people . . . and get into me, Ted, friends, mother and brother and father and family. The real world. Real situations, behind which the great gods play the dramas of blood, lust and death. (J 296)

It was in this period, as well, that Plath started writing more directly political poetry—the "real things" were, as I showed in the previous chapter, not only "real" personal experiences, but also actual events in and concerns about the social world (the world in which psychoanalysts seek to enable their patients to function). These intentions compare quite interestingly with Rose's effort to depersonalize and abstract Plath's work, "less personally, more pertinently." So it appears that Plath was using psychology, not only for its universally "validating" emblems, but as a way to write about "real things," behind which the melodramatic "drama" of the psyche functioned and fantasized. Later, introducing a BBC reading of poetry, she describes her recourse to the "storehouse" of archetypal imagery that psychoanalytic theory held in terms of using a set of images that appeared as "masks," but that were in fact able to express and communicate the "real" world.[89]

Yet on the other hand, Plath often views herself as victim rather than "master" of such a discourse. Psychoanalysis, while empowering, may also be perceived as victimizing—its recognition of the unconscious contradicted Plath's staunchly humanist beliefs in individualistic self-determination and free will. Also, as Eric Fromm notes in *Escape from Freedom* (a statement which Plath marked in her copy of the book), psychoanalysis, while potentially liberating, has also proved to work as an "instrument of the general trends in the manipulation of personality," constraining individuality and personality development."[90] When writing, in relation to the lost "Mummy" story, of the way the Jung case history "relates in a most meaningful way my instinctive images with perfectly valid psychological analysis," Plath goes on to declare that she, however, occupies the position of victim rather than analyst: "My 'fiction' is only a naked recreation of what I felt, as a child, must be true" (J 318). This conflict between Plath's objective and subjective attitudes toward psychoanalytic discourse (between her desire to stand back and "master" the discourse and her knowledge of her unconscious psychic involvement in it) is not, however, an expression of Plath's own psychological troubles. Rather, such a conflict is inherent in the discourse itself. As Felman asserts:

> The clear-cut opposition between madness and health, or between doctor and patient is unsettled by the odd functioning of the purloined letter of the unconscious, which no-one can possess or master. "There is no metalanguage," says Lacan: there is no language in which interpretation can escape the effects of the unconscious: the interpreter is not more immune than the poet to unconscious delusions and errors.[91]

It is often critics' ignorance of the instability of interpretation resulting from this lack of any metalanguage (whether psychoanalytic, structural, or whatever) that leads to banal, totalizing statements about Plath's life and work.

Plath's "victim-master" conflict is not confined to psychoanalysis. Her analysis of the Double in "The Magic Mirror," for instance, not only draws heavily on Freud's psychological theories, it also frequently refers to the mythic theories of James Frazer. Plath writes home at the time that her mother's gift of Frazer's *The Golden Bough* is a useful addition to her research on the double in its discussion of the soul or the ego symbolized as a shadow or reflection of the individual (LH 144–46). Like her readings of psychoanalysis, Plath also related her readings of myth (such as those collected by Frazer and Robert Graves) to her own life. She writes, for instance, in her journals, of finding in *The White Goddess* lots of potential and highly symbolic names for "our children whose souls haunt me" (J 221), who she sees as white goddesses and knights, and in relation to the semiautobiographical novel, *The Bell Jar*, describes the heroine, Judith Greenwood, as an enigmatic white goddess (J 168–69). Just as Plath uses Frazer and Graves as tools of both creative and academic work (between which, in any case, a definite line cannot be drawn), so with Jung and Freud. The boundary between myth and psychoanalysis is not absolute—Freud used myth as a metaphor for universal experiences such as the Oedipal complex, Jung was fascinated by the mythic properties of archetypes and the collective unconscious. Plath poetically treats the discourse of psychoanalysis as a myth itself—a myth of personal and universal origins and motivations, which enabled her to "get philosophy in" the universal statement, and also write about the "real."

It is Plath's combination of personal and universal (to which most poets aspire), her irreverent appropriation of, yet personal identification with, perhaps even victimization by the mythic power of Jung, Freud, Frazer, and Graves which, in Plath's case, confounds critics. True, Plath's use does not always produce good poetry, yet the single-mindedness of critics such as Holbrook (who applies psychoanalysis to Plath herself and sees the poetry as merely symptom of psychosis), Kroll (who sees *The White Goddess* as the central shaping force behind Plath's poetic development) and even Rose (who applies psychoanalysis seemingly to abstract rather than to elucidate Plath's writing) is ultimately of limited use in evaluating her poetry.

Fathers: Mythic, Literary, and "Real"

An awareness of the complexity of Plath's personal and intellectual treatment of psychoanalysis (her conflicting feelings of being both "master" and victim of such a discourse) is, then, crucial in any discussion of the figuring of the "family romance" in all of Plath's poetry. In other words, it is a mistake to perceive the figures of "mother" and "father" in her poems simply as either her "real" parents[92] or, on the other extreme, as just abstract treatments of a patriarchal social structure. As an example of this less frequent, but equally misleading extreme of abstraction, Ferrier writes, "While it is certainly true that Plath makes use of para-Freudian categories in many poems, especially in those dealing with her father, we must also be aware that she is using these ironically, saying, in effect, 'yes, well, this is what patriarchal psychology, even the mainstream tradition of literature itself at certain points makes of this'."[93] The evidence of Plath's conflicting attitudes toward psychoanalysis makes such a simplistic "mastery" of the discourse (that enables her to be confidently ironic about it) unlikely. Plath's treatment, then, of the father in her "family romance" lies between these extremes of abstraction and biographical "reality."

I have already explored an aspect of Plath's treatment of the mother with relation to "Poem for a Birthday" in terms of the problems of achieving an identity separate from her. Certainly, Plath treats this figure and related female figures throughout her career, most notably in "All the Dead Dears" (1957) and "Medusa" (1962). Yet, the father is also frequently treated, either within the same poem (as in "All the Dead Dears"), or, in both timing and theme, in companion works to the "mother-poems" ("The Disquieting Muses" [1957] and "On the Decline of Oracles" [1957]; "Lorelei" [1958] and "Full Fathom Five" [1958]; "The Colossus" [1959] and "Poem for a Birthday" [1959]; "Medusa" [1962] and "Daddy" [1962][94]). Notwithstanding her poetic interest in the mother (in relation both to her own mother and to her perception of herself as inhabiting that role in society—woman and mother), and, contrary to Bundtzen's simplistic feminist revision, the father is an equally, if not more powerful figure in Plath's poetry.[95] It is certainly the father to which her poetry returns more frequently. This is mainly because of Plath's awareness of herself as a writer in a predominantly male tradition. Despite her linking of female creativity with motherhood, the father stands, in a Bloomian sense, as the symbol and master of the literary heritage to which any poet aspires.

Biographically, the facts relating to Plath's relationship with her own father are well known. Briefly, Otto Plath was a professor in entomology at Boston University. He was considerably older than Plath's mother, a powerful, and, it appears, somewhat demanding man. Aurelia Plath gives an example of this. She writes that when Sylvia was born, Otto informed his colleagues, "'I hope for one more thing in life—a son, two and a half years from now!'" Sylvia's brother, Warren, was born exactly two and a half years later, and "Otto was greeted by his colleagues as 'the man who gets what he wants when he wants it'" (LH 12). In fact, all of Aurelia's introduction to *Letters Home* shows Otto as a powerful, if often benevolent, patriarchal figure of whom the young Syliva was very fond. He died when she was eight, and his physical absence translates into a powerful presence throughout Plath's poetry. Further, Otto Plath (in addition to standing for the general power of patriarchy), as the published author of a successful book on bumblebees, directly symbolized the *literary* power to which his daughter aspired—certainly, as Plath wrote to Cohen, she identified the creative-literary side of herself with her mother, but her professional ambitions centered on publication, in which her father was successful.[96] It was, as I noted in the introduction, the imagery of the bee, associated both with the might of Napoleon and with the literary authority of her father, which Plath developed as a revision of Blake's symbol of the potent striped tiger.

Indeed, critics have often seen Plath's oeuvre as expressing a struggle with, and final movement away from an oppressive father figure.[97] The development is generally perceived in terms of Plath's recognition, in her earlier poetry, of the oppressive, yet desirable power of the father figure (in poems such as "Full Fathom Five" [1958], "The Beekeeper's Daughter" [1959], "The Colossus" [1959], "Lament" [pre-1956], and "The Man in Black" [1959].) From this recognition, her poetry moves toward a final knowledge of, and freedom from the patriarchal figure (often husband as well as father), in poems of "the bee-sequence," "Daddy," "Purdah," "Lady Lazarus," "Fever 103," and "Ariel" (all 1962).[98] In this development, Plath's oeuvre may be viewed as similar in many ways to Elizabeth Barrett Browning's epic poem, *Aurora Leigh*, both being about the birth and development, not only of the female, but specifically of the daughter-poet.[99] Although Plath makes no direct mention of this work in her academic or private writings, she does, as I note in the introduction, class Barrett Browning as a literary "rival" to her position of "Poetess of America" (J 211) and must not have been blind to the parallels between Browning's life and her own—both had powerful fathers who encouraged their intellectual development, but who, for whatever reason (Barrett Browning's due to her marriage) were somehow "lost"; both married poets who were initially less publicly successful, but to whom they were devoted and supportive both poetically and personally. Leighton describes *Aurora Leigh* as a poem that "commemorates the figure of a father whom, in the end, [both poet and speaker] knows that she does not need. From this harsh disinheritance comes her woman's strength."[100] The beginnings of this disinheritance in *Aurora Leigh* is when the father dies, coincidentally at the time Aurora reaches adolescence, a time of molding of a separate identity from the father. To be a female poet means not only moving away from the sphere of influence which bestows love and praise, but actively threatening it. As Leighton asserts, "To be a woman and a poet is to threaten the father's power."[101] There are, however, two central difficulties with this, generally accepted, depiction of the movement away from the father in Plath's poetry: Plath's poetic treatment of the oppressive and unreachable power of the father, and the stability or simplicity of her final transcendence or appropriation of his power. Both these problems stem from the *literary* nature of this "family romance" and Plath's difficulties in positioning herself as a woman writer—as victim or "master" of the literary and psychoanalytic discourses she uses.

"Full Fathom Five": Mythic and Literary Fathers

"Full Fathom Five" is apparently a fairly standard treatment of the daughter's feelings toward the powerful, absent father. The figure of the father is godlike: huge, attractive, obscure, and potentially dangerous. As in *The Tempest* (from which Plath's title "Full Fathom Five" is drawn), the father is lost through drowning, but still powerful—at one with, rather than at the mercy of the sea. He is a vast figure, and, due to his size or age, possesses ancient knowledge to which the daughter desires access. The poem ends with the speaker declaring her desire to breathe water—a desire to return either to the father or to some pre-Oedipal state of powerlessness, because she realizes that she is "exiled to no good" (CP 93). The speaker exists in a situation of no good, somewhere she does not want to be (powerless without the ancient knowledge that the "father" possesses); she is also exiled to no good—exiled, but it makes no difference and does no good because she is still aware of and attracted to the sea-father, and carries within her the memory of and longing for childhood's perfect peace with the father. Simone de Beauvoir writes of this power of the father's mysterious prestige,

> If her father shows affection for his daughter, she feels that her existence is magnificently justified . . . she is fulfilled and deified. All her life she may longingly seek that lost state of plenitude and peace.[102]

Yet, as Angela Leighton notes in relation to Barrett Browning's *Aurora Leigh,*

> [The name of the father] stands for mastery . . . the sign of inherited right to power . . . The daughter poet's desire for her father is not only a desire to court his smile or speak his name: it is also a desire to overcome her fear and steal his thunder.[103]

Such conflicting attitudes are apparent in "Full Fathom Five." The daughter's dilemma is similar to that of the son's, characterized by Freud in terms of the Oedipus complex. Yet for the daughter, such feelings are exaggerated because of the complication that the father is the daughter's love object; she is not "meant" to desire his power, just him. Thus, the daughter's desire to gain access to his power either ends in his shrinking from her, or somehow hurts him, as she realizes that if she looks too long or too closely at the father his form appears warped and "seems to die." Thus this fairly simple reading of "Full Fathom Five" can be summed up in the ambivalence of the first line when the speaker calls the figure an old man, implying both reverence for the ancient power of the mythic man of the sea, but also contempt and distaste for the impotent geriatric whose rules and power the young ephebe desires. The specifically literary nature of this desire in "Full Fathom Five" is apparent in the poem's connotations: "Full Fathom Five" has an obvious connection to *The Tempest,* not only in terms of the poem's title, but also because the father figure appears as a kind of Prospero, jealously guarding his knowledge and magic, similar to the figure in Plath's earlier "On the Decline of Oracles" where, with his death, the father also disposed of his books. Indeed, Plath marked in her copy of *The Tempest* Caliban's advice about Prospero:

> Remember
> First to possess his books: for without them

He's but a sot, as I am, nor hath not
One spirit to command.

emphasizing the connection of magical power (literary creativity—
the spirit as muse) with literary knowledge.[104] Also, however, as
author of *The Tempest,* Shakespeare himself (the archetypal post-
classical mythic poet) may stand as the powerful old man of omni-
present influence depicted in Plath's poem. In relation to the
poem's hints at the "old man" figuring the poetic father, Plath's
sometime poetic god, T. S. Eliot, was fascinated by *The Tempest*'s
myths and imagery, returning to them frequently in the "Ariel
poems" (1927–54) and "The Waste Land" (1922), a link Plath
herself makes in her copy of the play, marking Ariel's song, "Full
Fathom Five," annotating "cf. T. S Eliot Wasteland." Plath, too,
perhaps from the early impact of a trip to see a performance of
The Tempest in 1945, appears intrigued by its image of the father
figure embodied in Prospero (and the related imagery of the
father's death by drowning), and the Ariel-Caliban (spirit-matter)
conflict. The playbill from this production, which the Plath family
visited on 8 January, remains among the collected memorabilia at
Smith College. With this playbill is Aurelia Plath's note that it was
her children's first trip to the theater and that they were entranced
by it. Plath explored this fascination in the poems "Full Fathom
Five," "On the Decline of Oracles," and "Ariel."[105]

Yet in a number of ways, the poem offers more than this quite
conventional attitude toward the father, both literary, mythic, and
"real." In terms of the poem's psychoanalytic overtones and traditional imagery, although the figure is Neptune-like (male) in his
connection to the sea, the gendered symbolism throughout the
poem is ambivalent. The sea and the father are often linked by
Plath, from "Electra on Azalea Path" through "All the Dead
Dears" to "Daddy." Yet she also uses the sea as a more traditional
female symbol in poems like "Medusa," "The Moon and the Yew
Tree," and "The Munich Mannequins," where its connection to
the moon and menstruation is suggested. The sea is traditionally
a feminine symbol, yet the speaker describes her attraction to the
father as a memory of his "shelled bed," a classical female image.
While the father's position is powerful, it is powerful in opposition
to the order of the world (the male Symbolic order), an essentially
traditional feminine disruptive power. Similarly in "On the Decline of Oracles," Plath also uses the classic female symbol of the
shell to describe the father's power. The speaker declares that
with his death the father disposed of his books and his shell: while

the symbolism of the books is clearly connected to the father's power in terms of the logos, the shell, a traditionally female symbol, destabilizes such gender distinctions, although it may, in fact, act in terms of the traditional literary structure as a symbol of the father's female muse (the father listens to the mysterious sound of the shell). In "Full Fathom Five," Plath could be combining the literary figures of both muse and precursor in the figure of the "father," or she could well be approaching the difficult task of placing the female infant in the Oedipus complex by trying to reverse all aspects of the Oedipal scenario—the father is desired and revolutionary (the traditional attributes of mother for the male infant)—yet it is *his* power in the world, in the Symbolic order, that the speaker desires. Father, then, encompasses both male and female symbols. This may work simply to emphasize his power; more likely, however, it functions as a destabilizing ambiguity, consolidated in the poem's ending where the daughter's desire to "breathe water" appears as a desire to return to the mother's womb as well as the father's sea (indeed in the womb, the "subject" is in a pre-Oedipal, and thus ungendered state). Whatever the "final" interpretation of the father figure in this poem, it is clear that Plath's attitude toward the father is neither as stable nor as straightforward as most readings of this poem suggest.

There is also, however, a more central ambiguity, relating to the *literary* aspect of the Oedipal conflict "Full Fathom Five" treats in the poem's use of a battery of erudite classical, literary, and psychoanalytic allusions. While "Full Fathom Five" might be dismissed as an "early" poem and thus merely a formal exercise, it can also be viewed as a self-conscious "masterpiece" in the original sense—a work that aims to prove to the father within it that the speaker is, in fact, in control of all the available mythic and literary symbols which he both symbolizes and to which he has access. In classical rhetorical terms, like the opening of Chaucer's "The Franklin's Tale," which Plath studied at Cambridge, the poet bewails his lack of literary skill in a highly skilled manner. Thus the poem that bewails the speaker's inability to find access to the father's mythic and literary power acts to prove that such an access has in fact been gained. The poem's title, with its confident appropriation of a past literary classic, strengthens the case that this is, in fact, a "masterpiece" by an apprentice poet. And just as "Full Fathom Five" is in ambivalent or, at least reflexive, relation to literary discourse, its relation to the discourse of psychoanalysis is equally ambiguous in its figurings of the traditional "family romance." Questions are raised about whether the speaker is either victim or "master" of such a discourse—does she speak it, or it speak her.[106] The psychoanalytic overtones of this project (that speaking of something frees oneself from it), and all its ambiguities about master and victim relations is more readily apparent in the later "Daddy."

Ambiguous Transcendence

The second difficulty with the perception of Plath's poetry as a linear movement from oppression to transcendence relates to the problems associated with the transcendental endings of Plath's late poems, examples of which are discussed both above and in previous chapters. Another aspect of this problem (important because many readings of Plath's oeuvre are based on a perception of her treatment of transcendence in the late poems) relates to the gendering of transcendence.

Kristeva sees a clear-cut choice between the "symbolic" of the father (language) and the "imaginary" of the mother (unintelligible sound or rhythm), and sees the daughter's entry into the symbolic as fraught with danger:

> the daughter . . . is rewarded by the symbolic order when she identifies with the father . . . [but she] has nothing to laugh about when the symbolic order collapses. She can take pleasure in it if, by identifying with the mother, the vaginal body, she imagines she is the sublime repressed forces which return through the fissures of the order. But she can just as easily die from this upheaval, as a victim or militant, if she has been deprived of a successful maternal identification and has found in the symbolic paternal order her one superficial, belated and easily severed link with life.[107]

Kristeva links her perception of the difficulties of female identification with the male symbolic order with Plath's textual family romance (a rarity, as Kristeva usually confines herself to commentary on male "feminine" or revolutionary writers). She writes, in a discussion of the suicides of twentieth-century female writers, Woolf, Maria Tsvetaeva, and Plath:

> For a woman, the call of the mother is not only a call from beyond time, or beyond the socio-political battle. With family and history at an impasse, this call troubles the word: it generates hallucinations, voices, "madness." . . . Once the moorings of the word, the ego, the superego, begin to slip, life itself can't hang on: death quietly moves in . . . I think of . . . Sylvia Plath, another of those women disillusioned

with meanings and words, who took refuge in lights, rhythms and sounds: a refuge that already announces, for those who know how to read her, her silent departure from life.[108]

While accepting the problematic aspects of Kristeva's theory (notably her identification of the "feminine" essence with the female body, and thus her seeming essentialism which implies that only men can be reasoned subjects), her argument is useful in relation to Plath's conscious struggles with writing and femininity. As the introduction showed, while Plath saw herself as apprenticed to male literary masters, consciously crafting her poetry in a desire to break into a male literary establishment, she also felt she was part of a female literary tradition: for her, being a female writer was similar to biological creativity (to which both her and Hughes' linking of her pregnancy with her writing attest), something both more earthy and due more to inspiration than the crafted nature of male literature. Obvious examples of this are from her journals (J 166, J 305), where, as I noted in the introduction, Plath criticizes Woolf's literary "emphemerality" as a result of not being a "complete woman," that is not having a strong husband and children. Also, much of Plath's later poetry (such as "Stillborn" [1960], "Barren Woman" [1961], "The Other" [1962], "Childless Woman" [1962], and "The Munich Mannequins" [1963]) makes more and less clear connections between female barrenness and lack of creativity. Her ambivalence about creativity and womanhood is also indicated by the fact that, although she wrote several articles about the need for social acceptance of the "whole" woman at Cambridge University (that is, both the "symbolic," rational side, but also the "imaginary," "feminine" side) she still, in her private correspondence, categorized all Cambridge women as being either intellectual blue-stockings or unthinking earth-mothers.[109]

Kristeva's theory, then, is useful in its mirroring of Plath's often conscious conflict between "masculine" and "feminine" ideas about her work as a writer and the resulting, gendered transcendence. For Kristeva, "transcendence" of the material world is a masculine attribute; femininity is characterized by "immanence" in the material world. As a writer, Plath saw transcendence of the "real world" as limiting. As Ronald Hayman speculates, she was in less than perfect sympathy with Hughes's lack of rootedness in everyday life:

When she talked to him [Hughes] about her depressions, he sometimes managed to cheer her up but she couldn't always accept his astrological diagnoses: he talked about the moon and Saturn 'to explain the curse which held me tight as a wire'. He never seemed rooted in their day-to-day existence, often saying he wanted to get clear of this life.[110]

This difference is supported in a sidelong fashion by my note (in chapter 2) about the difference between Plath's (worldly) and Hughes's (mythic) interpretations of his play, *The Harvesting*. In 1952 Plath also writes, as I noted in chapter 1, with irony about the idea of some otherworldly "inspiration" (J 55). In 1958 her skepticism toward the individual and uncontrollable mysteries of literary creation remains. She writes critically of the poet Ralph Rogers's apparent method of writing as throwing all his ideas into his unconscious from where, with little effort, complete poems proceed (J 209). For the female writer especially, Plath saw such disembodied transcendence of the practical, creative world of writing as damaging (viewing "man-imitator"s Teasdale and Gardner as being "too abstractionist" and judging Woolf's "limiting" ephemerality as the result of her childless state). The transcendental endings of "Lady Lazarus" and "Purdah," for example, are then ultimately ambiguous, because to transcend male oppression, the speaker has to collaborate with it, lose her femininity to it. In "Lady Lazarus," the speaker's apotheosis works not to rise above the victim-persecutor relationship of the patriarchal world, but merely transforms her into an aggressor, destroying men instead of becoming destroyed by them. In "Purdah," the speaker's power and violence is directed against the man, but is, finally, dependent upon him. The speaker declares, ambivalently, about the relationship between her powerlessness and her master that even when the master is gone she is stuck in the ever-repeating circle of stagnation (CP 243). Yet her destructive power, which climaxes in a mythic reference to the murder of Agamemnon by Clytemnestra, is only able to be loosened by his approach, as the second part of the poem builds up the speaker's power with every step toward her that the master takes (CP 243–44).

In "Ariel" the image of red, which signals apotheosis in both this poem and in the transformation of "Lady Lazarus," focuses Plath's final ambiguity toward transcendence. Red symbolizes blood, a female image for Plath, associated with menstruation and female creativity. The spilling of blood is, as the epigram of "Kindness" concludes, evidence of life, but also loses life in the process. Thus Plath's conflict is between a desire to gain entry into the symbolic order of the father, with its power over language and discourses, and a knowledge that to do this would conflict with or destroy her identity as a female or as a woman writer.

Thus both the usual critical description of Plath's initial oppression and final transcendence are flawed because they fail to take into account the literary side of Plath's "family romance"—the difficulties she encounters in her idea of herself as a writer and a woman, and her placement in a tradition of writers, which makes any simple biographical or purely textual figuring of the "family romance" impossible.

While, however, Kristeva's work provides an interesting way of theorizing or explaining the problems surrounding transcendence in Plath's poetry, the philosopher's disregard for real actions and conscious anxieties (as a necessary counterpart to symbolic fantasies and unconscious anxieties) makes such theories incomplete. Certainly, for example, Plath's later poetry is more rhythmically powerful, but her interest in rhythm occurred throughout her career and was linked to her apprenticeship interest in strict forms. Several years before her "late" poetry and the Peter Orr BBC interview that makes it sound as if her discovery of the sound of poetry occurred only in the last few years of her life, Plath declares her belief in the importance of music, be it beautiful or ugly (and she professes an attraction toward ugly sound effects) in poetry. Perhaps more interesting, however, is her response to Anderson's question about whether or not a writer needs to write in a strict form to get music indicates that for Plath, music and rhythm (Kristeva's Imaginary) are aligned with strict form (Kristeva's Symbolic). Plath declares that, like most novice poets, she started writing in strict forms as a way of getting "music ready made," but that currently she sees the strictness of the form like "a comfortable corset," believing that because she is "lyrically inclined" she "lean[s] very strongly towards forms which are, I suppose quite rigid, in comparison certainly to free verse. I'm much happier when I know that all my sounds are echoing in different ways throughout the poem than if I just forget about it."[111] In addition, it was her "male master" Hughes who encouraged her to write in freer rhythms, and Plath was keenly aware that such a style would, in the "symbolic" world of literary publishing, "make my name" (LH 468), as it had male writers such as Roethke and Lowell and Berryman. Plath wrote this letter on 16 October 1962, the period in which she wrote the poems which are generally seen to have "cut loose" from her social and poetic inhibitions and interests. Kristeva's strict distinction between the rhythmic, revolutionary, Imaginary, and strict form of the Symbolic, then, must be treated with an awareness of its practical limitations.

Psychoanalytic theory generally is useful, however, because of Plath's awareness of it as a symbolic discourse and how (consciously as well as unconsciously) she defines and structures her ideas of herself as a woman and a writer in its terms. Many aspects of this discourse are not confined to psychoanalysis—for example, Kristeva's rhythmic pre-Oedipal "semiotic" is remarkably similar to Eliot's description of the "auditory imagination"—part of a male-established literary arsenal. Plath's unresolved conflict, in psychoanalytic terms (as well as social) between what was male in her creativity and literary aspirations, what female, and her difficulties about what she should aspire to, is what makes her "family romance" interesting. This is because neither psychoanalysts nor feminist psychoanalysts (the problems with Kristeva's theory, one of the more interesting available, make this evident) are, finally, yet able to untangle what Freud perceived as the "riddle of femininity."[112]

Conclusion:
A Dialectic of Transcendence and Memory

My foulnesses peel from me . . .
Every day they do this.
        —Sylvia Plath, draft of "Years," 16 November, 1962

The carpet of recollections.
Green baize, civilized, grooved by time.
. . . .
The grasses are complaining of amnesia,
But keep their gentle nature in a landscape of brigands.
        —Sylvia Plath, draft, "The bald truth about:
                    Grass at Wuthering Heights

Plath's poetry is most usefully considered from the viewpoint of her subjective-objective conflict and in terms of her victim-master relationship with the discourses which inform her work. Not only (as I argued in the last chapter) is this struggle at the root of her relation with the discourses of psychoanalysis and myth, it is also central to her treatment of culture and literature. I have shown how her anxieties about the cultural situation of her poetry focus on a division between viewing poetry as the overflow of emotion (writing the personal because it is unavoidable), and perceiving it as an objective, committed pursuit (writing the personal in a reasoned strategy with a didactic purpose). In terms of her relationship with more aesthetic literary concerns, her conflict expresses itself both in a traditional Romantic concern about constructing a subjectively authentic yet objectively universal work and in her anxious relationship with her literary antecedents and contemporaries. In this way, Plath's "anxiety of influence" is rooted in her subjective-objective struggles—in a conflict between feeling merely subjectively interpolated by the heritage of discourses she uses or feeling able, quite consciously, to appropriate and gain power from them. Consequently, Plath's struggles with her "family romance" clearly extend beyond the biographical past which

175

transfixes so many critics (and which Plath treats using psychoanalytic discourse) to encompass her literary and cultural heri-
tages (with which she deals in relation to Romantic tradition and
the sociopolitical sphere, respectively).

An awareness of this broad nature of the influences operating
on Plath (covering the spheres of biographical, literary, and cultural pasts) and the resulting effort to avoid the extremes either
of abstraction or of biography is crucial to any valuable study of
her work. It permits a more balanced judgment of Plath's oeuvre
and creates space, away from fruitless debates about the relationship between her suicide and her poetry, to allow the proper perception of the central concerns of her poetry—transcendence and
memory—around which much of her work finds its focus.

Of all Plath's poetry, it is those late poems (such as "Lady Lazarus," "Daddy," "Fever 103°," and "Getting There") in which she
treats the theme of transcendence which tend to elicit the most
extreme positive and negative responses, and on the basis of which
her whole corpus is often evaluated. As I have shown in my return
to this theme in all the preceding chapters, her attitude toward it
is not straightforward, and examination of the drafts of her late
poems lends further support to this view. In a draft of "Lady
Lazarus," Plath's implicitly contradictory feelings about the purity
associated with transcendence are clearly evident, when the
speaker describes her rebirths: "Each time I rise, I rise a bloody /
blooming virgin / sweet whore."[1] Such images too closely resemble
the red-haired figure at the end of the poem to be dismissed as
simply descriptions of her previous unsuccessful attempts to rise
above the oppressions of life. In her first draft of "Years," Plath's
ambivalence about transcendence, still evident in the final version,
is more closely connected to the imagery of shedding before rebirth found in poems such as "Lady Lazarus," "Ariel," and "Fever
103°." In "Years," however, such imagery expresses a continuous
process, rather than a single apotheosis,

> My foulnesses peel from me . . .
> Every day they do this.[2]

Neither is Plath's interest in transcending life simply informed by
a personal reaction to difficult private circumstances, so fully to
understand the complexity of her treatment of transcendence, the
theme must be studied in relation to all three central influences
which inform her poetry. In terms of the private sphere, transcendence is problematic because it appears contrary to the material,

abject basis of life, and also because it appears to her as a particularly male project, inimical to the kinds of femininity with which much of her poetry deals. In relation to the literary sphere, Plath's attraction to the kinds of transcendence offered by Romantic traditions (most notably those expressed in works such as "Phoenix" and "The Woman Who Rode Away" by Lawrence) is tempered by the fact that, like Brontë, she appears only to have recourse to it as a negative reaction to the impingements of nature on femininity, and also, perhaps, by her characterization of a traditionally feminine Romantic's interest in the relational rather than the transcendental aim of living. In the context of the sociopolitical sphere, I have shown how Plath, in her approval of Nietzsche's philosophy of struggle, consequently sees transcendence as a negative response to the stringencies that need to be borne in pursuit of a creative life, and, in broader terms, views transcendence as explicitly set against the morally crucial purpose of cultural remembrance.

Plath's ultimate ambivalence toward transcendence lies in its apparent denial of memory—a theme whose importance for her may be judged by the fact that she treats it more broadly and returns to it more frequently than she does the theme of transcendence. Just as, however, her treatment of transcendence is informed by conflict, so, too, Plath's attitude toward memory and amnesia is divided. Again, the depth of such a conflict is exhibited in its extension to all the areas studied in this work. On one hand, she, like De Quincey, perceives memory as a crucial creative source, and in terms of her personal and political beliefs, sees it as morally necessary, leading both to a better society and to a stronger identity. Yet, on the other hand, in both personal and literary terms, memory often appears as an oppressive heritage, victimizing in the very act of empowering the individual through the necessary struggle that characterizes the "family romance."

As with her treatment of transcendence, the study of Plath's early drafts throws light on her attitude toward memory and amnesia. (Indeed, while Susan Van Dynne has undertaken interesting work on some of Plath's drafts,[3] detailed study of all the available drafts of her poems, similar to the brief examples in this chapter, is still necessary and would, in combination with an awareness of the broad bases of Plath's writing, work to achieve a more balanced appraisal of the sources of and conflicts in her poetry.) The depth and breadth of Plath's involvement with memory and amnesia finds further support, for example, in the recurrence of such concerns in many of the early drafts of poems whose final versions are less focused on the treatment of the past and memory. In early drafts of "The Moon and the Yew Tree," both the images of moon (as mother) and yew (as father) are more clearly associated with memory and the past. In a draft conclusion to the poem, the speaker explores the suffocating oppression of the shadows of the past, describing the yew tree as towering above the speaker, "stern/black and dumb, like a forgetful father," and viewing the comfortlessnes of the moon in terms of the past:

> Her mouth, a dead letter office, full of papers
> Centuries old, and staling.[4]

In the first drafts of "Last Words," two original versions of the image of the mirror becoming clouded over by breath explicitly describe the breath which clouds it as that of history.[5] In "Finisterre," the first draft opens out the concerns of the poem, not only to deal with the speaker's relationship with nature, but also to comment upon the problematic stasis of and resulting nostalgia about the past—especially when it concerns events such as war— by extending her comparison between the rocks and ancient soldiers to describe them as statues: "Paralysed bronze and greening with obsolescence."[6]

In the long, free-associative drafts Plath called "The Grass" and "The bald truth about: Grass at Wuthering Heights," which appear to be preparations for "Wuthering Heights" or "Two Views of Withens," memory and amnesia recur frequently. The epigraph to this chapter is one example, but throughout both pieces, lines describing the grass as either nostalgic or amnesic recur frequently.[7] The early drafts of "Wuthering Heights" are much closer in theme and content to her poem and story "All the Dead Dears" (explored in the introduction in terms of its dialogue with the past in relation to Emily Brontë's novel). Not only do the drafts deal more explicitly with the characters of Brontë's novel, they also focus less on the theme of the impingements of nature apparent in the final version and more on the concerns with memory and ghosts Plath explores in "All the Dead Dears." In draft 2, she notes the mindless presentness of aspects of the scene, describing the pools of bog which open up simply to reflect their surroundings. In draft 3, she is more explicit about the relation of the scene to the past (as the speaker describes searching in vain for the ghosts of Wuthering Heights), and about perceptions of durability:

> They [unpeopled spaces] see through the house as they saw
>   through her and through him
> Who thought love could be durable as these stones.

In much later drafts, after she had deleted much of the above, Plath was still concerned to include intimations of the past, memory, and ghosts. In drafts 5 and 6, there are five versions of a conclusion which describes the mists rising from the river as forming into ghosts.[8] In her first draft of "Little Fugue," the final version's reference to the necessary power associated with memory (when the speaker describes her lack of memory as a disability) is emphasized in a more extended dwelling on the ambivalent relationship between living and dead, past and present, when the speaker dwells on the traditional placement of the graveyard yew tree, each of whose many roots provides a mouthpiece for each of the dead.[9]

The drafts of "Private Ground" (1959), which Plath wrote around the same time as "Poem for a Birthday" during her stay at Yaddo, provide one of the more telling examples of the breadth and depth of Plath's treatment of the theme of memory, as well as show the usefulness of detailed study of her manuscripts. Examination of these drafts lends further support to the contentions that, not only was this theme a central one for Plath, but also that (of the three areas covered in this thesis) she does not privilege the personal above the literary and the political: rather, that she perceives the impossibility of establishing any clear boundary between them.

While the final version of "Private Ground" reads as a broad contemplation of old and new, death and life, all the preceding drafts show a more explicit reference to specific concerns about the ambiguous powers of personal, artistic, and cultural pasts. The first thirteen drafts of "Private Ground" contain two additional stanzas, fitting in the middle of the final poem. After the speaker's contemplation of the details of the estate—the imported Greek statues which are being boarded up for winter and the goldfish ponds which are being drained—the poem moves into a more explicitly personal mode in the two stanzas which were finally removed:

> White shadows melt and shrink.
> I try to forget my room.
> It's charitable and tidy as a room in an asylum.
> Off and on, now, my heart

Jumps in its hysterical chimney—
I can't hold onto it.

Your black firs drink my light. My bed extends.
One foot in the Tyrol and the other stubbed somewhere
In manic-depressive Prussia,
I'm almost at home, with gargoyles
Contorting your cabinets, and on your mantel
The ghost of Wagner glooming among the Bayreuth beersteins.[10]

Even after Plath finally deletes these two stanzas, she still retains the line "your black firs drink my light" in the concluding stanza, altering it only in the final copy she sent to the *Critical Quarterly* on the same day (25 February 1961) to the published version. In these earlier drafts, personal, cultural and, in the form of the reference to Wagner, artistic pasts are combined. The "black firs" which oppress the identity of the speaker signify not only the personal family tree (relating to the mother's Tyrolean and the father's Polish heritage), but also connote the broader European past which appears as oppressing modern America. Yet even within such doleful scenery, of Wagner's ghost "glooming," the gargoyles "contorting" the furniture, and Prussia's "manic-depressive" state, the dark melancholy of the past seems positive, both in comparison to the clean neatness of the speaker's room (connoting, perhaps, the speaker's identity, sealed off from her pasts, or, more specifically, her creative self, implied in draft two, when she describes the room, in two variants of "Walls, walls, blank as paper"[11]), and in contrast to the oppression of mechanized America, characterized by the isolating, deadening, and poisonous superhighways. The past or its memory, the speaker appears to say, be it personal, artistic, or cultural, may well be oppressive: its obverse, however, the state of memorylessness or pastlessness, is infinitely worse. Again, the past relates not only to the biographical heritage received from parents, but also encompasses the cultural heritage handed down from Europe which America must confront, a heritage which itself is both positive and negative, in the form of Wagner's art and the use made of it by Nazi ideology.

This broader framework, which takes into account personal, literary, and cultural influences on the writer, would allow a more balanced study of other strands in Plath's work—the most compelling being that of her treatment of a variety of (both western and eastern) religious frameworks and beliefs, and their relation to her conflicted attitude toward myth. Also, it provides a sound basis for the study of the relationship between Plath's poetic expression of her political interests and her immediately preceding precursors, the political poets of the 1930s (with whom, certainly at the start of her career, she was in great awe), as well as giving the necessary wideness of scope for a more complete account of the relation between the frequently luridly biographical interest in her poetry and Plath's own, often artfully concealed, intellectuality. While by no means a fan of Plath's work, Kenner did, however, in an early review, attempt to point out the relation between the two, writing "Obviously no one is meant to wonder how much work-over the poems in *Ariel* received. My guess would be, a good deal; and I'd add that some of them (notably the first and last in the volume) read rather like expert contrivances than like dictates from the black angel. On the death-poems, moreover, fingerprints of contrivance don't show, and I'd point to her mustering of the craft that was necessary in that harrowing time as the victory for which she deserves to be celebrated: that, and not the shrieking 'sincerity'."[12] His view, however, has not received the additional study it deserves. The counterargument to such a study (as indeed, to my own) may well go along the lines of "Well, why look at Plath's intellectuality, when it is other areas which have caught the public imagination?" I would respond by saying that, first, Jacqueline Rose (who, to a certain extent—in terms of the critical approach of "anxiety of influence" I have used—figures as my own precursor) has contributed to this interesting area; and second, that any study needs to be based on a more complete knowledge of the actual bases of Plath's work—a goal this work has attempted to achieve.

The broadness and consciously liberal nature of my approach has necessarily raised other, more general questions. Such questions that immediately spring to mind are those relating to the uses of psychoanalysis as a tool for interpreting poetry, and whether, as my use of the discourse in chapter 3 may appear implicitly to assert, psychoanalysis can only be used as a tool for literary elucidation if the writer him or herself has, in some way, had recourse to its symbolism. Also, the ethics and practicalities of any utilization of the Holocaust as an image, while dealt with in a way which necessarily does not do justice to its immensity, is a problem which continually demands attention. Linked to this problem is the question this work has implicitly raised, about the difficulty in distinguishing between, as it were, political poetry and poetry about politics, a problematic but important issue, relating to the need to determine the applications and limitations of the feminist adage that "the personal is political." Such questions, while not in the scope of this work to provide an answer (if, indeed simple answers exist), ultimately say something very positive about the range as well as the greater and lesser successes of Plath's poetry, in its ability to demand such dilemmas be readdressed.

Notes

INTRODUCTION: AN INTELLECTUAL BACKGROUND

1. Jan Montefiore, *Feminism and Poetry: Language, Experience, Identity in Women's Writing* (London: Routledge-Pandora, 1987), 5.
2. Many of such notebooks remain at both Smith and Lilly.
3. Sylvia Plath, notebook, Aurelia Plath ms. note on cover "Sylvia—Notes on Frogs etc.," Lilly.
4. Sylvia Plath, *The Poet Speaks: Interviews with Contemporary Poets*, ed. Peter Orr (London: Routledge & Kegan Paul, 1966), 167.
5. Sylvia Plath, Smith College Transcript, Smith. Smith Prospecti, 1951–56, Smith.
6. Sylvia Plath, "The Age of Anxiety and the Escape from Freedom," ts. essay, May 1954, Lilly; "Some Preliminary Notes on Plato and Popper: Concerning *The Republic*," ts. essay, 14 May 1956, Lilly; "Some Observations on Locke's 'Essay Concerning Human Understanding'," ts. essay, 4 February 1957, Lilly; "'Damn Braces, Bless Relaxes': Blake and Lawrence: A Brief Comparison and Contrast," ts. essay, 14 March 1957, Lilly.
7. Joanne Feit-Diehl, *Women Poets and the American Sublime* (Bloomington and Indianapolis: Indiana University Press, 1990), 112.
8. Ted Hughes, "Sylvia Plath," *Poetry Book Society Bulletin* no. 44, February 1965, 1.
9. Ted Hughes, "Notes on the Chronological Order of Sylvia Plath's Poems," *The Art of Sylvia Plath*, ed. Charles Newman (London: Faber, 1970), 188, 193.
10. William Wordsworth, "Preface to *Lyrical Ballads*," *Romantic Criticism 1800–1825*, ed. Peter Kitson (London: Batsford, 1989), 64.
11. Hughes, "Chronological Order," 190.
12. Sylvia Plath, "The Devil's Advocate," ts. essay, 24 March 1954, Lilly.
13. Sylvia Plath, "A New Idiom," ts. essay, 9 May 1951, Lilly.
14. Sylvia Plath, "The Tragedy of Progress," ts. essay, 19 March 1951, Lilly.
15. Sylvia Plath, "*Darwin, Marx, Wagner*: An Essay," ts. essay, ca.1951, Lilly.
16. David Lehman, *Signs of the Times: Deconstruction and the Fall of Paul de Man* (London: Andre Deutsch, 1991), 49.
17. Cleanth Brooks and Robert Penn Warren, *Understanding Poetry: An Anthology for College Students* (New York: Henry Holt, 1946), books from Sylvia Plath's Library, Smith; Cleanth Brooks, *The Well-Wrought Urn* (New York: Harcourt, ca.1947), Plath's Library, Smith; F. R. Leavis, *The Great Tradition* (N/A, 1954), Plath's Library, Smith; Leavis, *New Bearings in English Poetry* (N/A, 1954), Plath's Library, Smith; Leavis, *Revaluation* (N/A, 1953), Plath's Library, Smith; Leavis, *D. H. Lawrence: Novelist* (London: Chatto & Windus, 1955), books from Sylvia Plath's Library, Lilly; I. A. Richards, *Practical Criticism: A Study of Literary Judgement* (London: Routledge & Kegan Paul, 1954), Plath's Library, Lilly.

18. Terry Eagleton, *Literary Theory: An Introduction* (Oxford: Blackwell, 1983), 50.

19. Edward Lobb, *T. S. Eliot and the Romantic Critical Tradition* (London: Routledge & Kegan Paul, 1981), 5–6. Lobb convincingly contends that while "Eliot's dislike of Romanticism, and his sarcasms at the expense of the Romantic poets, are a matter of record," the "historical myth" of dissociation of sensibility which Eliot perceived, "was first put forward by the Romantics, and Eliot's use of it—in his own way and for his own purposes, *mutatis mutandis*—suggests that there is a considerable Romantic heritage in Eliot's literary criticism."

20. Brooks and Warren, *Understanding Poetry*, ix.

21. Brooks, *Urn*, 203.

22. Eagleton, *Literary Theory*, 48.

23. Richards, *Practical Criticism*, 223.

24. T. S. Eliot, "Tradition and the Individual Talent," *Selected Prose of T. S. Eliot*, ed. Frank Kermode (London: Faber, 1975), 42–43.

25. Patrick Parrinder, *Authors and Authority: English and American Criticism 1750–1990* (London: Macmillan, 1991), 215, 238.

26. Sylvia Plath, poetry reading and interview with Lee Anderson, Springfield, Mass. 18 April 1958, audiotape, Smith.

27. Sylvia Plath, "Fish in Unruffled Lakes," ts. Smith College essay, Lilly Library.

28. William Blake, *The Portable Blake*, ed. Alfred Kazin (New York: Viking Press, 1953), Plath's Library, Smith. Underlined with enthusiastic comments throughout, and discussed in depth in chapter 1. Thomas De Quincey, *Selected Writings of Thomas De Quincey*, ed. Philip Van Doren Stern (New York: Modern Library, 1949), Plath's Library, Lilly. De Quincey is also discussed in more depth in the next chapter. Sylvia Plath, "Religious Beliefs," ts. essay, ca.1952, Lilly, 1.

29. Sylvia Plath, ts. of *Letters Home*, ed. Aurelia Plath, 30 August 1955, Lilly.

30. Plath, poetry reading and interview with Lee Anderson.

31. Sylvia Plath, ed. "American Poetry Now: A Selection of the Best Poems by Modern American Writers," *Critical Quarterly* (poetry suppl. no. 2, 1962).

Sylvia Plath reviewing *Contemporary American Poetry*, ed. Donald Hall, transmission 10 January 1963 transcript, Smith; Plath, ts. of *Letters Home*, 19 November 1962. Such reviews included "Pair of Queens," *New Statesman*, 27 April 1962 (a review of *A Queen of Spain* by Peter De Polnay, and *Josephine* by Hubert Cole), and "Suffering Angel," *New Statesman*, 7 December 1962 (a review of *Lord Byron's Wife* by Malcolm Elwin). Plath also reviewed children's books for the same periodical (e.g., in "Oblongs," *New Statesman*, 18 May 1962).

32. Sylvia Plath, "Guess Where Its Heaven to Be a Girl," ts. ca.1956, Lilly.

33. Plath, ts. of *Letters Home*, 28 March 1956.

34. Plath, *Poet Speaks*, 171.

35. Betty Friedan, *The Feminine Mystique* (1963; Harmondsworth: Penguin, 1992), 151. Friedan quotes Helene Deutsch's psychoanalytic writings in the 1940s to emphasize her general point that women were encouraged to sacrifice their intellectual qualities on the altar of "femininity": "Woman's intellectuality is to a large extent paid for by the loss of valuable feminine qualities . . . All observations point to the fact that the intellectual woman is masculinized; in her warm, intuitive knowledge has yielded to cold unproductive thinking."

36. Margaret Dickie Uroff, *Sylvia Plath and Ted Hughes* (Urbana: University of Illinois Press, 1979).

37. Edward Cohen correspondence, letter to Plath, 3 January 1951, Lilly.

38. Plath, *Poet Speaks*, 168–69.

39. W. Jackson Bate, *The Burden of the Past and the English Poet* (Cambridge MA.: Harvard University Press, 1970), 3.

40. Harold Bloom, *The Anxiety of Influence: A Theory of Poetry* (London: Oxford University Press, 1973), 5, 8.

41. Bloom, *Anxiety*, 14.

42. Harold Bloom, *Criticism in Society*, ed. Imre Saluskinsky (London: Methuen, 1987), 51.

43. Bloom, *Anxiety*, 11.

44. Adrienne Rich, *On Lies, Secrets and Silence* (London: Virago, 1980), 35.

45. Bloom, *Anxiety*, 30.

46. Ibid., 11.

47. Bate, *Burden*, 9.

48. Harold Bloom, ed. and intro., *New Critical Views: Sylvia Plath* (New York: Chelsea House, 1989), 2.

49. Lionel Trilling, *Sincerity and Authenticity* (London: Oxford University Press, 1972), 6. In criticizing Plath's poetry as "sincere," Bloom appears to take Trilling's recognition of the debasement of the idea of sincerity to its most extreme conclusion. Trilling asserts that "The word itself [sincerity] has lost most of its former high dignity . . . To praise a work of literature by calling it sincere is now at best a way of saying that although it need be given no aesthetic or intellectual admiration, it was at least conceived in innocence of heart." Yet Bloom would deny even the value afforded by "innocence of heart" of the writer, by seeing "sincerity" as a tool manipulative of the "innocence of heart" of the reader.

50. Lehman, *Signs*, 28. Lehman neatly summarizes Bloom's idea of the School of Resentment: "He [Bloom] names some factions: these are the 'Lacanians, deconstructionists, Foucault-inspired New Historicisms, semioticians, neo-Marxists, and latest-model feminists.' All have their place in the School of Resentment, where literary criticism is used as a weapon on behalf of groups perceived as historical victims—its their way to get even with their oppressors."

51. Bloom, *Plath*, 3, 4.

52. Bloom, *Criticism*, 65.

53. Frank Lentricchia, *Criticism in Society*, ed. Imre Saluskinsky (London: Methuen, 1987), 196.

54. Jacqueline Rose, *The Haunting of Sylvia Plath* (London: Virago, 1990), 198.

55. Sandra M. Gilbert and Susan Gubar, *The Madwoman in the Attic* (New Haven and London: Yale University Press, 1979), 48.

56. Plath's dismissal of Moore is probably influenced by the poet's refusal to back Plath's application for a Saxton grant (J 250), which Plath could not have avoided comparing to the support Moore gave Hughes when she judged the *Harper's* contest (J 154), which resulted in the publication of Hughes's first book.

57. Joanne Feit-Diehl, "'Come slowly—Eden': An Exploration of Women Poets and Their Muse," *Signs* 3:3 (1978): 572–87. In exploring the relevance of Bloom's oedipal scenario to female writers and using Dickinson as an example, Feit-Diehl sets up a structure where the (traditional) male precursor and the female muse become a composite figure for the female poet, and where female precursor/muses become comforters and confidence-givers in opposition to the feelings of anxiety and desire aroused by male precursor/muses.

Alicia Suskin Ostriker, *Stealing the Language: The Emergence of Women's Poetry in America* (London: Women's Press, 1987), 192. Ostriker declares, affirming Feit-Diehl's revision, that "When women writers write of continuities from one writer, artist, or thinker to another, it is thus not, pace Harold Bloom, on the oedipal model of killing and superseding the precursor, but on the Demeter-Kore model of returning and reviving."

58. Ernest Jones, *Hamlet and Oedipus* (Garden City, NY: Doubleday, 1954), Plath's Library, Smith.

59. Ted Hughes, "Black Coat," *New Selected Poems: 1957–1994* (London: Faber, 1995), 298–99.

60. Sandra M. Gilbert and Susan Gubar, *No Man's Land: The Place of The Woman Writer in the Twentieth Century: vol. 1, The War of the Words* (New Haven and London: Yale University Press, 1988), 169.

61. Bloom, *Anxiety*, 96.

62. Bloom, *Criticism*, 50.

63. Gilbert and Gubar, *War of Words*, 199.

64. Feit-Diehl, "'Come Slowly—Eden,'" 573.

65. Juliet Mitchell, *Psychoanalysis and Feminism* (London: Penguin, 1990), 352, 354. Gilbert and Gubar's is an interesting fault because, as Juliet Mitchell notes, many feminist critiques of Freudian psychoanalysis—which forms the basis of Bloom's theoretical framework—also tend to ignore or deny the unconscious.

66. Gilbert and Gubar, *War of Words*, 200.

67. Ibid., 204.

68. Sylvia Plath, "A Walk to Withens," *Christian Science Monitor* 6 June 1959: 12 [cutting held at Smith]. Appearing as a prose version of "Two Views of Withens," the article describes two different routes, of varying difficulty, to the setting for *Wuthering Heights,* and is critical of those tourists to the area who feel they have experienced Withens and its historical and literary associations without actually making the pilgrimage across the moors. The interest of the piece lies in its relation to my later discussion of Plath's attitude toward the necessity of struggle and hardship fully to appreciate both the present and the past.

69. The provenance for this source of "All the Dead Dears" comes from the introduction Ted Hughes gave for his recently collected poem, "Anniversary," *New Selected Poems* 291–93, in a poetry reading on 25 February 1995 for the opening of the Bath Literary Festival at The Forum, Bath. He described how his mother had a kind of second sight, which meant that whenever someone she knew was about to die, she would see the ghost of her sister, Miriam, who died at eighteen years old; a situation that forms the background to, and is reflected in the experiences of, Nellie Meehan in Plath's short story.

70. Bloom, *Anxiety*, 14.

Chapter 1. Romantic Anxieties

1. Marjorie Perloff, "Angst and Animism in the Poetry of Sylvia Plath," *Critical Essays on Sylvia Plath*, ed. Linda W. Wagner (Boston: G. K. Hall, 1984), 109–23; Calvin Bedient, "Sylvia Plath: Romantic . . ." *Sylvia Plath: New Views on the Poetry*, ed. Gary Lane (Baltimore and London: Johns Hopkins University Press, 1979), 3–18; Joyce Carol Oates, "The Death Throes of Romanticism: The Poetry of Sylvia Plath," *Sylvia Plath: The Woman and the Work*, ed. Edward Butscher (London: Peter Owen, 1979), 206–24; Sandra Gilbert, "In Yeats' House: The Death and Resurrection of Sylvia Plath," *Critical Essays on Sylvia*

Plath, ed. Linda W. Wagner (Boston: G. K. Hall, 1984), 204–21; Barnett Guttenberg, "Plath's Cosmology and the House of Yeats," *Sylvia Plath: New Views on the Poetry,* ed. Gary Lane (Baltimore and London: Johns Hopkins University Press, 1979), 138–52.

2. Indeed, Gilbert's analysis, in "In Yeats' House," of Plath's debt to Yeats is based on Plath's own placement of him as a literary father.

3. Gareth Griffiths, *A Dictionary of Modern Critical Terms,* ed. Roger Fowler, rev. and enlarged ed. (London: Routledge & Kegan Paul, 1987), 209.

4. Clearly it would also be of value to consider American writers in the Romantic tradition, most notably Walt Whitman. Although it is unclear how familiar Plath was with Whitman's work, she reflects many of his attitudes and concerns.

5. Arthur K. Oberg, "Sylvia Plath and the New Decadence," *Sylvia Plath: The Woman and the Work,* ed. Edward Butscher (London: Peter Owen, 1979), 177; Edward Butscher, "In Search of Sylvia: An Introduction," *Sylvia Plath: The Woman and the Work,* ed. Edward Butscher (London: Peter Owen,1979), 4, 25; Gordon Lameyer, "Sylvia at Smith," *Sylvia Plath: The Woman and the Work,* ed. Edward Butscher (London: Peter Owen, 1979), 39.

6. Plath, *Poet Speaks,* 170.

7. Ibid., 169.

8. Blake, *Portable Blake.*

9. Plath, "'Damn Braces'."

10. Uroff, *Plath,* 69.

11. Blake, *Portable Blake,* 159.

12. Ibid., 252.

13. Vincent D. Balitas, "On Becoming a Witch: A Reading of Sylvia Plath's 'Witch Burning'," *Studies in the Humanities* 4 (February 1975): 27–30. Balitas's article, while somewhat limited in its discussion of "Witch Burning," is an otherwise engaging exploration of Plath's "uneasy identification with those tortured and murdered women [witches]."

14. Plath, ts. *Letters Home* 30 December 1955.

15. Margaret Mead, *Male and Female : A Study of the Sexes in a Changing World* (New York: William Morrow, 1952), Plath's Library, Lilly, 232, 375.

16. Rich, "When We Dead Awaken," 43.

17. Plath, ts. of *Journals,* Smith, 31 December 1958.

18. Christopher Fry, *The Lady's Not For Burning* (New York: Oxford University Press, 1950), Plath's Library, Lilly, 86. Note also, one of the only other places in which Plath annotates this play is when Jennet declares of society's perception of her witch's abilities, "They also say that I bring back the past;" (25)—linking the vision of the witch, not only to the future, but to the past; connecting, therefore, the witch and vision with one of Plath's main poetic themes, memory.

19. Blake, *Portable Blake,* 109.

20. Ibid., 250.

21. Ibid., 43.

22. Ibid., 84.

23. Ibid., 147.

24. Oates, "Death Throes," 211.

25. Bloom, *Anxiety,* 70. Bloom differentiates between conscious and unconscious influences, arguing that conscious influence does not really exist—"influence cannot be willed."

26. Plath, "Damn Braces."

27. Bedient, "Romantic . . . ," 2.

28. Claire Tomalin, "Everything But The Truth," *The Independent on Sunday* books review, 9 October 1994: 32. Tomalin writes, "it strikes me that certain notions about male-female bonding, loosely drawn from D. H. Lawrence via F. R. Leavis, coloured many young marriages of our generation."

29. D. H. Lawrence, *Selected Essays* (Harmondsworth: Penguin, 1954), Plath's Library, Smith, 45.

30. Plath, "Plato and Popper," 4.

31. Sylvia Plath, "D. H. Lawrence: The Tree of Knowledge Versus The Tree of Life," ts. essay, 18 February 1957, Lilly.

32. Gilbert, "Yeats' House," 215. Gilbert links Lawrence's tale to Plath's story, "Johnny Panic and the Bible of Dreams," in which the heroine is victimized by priest-like doctors because of her unauthorized access to the power of Johnny Panic. Gilbert notes direct similarities between the ages of the female protagonist (33 years old) and the number of attendants at each sacrifice, five priests in Lawrence's tale, and "Five false priests" in Plath's short story.

33. Kate Millett, *Sexual Politics* (London: Virago, 1977), 286. Millett, in her polemic attack on Lawrence, writes of his fear of the emancipated woman as a female who has "escaped the primitive condition others [Faulkner and Joyce are named] assume to be her nature. Drastic steps must be taken if she is going to be coerced back into it; her will must be broken, her newly found ego destroyed."

34. I describe this in chapter 2 in relation to her readings of Eric Fromm's *Escape from Freedom.*

35. Plath, "Ariel" draft 1, Smith.

36. Ibid.

37. Alan Richardson, "Romanticism and the Colonization of the Feminine," *Romanticism and Feminism,* ed. Anne K. Mellor (Bloom and Indianapolis: Indiana University Press, 1988), 22.

38. Plath, "Ariel" draft 1, Smith College.

39. Rosalind Miles, "A Baby God: The Creative Dynamism of Emily Brontë's Poetry," *The Art of Emily Brontë,* ed. Anne Smith (London: Vision Press, 1976), 85. As Rosalind Miles notes, "Emily Brontë is par excellence, our poet of nature's less benign aspects."

40. A. E. Dyson, "On Sylvia Plath," *The Art of Sylvia Plath,* ed. Charles Newman (London: Faber, 1970), 205.

41. Stevie Davies, *Emily Brontë: The Artist as a Free Woman* (Manchester: Carcanet Press, 1983), 63.

42. Emily Brontë, "Shall Earth No More Inspire Thee," *The Brontës: Selected Poems,* ed. Juliet R. V. Barker (London: Everyman-Dent, 1985), 62–63.

43. Emily Brontë, "The Night Wind," *The Brontës,* 59–60.

44. Richardson, "Colonization," 19.

45. Charlotte Brontë, "Biographical notice of Ellis and Acton Bell," *Wuthering Heights,* by Emily Brontë (London: Penguin, 1965), 30.

46. Hughes's attitude reflects that of Al Alvarez, who, Plath notes to her mother in 1962, declared she was the first woman poet he'd taken seriously since Emily Dickinson (LH 476).

47. Charlotte Brontë, "Editor's Preface to the New [1850] Edition of Wuthering Heights," *Wuthering Heights* by Emily Brontë (London: Penguin, 1965), 37.

48. Jacqueline Rose, in *The Haunting of Sylvia Plath,* has a fascinating chapter on Hughes's control of the Plath archive.

49. Brontë, "Biographical notice" 36, "Editors Preface" 39; Hughes, "Chronological Order," 187.

50. Samuel Taylor Coleridge, *The Oxford Authors*, ed. H. J. Jackson (Oxford: Oxford University Press, 1985), 27–29. His poem, "The Eolian Harp," is perhaps the best example of Coleridge's use of this image and idea, which occurs in a number of places in his work.

51. Wordsworth, "Preface," 59, 60 are examples of the general argument that threads throughout the preface. Wordsworth declares: "the Poet binds together by passion and knowledge the vast empire of human society, as it is spread over the whole earth, and over all time . . . The Poet is chiefly distinguished from other men by a greater promptness to think and feel without immediate external excitements, and a greater power in expressing such thoughts and feelings as are produced in him in that manner." In this statement, too, of the author's position as the triumphant source of his writing, is intimated the other central Romantic conflict, noted above, between ideals of the poet as a "man speaking to men" and as a man somehow superior to the rest of humanity, standing apart, because of his ability to grasp the "image," explored most completely in Frank Kermode's *Romantic Image* (London: Routledge & Kegan Paul, 1957).

52. Margaret Homans, *Women Writers and Poetic Identity* (Cambridge: Princeton University Press, 1980), 13, 15.

53. From *The Fact of a Doorframe: Poems Selected and New 1950–1984* (New York and London: Norton, 1984), 215–16.

54. Robin Grove, "'It would not do': Emily Brontë as Poet," *The Art of Emily Brontë* ed. Anne Smith (London: Vision Press, 1976), 47. Grove writes, "There are surprisingly few poems of landscape . . . Most of the time, after a stanza or two, the poems relinquish rapport with an outside world."

Miles, "Baby God," 86. Miles concurs, "On the whole . . . nature is present rather as the essential background and preconditioning factor without which the thoughts of the poem could not have birth, rather than as a subject in itself."

55. Plath's treatment of nature as nonsubject as either narrow, egotistical, or due to unique sense of connection is discussed by, among others, Hughes in "Chronological Order" 187–95, Perloff in "Angst" 109–24, and Seamus Heaney in "The Indefatigable Hoof-taps: Sylvia Plath," *The Government of the Tongue* (London: Faber, 1989), 148–70.

56. Annette Kolodny, *The Lay of the Land: Metaphor as Experience and History in American Life and Letters* (Chapel Hill: University of North Carolina Press, 1975), 5. Kolodny describes the importance of the psychic (rather than purely literary traditional) connection between landscape and the mother: "Paul Shepard undoubtedly has a point when he claims that 'we have yet to recognise the full implication of the mother as primary landscape,' especially since, as psychiatrist Joel Kovel has argued, 'the life of the body and the experiences of infancy . . . are the reference points of human knowledge and the bedrock of the structures of culture'."

57. Wordsworth, "Preface," 50.

58. Kolodny, *Lay of the Land*, 4, 7.

59. Homans, *Identity*, 141.

60. Bloom, *Anxiety*, 70. Indeed, Bloom asserts, that "an ephebe's best misinterpretations may well be of poems he has never read."

61. Thomas De Quincey, *Confessions of an English Opium-Eater and Other Writings*, ed. Grevel Lindop (Oxford: Oxford University Press, 1985), iv. Lindop's

apt description of the tone of "Confessions" as "wry urbanity and quizzical self-dramatization, rising to climactic passages of the pathetic and the bizarre" seems equally well-fitted to Plath's own combination of reflexive knowingness and piercing intensity.

62. Examples of these include *"On the Elevation of Reason:* Some Notes Concerning the Cambridge Platonists, Whichcote and Smith," ts. essay, 26 October 1956, Lilly; "Literature versus Dogma," ts. essay, 4 December 1956, Lilly; "Some Notes on Coleridge's *Aids to Reflection,* ts. essay, 22 January 1957, Lilly; "Locke," and "D. H. Lawrence."

63. De Quincey, *Selected,* 11.

64. Ibid., 13.

65. Ibid., 22.

66. Plath, *Poet Speaks,* 170.

67. De Quincey, *Selected,* 1099.

68. Ibid., 1090.

69. Ibid., 16, 18.

70. De Quincey, *Confessions,* xiii. Lindop notes that De Quincey offers "On the Knocking at the Gate in Macbeth" as "psychological criticism."

71. Ibid., ix. The editor describes De Quincey's writing as "a remarkable blend of autobiography and visionary fantasy."

72. De Quincey, *Selected,* 16.

73. De Quincey, *Confessions,* 145–46.

74. Aldous Huxley, *The Doors of Perception and Heaven and Hell* (London: Grafton: HarperCollins, 1977), 71.

75. Aldous Huxley, *Heaven and Hell* (London: Chatto and Windus, 1956), Plath's Library, Lilly, 12.

76. De Quincey, *Confessions,* 146.

77. Sylvia Plath, "Some Few Observations on 'Disagreeables' in the Plays of Webster and Tourneur," ts. essay, 12 March 1956, Lilly.

78. De Quincey, *Selected,* 18.

79. Plath, *Poet Speaks,* 169.

80. See note 77.

81. Bloom, *Anxiety,* 14.

82. Ibid., 14.

83. Class notes for Smith teaching, Lilly.

84. Plath, "The Living Poet," transcript of radio program, transmission 8 July 1961, BBC Third Programme, Smith.

85. De Quincey, *Selected,* 900.

86. De Quincey, *Confessions,* 158. An additional link between Plath's Arthurian setting and De Quincey's piece occurs when De Quincey refers to Arthurian myth in the form of Arthur's sister, Morgan-La-Fay, when he describes Savannah-La-Mar as "fascinat[ing] the eye with a Fata-Morgana revelation."

87. De Quincey, *Confessions,* 250.

88. Plath, drafts 1 and 2 of "Amnesiac—The Man With Amnesia," Smith College.

89. Plath, "Plato and Popper," 3, 4.

90. De Quincey, *Confessions,* 159.

91. De Quincey, *Selected,* 980.

92. Ibid., 914.

93. Ibid., 14.

94. De Quincey, *Confessions*, 194.

Chapter 2. Politics—History—Myth

1. Plath, *Poet Speaks*, 169.

2. Linda Wagner-Martin, *Sylvia Plath—A Biography* (London: Cardinal-Sphere, 1990), 45.

3. Ruth Inglis, "Alma Mater of Private Pain and Public Death," *Jewish Chronical*, lit. suppl. (5 February 1993): iv.

4. See my comments below about Plath's treatment of the "gaze" in the poems "Lady Lazarus" and "Daddy."

5. Wagner-Martin, *Biography*, 64.

6. Ibid., 58.

7. Ibid., 64.

8. Sylvia Plath and Perry Norton, "Youth's Plea for World Peace," *The Christian Science Monitor* (Boston), 16 March 1950: 19, Smith.

9. Plath, Smith TS.; Smith Prospecti, 1951–56, Smith. See my comments in the introduction.

10. Plath, TS. of *Letters Home*, 6 November 1952.

11. Ibid.

12. Sylvia Plath, "Leaves from a Cambridge Notebook," TS., ca.1956, Lilly, 5.

13. Plath, TS. of *Letters Home*, 25 September 1955.

14. Ibid., 9 October 1955.

15. Ibid., 25 February 1960.

16. Ibid., 21 April 1960, 13 September 1960.

17. Plath, "Age of Anxiety."

18. Plath, "Damn Braces," 3.

19. Plath, "Plato and Popper," 6, 8.

20. Plath, "Devil's Advocate," 7.

21. Sinclair Lewis, *Babbitt* (New York: Harcourt Brace, 1922), Plath's Library, Lilly. 39. D. H. Lawrence, "Democracy," *Selected Essays* (Harmondsworth, Essex: Penguin, 1954), Plath's Library, Smith.
To Secure These Rights: The Report of the President's Commitee on Civil Rights (New York: Simon and Schuster, 1947), Plath's Library, Lilly, 49, 165.

22. "John Mason Brown Lectures on Writer's Responsibility," *The Daily Hampshire Gazette*, n.d., cutting, Smith.

23. Ted Hughes, "Context," *London Magazine* 1 : 11 (11 February 1962): 4–6.

24. Jose Ortega y Gassett, *The Revolt of the Masses* (New York: New American Library, 1951), Plath's Library, Lilly, 11; Eric Fromm, *Escape from Freedom* (New York: Rinehart, ca.1941), Plath's Library, Smith, 158.

25. Fromm, *Escape*, 273.

26. Plath, *Poet Speaks*, 169.

27. Richard Gray, *American Poetry of the Twentieth Century* (Harlow: Longman, 1990), 216; David Caute, *The Great Fear: The Anti-Communist Purge Under Truman and Eisenhower* (London: Secker & Warburg, 1978), 541.

28. Robert von Hallberg, *American Poetry and Culture 1945–1980* (Cambridge, MA and London: Harvard University Press, 1985), 133.

29. Robert Jay Lifton and Eric Markussen, *The Genocidal Mentality: Nazi Holocaust and Nuclear Threat* (London: Macmillan, 1991), 37.

30. Lynda B. Salamon, "Double, Double: Perception in the Poetry of Sylvia Plath," *Spirit* 38 (1970): 34–39. Salamon perceives this "double vision," the "contrast between real terror and apparent safety," as central to Plath's poetry and at the root of the horror it often expresses.

31. Plath, "I Am An American," Smith.

32. Wagner-Martin, *Biography*, 45. Wagner-Martin believes it was written at high school, when she describes one of Plath's "creative writing" political pieces as dealing with the theme of "being an American."

33. Caute, *Great Fear*, 507.

34. Ibid., 12. Caute writes, "While many American citizens who criticised American foreign policy were deprived of passports, of the right to travel, aliens who were deemed too subversive to enter were held on Ellis Island. So few foreign scientists were admitted to the land of the free that one international conference after another had to be cancelled."

35. Edward Butscher, *Sylvia Plath: Method and Madness* (New York: Seabury Press, 1976), 94.

36. Plath, "Collage," Smith.

37. Plath, "Religion As I See It," TS. essay, 3 May 1952, Lilly.

38. Plath, "Religious Beliefs."

39. Ortega y Gassett, *Revolt*, 72.

40. J. A. Corry, *Elements of Democratic Government* (New York: Oxford University Press, 1951), Plath's Library, Lilly, 28.

41. Fromm, *Escape*.

42. David Riesman, Nathan Glazer, Reul Denney, *The Lonely Crowd*, abridged by the authors (New York: Doubleday, 1953), Plath's Library, Smith, 122.

43. See notes 17–20.

44. Fromm, *Escape*, 5.

45. Ibid., 155.

46. Ibid., 186.

47. Ibid., 208.

48. Ibid., 221.

49. See note 24.

50. In her use of the "holy fire," Plath may well be responding to Yeats's "Sailing to Byzantium," which mentions "holy fire" in relation to his ambivalence toward the idea of some perfect state, abstracted from life. In her essay "Plato and Popper," as I note below, Plath identifies this ambivalence about art and life as the "central problem" of Yeats's poetry. For Yeats in "Sailing to Byzantium," this perfect state is related to art; in "Mary's Song," it is related to man's technological achievements.

51. This line also relates to the pagan rituals described in Frazer's *The Golden Bough*, a book Plath read at Smith for her thesis on Dostoevsky but which influenced her poetry throughout her life.

52. This concern with the destructive power of "progress" is also seen in Robert Lowell's "For the Union Dead," written about two years later (published in 1964), and showing the widespread nature of such anxieties. Note, however, Perloff, "Angst," 57, who contrasts the two poems and asserts that "For the Union Dead" possesses a sense of history lacking in Plath's *Ariel* poems: "The sense of history, both personal and social, found in a poem like 'For the Union Dead' is conspicuously absent from the *Ariel* poems. This is not a mere coinci-

dence: for the oracular poet, past and future are meaningless abstractions; emotion, as Northrup Frye has observed, is 'maintained at a continuous present'. For Sylvia Plath there is only the given moment, only now." Perloff's argument is interesting in its location of the central problem in Plath's political poetry in the question of time. In trying, however, to so rigidly place Plath in a literary tradition (of ecstatic poets), Perloff ignores the social context of Plath's poetry and the impact of the recent events of World War II, which were the main contributory factors in Plath's mythologizing (giving a property of timelessness to) of history.

53. Robyn Marsack, *Sylvia Plath : Open Guides to Literature* (London: Open University Press, 1992), 31–32.

54. Heaney, "Hoof-taps," 159.

55. Perloff, "Angst," 110.

56. Ibid., 111–12.

57. Ibid., 119.

58. Rose, *Haunting*, 8.

59. Plath, *Poet Speaks*, 169.

60. Rose, *Haunting*, 196.

61. Nancy Hunter Steiner, *A Closer Look at Ariel: A Memory of Sylvia Plath* (London: Faber, 1974), 19.

62. Perloff, "Angst," 122.

63. "Context," *London Magazine*, 27.

64. Gray, *American Poetry*, 221.

65. Ibid., 223.

66. Ibid.

67. Judith Kroll, *Chapters in a Mythology* (London: Harper & Row, 1976), 160.

68. Lewis, *Babbitt*, 100.

69. The Krupp business flourished in the nineteenth and twentieth centuries: instrumental in helping Nazi Germany re-arm, after the war, Krupp was jailed as a war criminal, but was later released and returned to run the company.

70. Uroff, *Plath*, 154.

71. In "Daddy," the importance of the speaker's amnesia, in not knowing her father's history (and so unable to break out of his influence) is linked to cultural amnesia and nationalism—lack of knowledge of the past is seen as contributing to stereotypical views of past and present culture.

72. Ortega y Gassett, *Revolt*, 39.

73. Cary Nelson, *Repression and Recovery: Modern American Poetry and the Politics of Cultural Memory 1910–1945* (Madison: University of Wisconsin Press, 1989), 165–66. Nelson writes, "Imagining that radical political poetry as a whole came to an end in America in 1939—showing no evidence of vitality in the 1940s and 1950s—requires a whole series of fragmentations, repressions, and redefinitions. A number of highly interested interpretative moves, in other words, need to be installed as facts of nature . . . when Robert Lowell and Sylvia Plath, among others, appear, they need to be contained within autobiographical confession, their interests in history and sexual difference turned back on themselves rather than outward on American culture." If this is the case, irony can be found in Plath's interest in the warping nature of cultural amnesia; her concern proves to have been justified in her own critical reception.

74. Hannah Arendt, *Eichmann in Jerusalem: A Report on the Banality of Evil* (1963; Harmondsworth: Penguin, 1977), 85.

75. Fromm, *Escape*, 274.

76. James Frazer, *The Golden Bough: A Study in Magic and Religion,* abridged ed. (1922; New York: Macmillan, 1952), Plath's Library, Smith, 293, 284; Sigmund Freud, *The Basic Writings of Sigmund Freud,* ed. Dr A. A. Brill (New York: Modern Library, ca.1938), Plath's Library, Smith, 870.

77. Christopher Norris and Ian Whitehouse, "The Rhetoric of Deterrence," *Styles of Discourse,* ed. Nikolas Coupland (London: Croom Helm, 1988), 293.

78. Paul Chilton, "Nukespeak: Nuclear Language, Culture and Propoganda," *Nukespeak—The Media and the Bomb,* ed. Crispin Audrey (London: Comedia, 1982), 96–97.

79. Norris and Whitehouse, "Deterrence," 313, 317.

80. Ibid., 316. The authors describe the effect of nuclear, Cold War rhetoric in America as "the naturalization of an attitude, a way of life, a mode of imagining which evades the requirements of rational, enlightened discourse. And yet this perfectly 'natural' way of conducting one's affairs is so intricately bound up with a mythic national identity that any inquiry into the logic or nature of its premises is taken as a well-nigh treacherous affront to both one's person and one's sense of communal belonging."

81. Plath, *Poet Speaks,* 169.

82. Pamela Annas, "The Self in the World: the Social Context of Sylvia Plath's Late Poems," in *Critical Essays on Sylvia Plath,* ed. Linda W. Wagner (Boston: G. K. Hall, 1984), 135.

83. Ronald Hayman, *The Death and Life of Sylvia Plath* (London: Mandarin-Minerva, 1992), 85.

84. Eileen Aird, *Sylvia Plath* (Edinburgh: Oliver & Bryd, 1973), 10.

85. Many such lists of poem subjects are held at Smith, the most fascinating being one in which, among other suggestions, all the titles for the sections of "Poem for a Birthday" and many of the subjects and themes are contained in Hughes's handwriting and summarized in Plath's.

86. Plath, TS. of *Letters Home,* 24 December 1960.

87. Poetry reading and interview with Lee Anderson.

88. Friedan, *Mystique,* 41–42.

89. Ibid., 53–54.

90. Al Alvarez, *The Savage God: A Study of Suicide* (Harmondsworth: Penguin, 1974), 22–23.

91. Plath, TS. of *Letters Home,* 16 October 1962, 23 October 1962.

92. Hughes, "Chronological Order," 190.

93. Ibid.

94. See chapter 3 for a full exploration of this.

95. Plath utilizes resonances of this scene at the end of "Purdah" (1962).

96. Heaney, "Hoof-taps," 165, 168.

97. Ibid., 168.

98. Robert Graves, *The White Goddess* (1948; London: Faber, 1961).

99. Kroll has exhaustively studied Plath's debt to Graves's *The White Goddess* and what she sees as Plath's resulting personal "system" of moon, sea, and blood imagery. This "system" (which Heaney admires) is, however, neither itself stable, nor describes the stable and linear progression toward transformation and transcendence of the difficulties of life that Kroll perceives.

100. Graves, *White Goddess,* 101, 443.

101. Ibid., 459. See also my comment in the introduction on Plath's conscientious note-taking on mythic subjects.

102. Rose, *Haunting,* 163.

103. Jon Harris, "An Elegy for Myself: British Poetry and the Holocaust," *English* (January 1993) : 220.

104. Rose, *Haunting,* 216. Rose suggests an interesting, if somewhat fanciful, parallel between the timing of Plath and survivors' writings about the Holocaust: "If, therefore, the Holocaust appears as historical reference only in the last years of Plath's writing, the delay is coincident with the memory of the survivors themselves. Her tardiness mimics, or chimes in with, their own." Even such famous writers as Primo Levi, while writing poetry directly after his experiences, did not publish it until much later.

105. Harris, "Elegy," 213.

106. Plath, *Poet Speaks,* 170.

107. Katherine Anne Porter was a short story writer whose career Plath followed with interest, writing about her stories with approval in her journal on 26 September 1959 at Yaddo (J 314).

108. Hayman, *Death and Life,* 3.

109. Al Alvarez, "The Literature of the Holocaust," *Commentary* 64 November 1964: 65.

110. Insdorf, *Indelible Shadows,* 10

111. Elie Wiesel, quoted in *Genocidal Mentality,* Lifton and Markussen, 1.

112. Ibid., 9.

113. Ibid., 13.

114. Aharon Applefield, "After the Holocaust," *Writing and the Holocaust,* ed. Berel Lang (New York: Holmes & Meier, 1988), 92.

115. Irving Howe, "Writing and the Holocaust," *Writing and the Holocaust,* ed. Berel Lang (New York: Holmes & Meier, 1988), 175.

116. Harris, "Elegy," 213.

117. Annette Insdorf, *Indelible Shadows: Film and the Holocaust,* 2d ed. (Cambridge: Cambridge University Press, 1989), 4.

118. Insdorf, *Indelible Shadows,* 6–7.

119. James E. Young, "'I may be a bit of a Jew'; The Holocaust Confessions of Sylvia Plath," *Philological Quarterly* 6 (1987): 140. Young writes: "To question whether or not the suffering of the Holocaust should be cast as a type implies that we have some sort of legislative control over which events figure other, which events enter consciousness."

120. Ibid., 132.

121. Edward Alexander, "Stealing the Holocaust," *Midstream* (November 1980): 48, 50.

122. Laurence Langer, *The Holocaust and the Literary Imagination* (New Haven and London: Yale University Press, 1975), 171. Langer writes, "According to the research of a psychologist, reports Ortega Y Gassett [in "The Dehumanization of Art"], one of the roots of metaphor lies in the spirit of the taboo. Certain objects or beings—the ancient Jahweh comes to mind—are too awful to name; but since they exist and cannot be avoided, they must somehow be approached, through symbolic action as well as through language. 'Such an object' says Ortega, 'has to be alluded to by a word denoting something else and thus appears in speech vicariously and surreptitiously'."

123. Langer, *Holocaust,* 175.

124. Teresa De Laurentis, *Alice Doesn't: Feminism, Semiotics, Cinema* (London: Macmillan, 1984), 139, 206. De Laurentis outlines, in cinematic terms, how the woman resists "confinement in that symbolic space [as object of the gaze]," quoting Laura Mulvey regarding one of these ways, the reversal of gaze: "a form of

direct address to the viewer, an 'articulation of images and looks [between characters, from viewers, from camera] which brings into play the position and activity of the viewer . . . then the viewer runs the risk of becoming the object of the look, of being overlooked in the act of looking'."

125. Judith Butler, *Gender Trouble: Feminism and the Subversion of Identity* (London: Routledge, 1990), 139.

126. George Steiner, "Dying is an Art," *Language and Silence* (London: Faber, 1967), 330. Steiner writes in approval, "Perhaps it is only those who had no part in the events who *can* focus on them rationally and imaginatively; to those who experienced the thing, it has lost the hard edges of possibility, it has stepped outside the real . . . In 'Daddy' she wrote one of the very few poems I know of in any language to come near the last horror. It achieves the classic act of generalization, translating a private, obviously intolerable hurt into a code of plain statement, of instantaneously public images which concern us all. It is the 'Guernica' of modern poetry. And it is both histrionic and, in some ways, 'arty' as is Picasso's outcry." The second reference, when Steiner was writing in 1969, is from his essay "In Extremis," cited in *Sylvia Plath and Anne Sexton: A Reference Guide* by Cameron Northouse and Thomas P. Walsh (Boston: G. K. Hall, 1974), 52.

127. Hughes, "Chronological," 187.

128. Kroll, *Mythology*, 2.

129. Ibid., 3.

130. Ibid., 210.

131. Plath, "Religion As I See It," 5.

132. Plath, "Plato and Popper," 4.

133. D. H. Lawrence, "Phoenix," *The Complete Poems of D. H. Lawrence* (London: Heineman, 1957), Plath's Library, Smith, 176.

134. Plath, "Devil's Advocate," 9.

135. The ambiguities inherent in Plath's use of witch imagery, explored in the previous chapter, are linked to this ambivalence toward such "easy" transcendence.

136. A similar exploration of the symbiotic "master-slave" relationship appears in "Daddy" and "The Jailor."

Chapter 3. The Psychoanalyzing of Sylvia

1. Early examples include P. N. Furbank, "New Poetry," *The Listener* 11 March 1965: 379, "It is no good pretending that Sylvia Plath's is not sick verse"; James F. Hoyle, "Sylvia Plath: A Poetry of Suicidal Mania," *Literature and Psychology* 18 (1968): 187–203, "Like Freud's achievement, [Plath's] is thoroughly rooted in the family and its problems." Later examples include Timothy Materer, "Occultism As Source and Symptom in Sylvia Plath's 'Dialogue Over a Ouija Board'," *Twentieth Century Literature* 37 (Summer 1991): 131–47; Patrick Wakeling, "Sylvia Plath, A Balance of Loss and Gain," *Contemporary Review* 25 (September 1991): 142–46.

2. Alicia Ostriker, "The Americanization of Sylvia," *Critical Essays on Sylvia Plath,* ed. Linda W. Wagner (Boston: G. K. Hall, 1984), 109.

3. Elizabeth Hardwick, "On Sylvia Plath," *Ariel Ascending: Writings about Sylvia Plath,* ed. Paul Alexander (New York: Harper & Row, 1985), 100.

4. Shoshana Felman, *Jacques Lacan and the Adventure of Insight: Psychoanalysis in Contemporary Culture* (Cambridge: Harvard University Press, 1987), 15.

5. Marsack, *Plath*, 21. For example, Marsack notes the images of orality in "Poem for a Birthday" and sees them as signifying that the speaker inhabits "the oral stage [which is] pre-Oedipal, before the child begins to assume a separate identity from the mother."

6. Felman, *Lacan*, 11.

7. While Laing is not generally classed as an object-relations theorist, his interest in the relational nature of subject-formation and his concentration on the mother-child dyad reveal the general similarities of his work with theorists such as Winnicott. (In addition, Winnicott, Klein, and Laing all spent considerable periods working at the Tavistock Clinic, a center for interest in object-relations theory and practice.)

8. Lynda K. Bundtzen, *Plath's Incarnations: Woman and the Creative Process* (Ann Arbor: University of Michigan Press, 1988), 42.

9. Bundtzen, *Incarnations*, 41.

10. Stephen Gould Axelrod, *Sylvia Plath: The Wound and the Cure of Words* (Baltimore and London: Johns Hopkins University Press, 1990), 5.

11. David Holbrook, *Sylvia Plath: Poetry and Existence* (London: Athlone Press, 1976), 23.

12. Ibid., 24.

13. Ibid., 27–28.

14. Ibid., 42.

15. Felman, *Lacan*, 35.

16. Ibid.

17. Ibid., 36, 37.

18. "Psychoanalytic Criticism," *The Fontana Dictionary of Modern Thought*, ed. Alan Bullock, Oliver Stallybrass, and Stephen Trombley, 2d ed. (London: HarperCollins-Fontana, 1988), 696.

19. Lynne Salop, *Suisong* (New York: Vantage Press, 1978). A well-researched book, weakened by a sentimental pop psychoanalysis of Plath's "tortured soul."

20. Alicia Ostriker, "Americanization," 98.

21. Felman, *Lacan*, 36.

22. Butscher, *Method and Madness*. Although Butscher's critical biography sees Plath's late "bitch goddess" persona in a favorable light, the terms of his description still imply censure, a censure in which other critics are more than happy to collude.

23. Felman, *Lacan*, 38, writes: "As do its opponents, so does applied psychoanalysis itself fail precisely to account for the dynamic interaction between the unconscious and the conscious elements of art."

24. Rose, *Haunting*, 49.

25. Axelrod, *Wound*, 63.

26. See my comments in the introduction on Plath's belief in the importance of physical fertility to the female writer.

27. Hughes, *Chronological Order*, 191.

28. Al Alvarez, "Sylvia Plath: A Memoir," *The Art of Sylvia Plath: A Symposium*, ed. Charles Newman (London: Faber, 1970), 58.

29. Sylvia Plath, "Jung: Notes," Smith College. Although these notes are undated, they appear to have been written in late 1959, because they include details of the Jung case history to which Plath refers in her journal on 4 October.

30. Bundtzen, *Incarnations*, 242; Kroll, *Mythology*, 91.

31. Bundtzen, *Incarnations*, 242–43.

32. Marsack, *Plath*, 21.

33. Bundtzen, *Incarnations*, 51.

34. Nancy Chodorow, *Feminism and Psychoanalytic Theory* (New Haven and London: Yale University Press, 1989), 110.

35. Lynne Segal, *Is the Future Female?* (London: Virago, 1987), 148.

36. Rose, *Haunting*, 52.

37. Julia Kristeva, *Powers of Horror: An Essay on Abjection* (New York: Columbia University Press, 1982), 12.

38. Elizabeth Grosz, "Julia Kristeva," *Feminism and Psychoanalysis: A Critical Dictionary*, ed. Elizabeth Wright (London: Blackwell, 1992), 198.

39. This conflation of womb and stomach can be seen as describing the infantile state of the speaker, frequently noted by Melanie Klein in her studies of children. Yet, as has been shown, the speaker's position as either mother or infant is never stable.

40. Kristeva, *Abjection*, 12.

41. Elizabeth Grosz, "The Body of Signification," *Abjection, Melancholia and Love: the Work of Julia Kristeva*, ed. John Fletcher and Andrew Benjamin (London: Routledge, 1990), 90.

42. Kristeva, *Abjection*, 2.

43. Ibid., 3.

44. Elizabeth Grosz, *Sexual Subversions: Three French Feminists* (Sydney: Allen & Unwin, 1989), 75.

45. Grosz, "Kristeva," 198.

46. Mary Douglas, *Purity and Danger: An Analysis of the Concept of Pollution and Taboo* (London: Routledge & Kegan Paul-Ark, 1984), 161.

47. Kristeva, *Abjection*, 3.

48. An interesting adjunct to this is Irigaray's theories of women's lesser status in society, explored by Grosz, *Subversions*, chaps. 4 & 5, where Irigaray postulates that if man defines himself by the material waste, the other, he expels, the woman (other) is necessarily defined as abject, or waste.

49. Marsack, *Plath*, 23.

50. Rose, *Haunting*, 54.

51. Kristeva, *Abjection*, 3.

52. Plath, "Living Poet." Plath's description of "The Stones" is interesting. Her ambiguous attitude toward rebirth and transcendence is clear, as she describes the speaker's rebirth (implicitly natural) using the mechanical image of the reconstruction of an ancient statue. Her knowledge of and interest in psychology is also clear in the statement. She describes the speaker as lacking an identity and sense of relationship with the world, and needing to accept the "frightening yet necessary" ties of love.

53. Julia Kristeva, "Among Chinese Women," *The Kristeva Reader*, ed. Toril Moi (Oxford: Blackwell, 1986), 152–53.

54. Douglas, *Purity*, 2.

55. Kristeva, "Chinese Women," 156.

56. See my discussion below of the problems associated for the woman with the alternate claims of female "materiality" or immanence and male "transcendence" and the difficulties with Kristeva's theorization of this.

57. Kristeva, "Chinese Women," 153.

58. Kristeva, *Abjection*, 12.

59. Gross, "Body," 93.

60. Marsack, *Plath*, 21.

61. Plath uses the barnyard image in a poem she wrote immediately before this sequence, "The Colossus," in similar terms of the echolalia before speech, but in "The Colossus" it is the father rather than the infant who is subject to this presubjective communication.

62. The pre-eminence of Plath's connection between language and subjectivity in "Poem for a Birthday" meaningfully relates to Plath's need to claim her own writing, rather than offer it up for appropriation by mother or husband, noted above.

63. Rose, *Haunting*, 57.

64. It is ironic that Rose perceives such extremes in Plath criticism, as she, too, is subject to another type of extreme in her abstraction.

65. Rose, *Haunting*, 58.

66. Ibid.

67. Ibid., 57.

68. Ibid., 36.

69. Ibid., 61.

70. Ibid.

71. Grosz, *Subversions*, 81.

72. Ibid., 79.

73. Rose, *Haunting*, 56.

74. Ibid., 63.

75. Grosz, *Subversions*, 71.

76. Butscher, *Method and Madness*, 152.

77. Aurelia Plath, TS. of *Letters Home*, preface to spring 1953 collection of correspondence.

78. Cohen correspondence, 13 March 1951, 26 January 1953, Lilly.

79. Sylvia Plath, "Smith Class Notes," 1951–52, English 211, twentieth-century literature, Smith. Plath notes her lecturer, Miss Drew's points about the importance of psychoanalysis and myth to the writers of the 1920s, which conclude: "Inner territory where thought and feeling translate themselves into symbol, 'logic of imagination'." This last part of the notes is especially interesting in relation to the "intellect-emotion" conflict that affected both Plath and her generation, described in the introduction.
Plath, "Plato and Popper," 10. Plath makes the connection between Plato's concerns and those of Freud explicit. She quotes Plato's description of the "lawless wild-beast nature, which peers out in sleep" that is a part of every person and makes the link between this and Freud's description of repression.

80. Plath, "Magic Mirror," 10. The bibliography includes: Stanley M. Coleman, "The Phantom Double. Its Psychological Significance," *British Journal of Medical Psychology* 14 (1934); Otto Rank, "The Double as Immortal Self," *Beyond Psychology;* Otto Rank, "The Double," *Psychoanalytic Review* 6 (1919); Sigmund Freud, "Doestoevsky and Parricide," *Collected Papers*, vol. 5; Freud, "A Neurosis of Demonical Possession in the 17th Century," *Collected Papers*, vol. 4; Freud, "The Uncanny," *Collected Papers*, vol. 4.

81. David Holbrook, "The 200–inch Distorting Mirror," *New Society* 11 July 1968: 57–58; David Holbrook, "R. D. Laing and the Death Circuit," *Encounter* August 1968: 35–45; Marjorie Perloff, "'A Ritual for Being Born Twice': Sylvia Plath's *The Bell Jar,*" *Contemporary Literature* 12 (1972): 507–22.

82. Plath, "Magic Mirror," 5.

83. Ernest Jones, *Hamlet and Oedipus* (ca. 1949; Garden City, NY: Doubleday, 1954), Plath's Library, Smith. The cover blurb to Plath's copy of Jones's emphasizes the increasing popularity of psychoanalytic approaches to literature. It reads, "Of the great number of psychoanalytic studies of literary subjects that have appeared during the recent past, this work by Freud's biographer and his greatest living disciple is by far the best."

84. Sylvia Plath, "New Comment 2—Sylvia Plath on Contemporary American Poetry," TS., transmission 10 January 1963, BBC Third Programme, Smith.

85. Mary Louise Aswell, ed., *The World Within: Fiction Illuminating the Neuroses of our Time*, intro. and notes, Frederic Wertham, MD (New York: McGraw-Hill, 1947), Plath's Library, Lilly.

86. Ibid., 300.

87. Sylvia Plath, "Hospital Notes," Journal 1958–59, Smith. 3.

88. Plath, "Jung: Notes."

89. Plath, "Living Poet."

90. Fromm, *Escape*, 246.

91. Felman, *Lacan*, 48.

92. Carl Jung, *Selected Writings*, ed. Antony Storr (London: Fontana 1983), 115. Even if Plath's poetic mention of the father is treated purely biographically, it is important to bear in mind Jung's qualification of such "knowledge": "Up till now, everybody has been convinced that the idea of 'my father' 'my mother' etc. is nothing but a faithful reflection of the real parent, corresponding in every detail to the original, so that when someone says 'my father' he means no more and no less than what his father is in reality. This is actually what he supposes he does mean, but a supposition of identity by no means brings that identity about. This is where the fallacy of . . . 'the veiled one' . . . comes in . . . X's idea of his father is a complex quantity for which the real father is only in part responsible, an indefinitely larger share falling to the son."

93. Carole Ferrier, "The Beekeeper's Apprentice," *Sylvia Plath: New Views on the Poetry*, ed. Gary Lane (Baltimore and London: Johns Hopkins University Press, 1979), 205.

94. Plath did not really start consistently dating her poems until late 1959, so the timing of the early pieces has to go on the order of their appearance in the *Collected Poems*. Certainly though, the frequency with which a poem dealing with either the mother or father is accompanied by its companion makes such a doubling more than coincidence.

95. To try and determine which figure is the more important is a pointless exercise, as the importance of Plath's figurings of both "mother" and "father" lies in how she situated herself in this "family romance" (broadly, as either mother- or father-identified) in terms of her conflict in her view of herself as a female writer keen to break into the male worlds of publishing and literary greatness.

96. Cohen correspondence, 11 August 1950.

97. Robert Phillips, "The Dark Funnel: A Reading of Sylvia Plath," *Modern Poetry Studies* 3 (1972): 49–74. Phillips sees the theme of the death and rejection of the father-figure apparent throughout Plath's work. He claims the father-figure becomes, in a Jungian sense, the chief archetypal configuration with which Plath identifies, making her into a "modern Electra." More recently, critics frequently return to this theme, perceived in both Plath's poetry and fiction. Examples include K. G. Srivnstava, "Plath's Daddy," *The Explicator* 50 (Winter 1992): 126–28; Mary G. De Jong, "Sylvia Plath and Sheila Ballantyne's Imaginary Crimes," *Studies in American Fiction* 16 (Spring 1988): 27–38; Sally Greene, "Fa-

thers and Daughters in Sylvia Plath's Blossom Street," *Studies in American Fiction* 18 (Autumn 1990): 225–31. [Greene's connection of Plath's writing with the influence of T. S. Eliot is interesting in terms of my discussion of "Full Fathom Five" below]; Jahan Ramazani, "'Daddy, I have had to kill you': Plath, Rage and the Modern Elegy," *PMLA* 108 (1993): 1142–56.

98. Ferrier in "Beekeeper's Apprentice" provides the most systematic argument of this progression.

99. Linda W. Wagner, "Plath's *The Bell Jar* as female Bildungsroman," *Women's Studies* 12 : 1 (1986): 55–68. Arguably, *The Bell Jar* reflects, in novel form, a similar movement throughout Plath's whole oeuvre.

100. Angela Leighton, *Elizabeth Barrett-Browning* (Brighton: Harvester, 1986), 54.

101. Ibid., 52.

102. Simone de Beauvoir, *The Second Sex* (Harmondsworth: Penguin, 1974), 315.

103. Barrett-Browning wrote a poem, "The Tempest," in which a similar "family romance," with all its ambiguities about the position of the father as precursor or muse, is figured.

104. William Shakespeare, *Complete Works,* ed. William Allan Neilson and Charles Jarvis Hill (Boston: Houghton Mifflin, ca.1942), Plath's Library.

105. As such, William V. Davis's argument in "Sylvia Plath's "Ariel," *Modern Poetry Studies* 3 (1979): 176–84, is inaccurate. Davis states that "Ariel"'s three references are the biographical horse she rode in Devon, the biblical term for Jerusalem, and the literary *The Tempest,* and that of these three the biographical and biblical connections are the most significant. Not only, however, is *The Tempest* an equally important allusion in Plath's poem, but Davis misses the point (about the complex nature of Plath's influences) by trying to assign them to a stable rank order.

106. Elizabeth Butler Cullingford, "A Father's Prayer, A Daughter's Anger: W. B. Yeats and Sylvia Plath," *Daughters and Fathers,* ed. Lynda E. Boose and Betty S. Flowers (Baltimore: Johns Hopkins University Press, 1989), 245. Cullingford writes, "While her hostility to Otto Plath eventually became overt and her loyalty to her literary father, Yeats, was tempered by considerable criticism she seems never to have questioned the powerfully seductive and patriarchal claims of psychoanalysis itself." Cullingford's assertion ignores the difficulty in defining boundaries between literary, psychoanalytic, and "real" fathers in Plath's treatment of the "father" in her poetry. She also simplifies the relationships as being either unquestioning or hostile and so ignores the more important and ambiguous nature of Plath's victim-master attitude toward such patriarchal discourses.

107. Kristeva, "Chinese Women," 150.

108. Ibid., 156–57.

109. Butscher, *Method and Madness,* 181.

110. Hayman, *Death and Life,* 103.

111. Plath, poetry reading and interview with Lee Anderson.

112. Teresa Brennan, *The Interpretation of the Flesh: Freud and Femininity* (London: Routledge, 1992), 6. Brennan puts Freud's recognition of the problem of femininity in its proper context (a context that should not be seen to reinforce the traditionally romanticized notion of the feminine as mysterious, hidden, and somehow outside rational discourse). She writes: "In some of his last words on the subject, he quotes Heine's *Nordsee,* noting that, for generations, 'sweating,

human heads have been knocking against . . . the riddle of femininity'. Yet, in the context of this appeal to Heine, Freud also makes it plain that he regards femininity as a problem to be solved, something he knew too little about."

Mitchell, *Psychoanalysis and Feminism*, 129. Mitchell declares that from the early part of this century, when Freud declared that those after him should look more closely into female psychology: "the disagreement on the psychological distinction between the sexes had settled into a rut from which it never really freed itself."

CONCLUSION: A DIALECTIC OF TRANSCENDENCE AND MEMORY

1. Sylvia Plath, draft 2 of "Lady Lazarus," Smith.
2. Sylvia Plath, draft 1 of "Years," 16 November 1962, Smith.
3. Susan Van Dyne, "'More Terrible Than She Ever Was': The Manuscripts of Sylvia Plath's Bee Poems," *Critical Essays on Sylvia Plath*, ed. Linda W. Wagner (Boston: G. K. Hall, 1984), 154–70; "Fueling the Phoenix Fire: The Manuscripts of Sylvia Plath's 'Lady Lazarus,'" *Modern Critical Views: Sylvia Plath*, ed. Harold Bloom (New York: Chelsea House, 1989), 133–48.
4. Sylvia Plath, draft 3 of "The Moon and the Yew Tree," initially titled "Moon and Yew," Lilly.
5. Sylvia Plath, "Last Words," originally untitled, 21 October 1961, Lilly.
6. Sylvia Plath, draft 1 of "Finisterre," Lilly.
7. Sylvia Plath, "The Grass" and "The bald truth about: Grass at Wuthering Heights," Lilly.
8. Sylvia Plath, drafts "Wuthering Heights," initially titled "Withens," Lilly.
9. Sylvia Plath, draft 1 of "Little Fugue," 2 April 1962, Smith.
10. Sylvia Plath, draft 13 of "Private Ground," 25 February 1961, Lilly.
11. Plath, draft 2 of "Private Ground," untitled, Lilly.
12. Hugh Kenner, "*Ariel*, by Sylvia Plath," *Triumph* 1 (1966): 34.

Bibliography

By Sylvia Plath (Arranged Chronologically)

With Perry Norton. "Youth's Plea for World Peace." *Christian Science Monitor,* 16 March 1950: 19.

"*Stones of Troy.*" Review of collection of poetry by C. A. Trypanis. *Gemini* 2 (1957): 98–103.

"A Walk to Withens." *Christian Science Monitor,* 6 June 1959: 12.

American Poetry Now : A Selection of the Best Poems by Modern American Writers. Edited by Sylvia Plath. *Critical Quarterly,* poetry suppl. no. 2 (1961).

"General Jodpur's Conversion." Review of *The General* by Janet Charters, *A Wish for Little Sister* by Jacqueline Ayer, *Joba and the Wild Boar* by Gaby Baldner, and others. *New Statesman* (10 November 1961): 696, 698.

"Pair of Queens." Review of *A Queen of Spain* by Peter de Polnay and *Josephine* by Hubert Cole. *New Statesman* (27 April 1962): 602–3.

"Oblongs." Review of *The Emperor's Oblong Pancake* by Peter Hughes, *The Three Robbers* by Tomi Ungerer, *The Funny Thing* by Wanda Gag, and *Dr. Spock Talks with Mothers. New Statesman* (18 May 1962): 724.

"Oregonian Original." Review of *Opal Whitelely* by E. S. Bradburne, *The Wonderful Button* by Evan Hunter, *Little Blue and Little Yellow* by Leo Lionni, and *Punch and Judy Carry On* by Elizabeth and Gerald Rose. *New Statesman* (9 November 1962): 660.

"Suffering Angel." Review of *Lord Byron's Wife* by Malcolm Elwin. *New Statesman* (7 December 1962): 828–29.

The Bell Jar. 1963. London: Faber, 1966.

"Sylvia Plath." *The Poet Speaks: Interviews with Contemporary Poets.* Edited by Peter Orr. London: Routledge & Kegan Paul, 1966, 167–72.

Johnny Panic and the Bible of Dreams and Other Prose Writings. London: Faber, 1977.

Letters Home: Correspondence 1950–1963. Edited by Aurelia Plath. London: Faber, 1978.

Collected Poems. Edited by Ted Hughes. London: Faber, 1981.

The Journals of Sylvia Plath. Edited by Ted Hughes and Frances McCullough. New York: Ballantine, 1982.

Also unpublished material from The Sylvia Plath Collection, Lilly Library, Indiana University, Bloomington, Indiana; and from The Sylvia Plath Collection, Smith College Library Rare Book Room, Northampton, Massachusetts.

Books from Plath's Library
(Collections at Lilly & Smith)

Aswell, Mary Louise, ed. *The World Within: Fiction Illuminating Neuroses of Our Time.* New York: McGraw Hill, ca.1947.

Barzun, Jacques. *Darwin, Marx and Wagner.* Boston: Little Brown, 1947.

Blake, William. *The Portable Blake.* Edited by Alfred Kazin. New York: Viking, 1953.

Brooks, Cleanth. *The Well-Wrought Urn: Studies in the Structure of Poetry.* New York: Harcourt Brace, ca.1947.

Brooks, Cleanth, and Robert Penn Warren. *Understanding Poetry: An Anthology for College Students.* New York: Henry Holt, 1946.

Campbell, Oscar James, Justine Van Gundy, and Caroline Shrodes. *Patterns for Living.* New York: Macmillan, 1949.

Ciardi, John, ed. *Mid-Century American Poets.* New York: Twayne, 1952.

Corry, J. A. *Elements of Democratic Government.* New York: Oxford University Press, 1951.

De Quincey, Thomas. *Selected Writings of Thomas De Quincey.* Edited by Philip Van Doren Stern. New York: Modern Library, 1949.

Frazer, J. A. *The Golden Bough: A Study in Magic and Religion.* 1922. New York: Macmillan, 1952.

Freud, Sigmund. *The Basic Writings of Sigmund Freud.* Translated and edited by Dr. A. A. Brill. New York: Modern Library, ca.1938.

Fromm, Eric. *Escape from Freedom.* New York: Rinehart, 1941.

Fry, Christopher. *The Lady's Not For Burning.* New York: Oxford University Press, 1950.

Huxley, Aldous. *Heaven and Hell.* London: Chatto & Windus, 1956.

Jarrell, Randall. *Poetry and the Age.* New York: Vintage, 1955.

Jones, Ernest. *Hamlet and Oedipus.* Garden City, NY: Doubleday, 1954.

Lawrence, D. H. *The Complete Poems of D. H. Lawrence.* London: Heinemann, 1957.

———. *Selected Essays.* Harmondsworth, Middlesex: Penguin, 1954.

Lewis, Sinclair. *Babbitt.* New York: Harcourt Brace, 1922.

Mead, Margaret. *Male and Female: A Study of the Sexes in a Changing World.* New York: William Morrow, 1952.

Ortega y Gassett, Jose. *The Revolt of the Masses.* 1930. New York: New American Library, 1951.

Richards, I. A. *Practical Criticism: A Study of Literary Judgment.* London: Routledge & Kegan Paul, 1954.

Riesman, David, Nathan Glazer, and Reul Denney. *The Lonely Crowd.* 1950. Garden City, NY: Doubleday, 1953.

Sitwell, Edith. *The Collected Poems of Edith Sitwell.* New York: Vanguard Press, 1954.

Wood, Clement, ed. *The Complete Rhyming Dictionary and Poet's Craft Book.* Garden City, NY: Garden City Books, ca. 1936.

Books and Articles On Sylvia Plath

Aird, Eileen. "'Poem for a Birthday' to 'Three Women': Development in the Poetry of Sylvia Plath." *Critical Quarterly* 21 (1979): 63–72.

———. *Sylvia Plath.* Edinburgh: Oliver and Boyd, 1973.

Alexander, Paul, ed. *Ariel Ascending: Writings about Sylvia Plath.* New York: Harper & Row, 1985.

Alvarez, Al. "Prologue: Sylvia Plath." *The Savage God: A Study of Suicide,* 19–57. Harmondsworth, Middlesex: Penguin, 1974.

———. "Sylvia Plath." In *The Art of Sylvia Plath: A Symposium,* edited by Charles Newman, 56–68. London: Faber, 1970.

Ames, Lois. "Notes Towards a Biography." In *The Art of Sylvia Plath,* edited by Charles Newman, 155–73. London: Faber, 1970.

Annas, Pamela J. "The Self in the World: The Social Context of Sylvia Plath's Last Poems." In *Critical Essays on Sylvia Plath,* edited by Linda W. Wagner, 130–39. Boston: G. K. Hall, 1984.

Ashford, Deborah. "Sylvia Plath's Poetry: A Complex of Irreconcilable Antagonisms." *Concerning Poetry* 7 (1974): 62–69.

Axelrod, Steven Gould. *Sylvia Plath: The Wound and the Cure of Words.* Baltimore and London: Johns Hopkins University Press, 1990.

Balitas, Vincent D. "On Becoming a Witch: A Reading of Sylvia Plath's 'Witch Burning'." *Studies in the Humanities* 4 (1975): 27–30.

Bannerjee, Jacqueline. "Grief and the Modern Writer." *English* 43.175 (1994): 17–36.

Barnard, Caroline King. *Sylvia Plath.* Boston: Twaine-G. K. Hall, 1978.

Bassnett, Susan. *Sylvia Plath.* London: Macmillan, 1987.

Bedient, Calvin. "Sylvia Plath: Romantic . . ." In *Sylvia Plath: New Views on the Poetry,* edited by Gary Lane, 3–18. Baltimore and London: Johns Hopkins University Press, 1979.

Bennett, Paula. *My Life a Loaded Gun: Dickinson, Plath, Rich and Female Creativity.* Urbana and Chicago: University of Illinois Press, 1990.

Berman, Jeffrey. "Sylvia Plath and the Art of Dying: Sylvia Plath: 1932–1963." *University of Hartford Studies in Literature* 10 (1978): 137–55.

Blodgett, E. D. "Sylvia Plath: Another View." *Modern Poetry Studies* 2.3 (1971): 97–106.

Bloom, Harold. "Editor's Note and Introduction." In *Modern Critical Views: Sylvia Plath,* edited by Harold Bloom, vii–4. New York: Chelsea House, 1989.

Broe, Mary Lynn. "'Enigmatical, Shifting my Clarities'." In *Ariel Ascending: Writings about Sylvia Plath,* edited by Paul Alexander, 80–93. New York: Harper & Row, 1985.

———. *Protean Poetic: The Poetry of Sylvia Plath.* Columbia and London: University of Missouri Press, 1980.

Buell, Frederic. "Sylvia Plath's Traditionalism." In *Critical Essays on Sylvia Plath,* edited by Linda W. Wagner, 140–54. Boston: G. K. Hall, 1984.

Bundtzen, Lynda K. *Plath's Incarnations: Woman and the Creative Process.* Ann Arbor: University of Michigan Press, 1988.

Butler, C. S. "Poetry and the Computer: Some Quantitive Aspects of the Style of Sylvia Plath." *Proceedings of the British Academy* 65 (1979): 291–312.

Butscher, Edward. "In Search of Sylvia: An Introduction." In *Sylvia Plath: The Woman and the Work,* edited by Edward Butscher, 3–29. London: Peter Owen, 1979.

———. *Sylvia Plath: Method and Madness.* New York: Seabury Press, 1976.

————, ed. *Sylvia Plath: The Woman and the Work.* London: Peter Owen, 1979.

Campbell, Wendy. "Remembering Sylvia." In *The Art of Sylvia Plath,* edited by Charles Newman, 182–86. London: Faber, 1970.

Cleverdon, Douglas. "On 'Three Women'." In *The Art of Sylvia Plath,* edited by Charles Newman, 227–29. London: Faber, 1970.

Cluysenaar, Anne. "Post-culture: Pre-culture?" In *British Poetry Since 1960: A Critical Survey,* edited by Micheal Schmidt and Grevel Lindop, 215–32. Oxford: Carcanet, 1972.

Cooley, Peter. "Autism, Autoeroticism, Auto-Da-Fe: The Tragic Poetry of Sylvia Plath." *Hollins Critic* 10 (1973): 1–15.

Cox, C. B., and A. R. Jones. "After the Tranquilized Fifties: Notes on Sylvia Plath and James Baldwin." *Critical Quarterly* 6 (1964): 107–22.

Drake, Barbara. "'Perfection is Terrible: It Cannot Have Children'." In *Critical Essays on Sylvia Plath,* edited by Linda W. Wagner. Boston: G. K. Hall, 1984.

Dyson, A. E. "On Sylvia Plath." *The Art of Sylvia Plath,* 204–10. London: Faber, 1970.

Feit-Diehl, Joanne. "Plath's Bodily Ego: Restaging the Sublime," *Women Poets and the American Sublime,* 111–41. Bloomington and Indianapolis: Indiana University Press, 1990.

Ferrier, Carole. "The Beekeeper's Apprentice." In *Sylvia Plath: New Views on the Poetry,* edited by Gary Lane, 203–17. Baltimore and London: Johns Hopkins University Press, 1979.

Gilbert, Sandra M. "'A Fine, White Flying Myth': The Life/Work of Sylvia Plath." *Shakespeare's Sisters: Feminist Essays on Women Poets,* 245–60. Bloomington and London: Indiana University Press, 1979.

————. "In Yeats' House: The Death and Resurrection of Sylvia Plath." In *Critical Essays on Sylvia Plath,* edited by Linda W. Wagner, 204–22. Boston: G. K. Hall, 1984.

Greene, Sally. "Fathers and Daughters in Sylvia Plath's Blossom Street." *Studies in American Fiction* 18 (1990): 225–31.

————. "The Pull of the Oracle: Personalized Mythologies in Plath and De Chirico." *Mosaic* 25 (1992): 107–20.

Guttenberg, Barnett. "Plath's Cosmology and the House of Yeats." In *Sylvia Plath: New Views on the Poetry,* edited by Gary Lane, 138–52. Baltimore and London: Johns Hopkins University Press, 1979.

Hardwick, Elizabeth. "Victims and Victors." *Seduction and Betrayal: Women and Literature,* 104–24. London: Weidenfield & Nicholson, 1970.

————. "On Sylvia Plath." In *Ariel Ascending: Writings about Sylvia Plath,* edited by Paul Alexander, 100–115. New York: Harper & Row, 1985.

Hardy, Barbara. "Enlargement or Derangement?" In *Ariel Ascending: Writings about Sylvia Plath,* edited by Paul Alexander, 61–79. New York: Harper & Row, 1985.

Hawthorn, Jeremy. "The Bell Jar and Larger Things." *Multiple Personality and the Disintegration of Literary Character from Oliver Goldsmith to Sylvia Plath,* 117–34. London: Edward Arnold, 1983.

Hayman, Ronald. *The Death and Life of Sylvia Plath.* London: Mandarin-Minerva, 1992.

Heaney, Seamus. "The Indefatibable Hoof-taps: Sylvia Plath." *The Government of the Tongue*, 148–70. London: Faber, 1989.

Holbrook, David. "Out of the Ash: Different Views of the 'Death Camp': Sylvia Plath, Al Alvarez and Viktor Frankl." *Human World* 5 (1971): 22–39.

———. "R. D. Laing and the Death Circuit." *Encounter* 31 (1968): 35–45.

———. "Sylvia Plath, Pathological Morality, and the Avant-Garde." In *Pelican Guide to English Literature: The Modern Age*, vol. 7, edited by Boris Ford, 433–49. Harmondsworth, Middlesex: Penguin, 1973.

———. *Sylvia Plath: Poetry and Existence*. London: Athlone Press, 1976.

———. "The 200–Inch Distorting Mirror." *New Society* 11 July 1968: 57–58.

Homberger, Eric. *A Chronological Checklist of the Periodical Publications of Sylvia Plath*. Exeter, Devon: University of Exeter American Arts Documentation Centre, 1970.

Howard, Richard. "Sylvia Plath: 'And I Have No Face, I Have Wanted To Efface Myself . . .'." In *The Art of Sylvia Plath*, edited by Charles Newman, 77–78. London: Faber, 1970.

Howe, Irving. "The Plath Celebration. A Partial Dissent." In *Sylvia Plath: The Woman and the Work*, edited by Edward Butscher, 225–35. London: Peter Owen, 1979.

Hoyle, James F. "Sylvia Plath: A Poetry of Suicidal Mania." *Literature and Psychology* 18 (1968): 187–203.

Hughes, Ted. "Forward." *The Journals of Sylvia Plath* by Sylvia Plath, edited by Ted Hughes and Frances McCullough, xi–xiii. New York: Ballantine, 1982.

———. "Introduction." *Johnny Panic and the Bible of Dreams and Other Prose Writings*, by Sylvia Plath, 11–13. London: Faber, 1977.

———. "Sylvia Plath's 'Crossing the Water': Some Reflections." *Critical Quarterly* 13 (1971): 165–71.

———. "Notes on the Chronological Order of Sylvia Plath's Poems." In *The Art of Sylvia Plath*, edited by Charles Newman, 187–95. London: Faber, 1970.

———. "Sylvia Plath and Her Journals." In *Ariel Ascending: Writings about Sylvia Plath*, edited by Paul Alexander, 152–64. New York: Harper & Row, 1985.

Inglis, Ruth. "Alma Mater of Private Pain and Public Death." *Jewish Chronicle— Literary Supplement*, 5 February 1993: iv.

Jones, A. R. "Necessity and Freedom: The Poetry of Robert Lowell, Sylvia Plath and Anne Sexton." *Critical Quarterly* 7 (1965): 11–30.

———. "On 'Daddy'." In *The Art of Sylvia Plath*, edited by Charles Newman, 230–36. London: Faber, 1970.

Juhasz, Suzanne. "'The Blood Jet': The Poetry of Sylvia Plath." *Naked and Fiery Forms: Modern American Poetry by Women, A New Tradition*, 85–116. New York: Harper & Row, 1976.

Kenner, Hugh. "Sincerity Kills." In *Sylvia Plath: New Views on the Poetry*, edited by Gary Lane, 33–44. Baltimore and London: Johns Hopkins University Press, 1979.

Kopp, Jane Baltzell. "'Gone, Very Gone Youth': Sylvia Plath at Cambridge, 1955–57." In *Sylvia Plath: The Woman and the Work*, edited by Edward Butscher, 61–80. London: Peter Owen, 1979.

Kroll, Judith. *Chapters in Mythology: The Poetry of Sylvia Plath*. New York: Harper & Row, 1976.

Krook, Dorothea. "Recollections of Sylvia Plath." In *Sylvia Plath: The Woman and the Work,* edited by Edward Butscher, 49–60. London: Peter Owen, 1979.

Kumar, Sukrita Paul. "Sylvia Plath: A Self in 'Halflighted Castles'." In *Existentialism in American Literature,* edited by Ruby Chatterji, 71–79. Atlantic Highlands, NJ: Humanities Press, 1983.

Lameyer, Gordon. "Sylvia at Smith." In *Sylvia Plath: The Woman and the Work,* edited by Edward Butscher, 32–41. London: Peter Owen, 1979.

———. "The Double in Sylvia Plath's *The Bell Jar.*" In *Sylvia Plath: The Woman and the Work,* edited by Edward Butscher, 143–65. London: Peter Owen, 1979.

Lane, Gary. "Influence and Originality in Plath's Poems." In *Sylvia Plath: New Views on the Poetry,* edited by Gary Lane, 116–37. Baltimore and London: Johns Hopkins University Press, 1979.

———, ed. *Sylvia Plath: New Views on the Poetry.* Baltimore and London: Johns Hopkins University Press, 1979.

Larkin, Phillip. "Horror Poet." *Required Writing: Miscellaneous Pieces 1955–1982.* London: Faber, 1983, 278–81.

Lavers, Annette. "The World as Icon: On Sylvia Plath's Themes." In *The Art of Sylvia Plath,* edited by Charles Newman, 100–135. London: Faber, 1970.

Lucie-Smith, Edward. "A Murderous Art?" *Critical Quarterly* 6 (1964): 355–63.

———. "Sea-imagery in the Work of Sylvia Plath." In *The Art of Sylvia Plath: A Symposium,* edited by Charles Newman, 91–99. London: Faber, 1970.

McClatchy, J. D. "Short Circuits and Folding Mirrors." In *Sylvia Plath: New Views on the Poetry,* edited by Gary Lane, 19–32. Baltimore and London: Johns Hopkins University Press, 1979.

———. "Staring from her hood of bone: Adjusting to Sylvia Plath." In *American Poetry Since 1960: Some Critical Perspectives,* edited by Robert B. Shaw, 155–66. Cheadle, Cheshire: Carcanet, 1973.

Mckay, D. F. "Aspects of Energy in the Poetry of Dylan Thomas and Sylvia Plath." In *Modern Critical Views: Sylvia Plath,* edited by Harold Bloom, 17–32. New York: Chelsea House, 1989.

McPherson, Patricia. "The Puzzle of Sylvia Plath." *Womens Studies Occasional Papers* 4. Canterbury, Kent: University of Kent at Canterbury, 1983.

Markey, Janice. *A Journey into the Red Eye: the Poetry of Sylvia Plath—A Critique.* London: Womens Press, 1993.

Marsack, Robyn. *Sylvia Plath: Open Guides to Literature.* London: Open University Press, 1992.

Mazzaro, Jerome. "Sylvia Plath and the Cycles of History." In *Sylvia Plath: New Views on the Poetry,* edited by Gary Lane, 218–40. Baltimore and London: Johns Hopkins University Press, 1979.

Melander, Ingrid. "The Poetry of Sylvia Plath: A Study of Themes." *Gothenberg Studies in English* 25. Stockholm: Almqvist & Wiksell, 1972.

Miller, Karl. "Who is Sylvia?" *Doubles: Studies in Literary History.* Oxford: Oxford University Press, 1985, 318–28.

Murdoch, Brian. "Transformations of the Holocaust: Auschwitz in Modern Lyric Poetry." *Comparative Literature Studies* 11 (1974): 123–50.

Nance, Guinevara A., and Judith P. Jones. "Doing Away with Daddy: Exorcism and Sympathetic Magic in Plath's Poetry." In *Critical Essays on Sylvia Plath,* edited by Linda W. Wagner, 124–30. Boston: G. K. Hall, 1984.

Newlin, Margaret. "The Suicide Bandwagon." *Critical Quarterly* 14 (1972): 367–78.

Newman, Charles, ed. *The Art of Sylvia Plath: A Symposium.* London: Faber, 1970.

―――. "Candor Is The Only Wile: The Art of Sylvia Plath." In *The Art of Sylvia Plath,* edited by Charles Newman, 21–55. London: Faber, 1970.

Nims, John Frederick. "The Poetry of Sylvia Plath: A Technical Analysis." In *Ariel Ascending: Writings about Sylvia Plath,* edited by Paul Alexander, 46–60. New York: Harper & Row, 1985.

Northouse, Cameron, and Thomas P. Walsh. *Sylvia Plath and Anne Sexton: A Reference Guide.* Boston: G. K. Hall, 1974.

Oates, Joyce Carol. "The Death Throes of Romanticism." In *Sylvia Plath: The Woman and the Work,* edited by Edward Butscher, 206–24. London: Peter Owen, 1979.

Oberg, Arthur K. "Sylvia Plath and the New Decadence." In *Sylvia Plath: The Woman and the Work,* edited by Edward Butscher, 177–85. London: Peter Owen, 1979.

O'Hara, J. D. "Plath's Comedy." In *Sylvia Plath: New Views on the Poetry,* edited by Gary Lane, 75–96. Baltimore and London: Johns Hopkins University Press, 1979.

Ostriker, Alicia. "The Americanization of Sylvia." In *Critical Essays on Sylvia Plath,* edited by Linda W. Wagner, 97–109. Boston: G. K. Hall, 1984.

Perloff, Marjorie. "Angst and Animism in the Poetry of Sylvia Plath." In *Critical Essays on Sylvia Plath,* edited by Linda W. Wagner, 109–24. Boston: G. K. Hall, 1984.

―――. "On the Road to *Ariel:* The 'Transitional' Poetry of Sylvia Plath." In *Sylvia Plath: The Woman and the Work,* edited by Edward Butscher, 125–42. London: Peter Owen, 1979.

―――. "Sylvia Plath's 'Sivvy' poems: A Portrait of the Poet as Daughter." In *Sylvia Plath: New Views on the Poetry,* edited by Gary Lane, 155–78. Baltimore and London: Johns Hopkins University Press, 1979.

―――. "The Two Ariels: The (Re)making of the Sylvia Plath Cannon." *Poetic License,* 175–97. Evanston, Ill.: Northwestern University Press, 1990.

Phillips, Robert. "The Dark Funnel: a Reading of Sylvia Plath." In *Sylvia Plath: The Woman and the Work,* edited by Edward Butscher, 186–205. London: Peter Owen, 1979.

Plath, Aurelia. "Introduction" and notes. *Letters Home: Correspondence 1950–1963* by Sylvia Plath, edited by Aurelia Plath, 3–41. London: Faber, 1978.

―――. "Letter Written in the Actuality of Spring." In *Ariel Ascending: Writings about Sylvia Plath,* edited by Paul Alexander, 214–17. New York: Harper & Row, 1985.

Plumley, Stanley. "What Ceremony of Words." In *Ariel Ascending: Writings about Sylvia Plath,* edited by Paul Alexander, 13–25. New York: Harper & Row, 1985.

Quinn, Sister Bernetta. "Medusan Imagery in Sylvia Plath." In *Sylvia Plath: New Views on the Poetry,* edited by Gary Lane, 97–115. Baltimore and London: Johns Hopkins University Press, 1979.

Ramazani, Jahan. "'Daddy, I have had to kill you': Plath, Rage, and the Modern Elegy." *PMLA* 108 (1993): 1142–56.

Robins, Corrine. "Four Young Poets." *Mademoiselle* 48 (1959): 34–35, 85.

Roche, Clarissa. "Sylvia Plath: Vignettes from England." In *Sylvia Plath: The Woman and the Work,* edited by Edward Butscher, 81–96. London: Peter Owen, 1979.

Rose, Jacqueline. *The Haunting of Sylvia Plath.* London: Virago, 1991.

Rosenblatt, Jon. *Sylvia Plath: The Poetry of Initiation.* Chapel Hill: University of North Carolina Press, 1979.

Rosenfeld, Alvin. "Exploiting Atrocity." *A Double Dying: Reflections on Holocaust Literature.* Bloomington: Indiana University Press, 1980.

Rosenthal, M. L. "Poetic Theory of Some Contemporary Poets." *Salmagundi* 1 (1966–67): 69–77.

———. "Sylvia Plath and Confessional Poetry." In *The Art of Sylvia Plath,* edited by Charles Newman, 69–76. London: Faber, 1970.

Rosenthal, M. L., and Sally M. Gall. "Sylvia Plath's 'Final' Poems and Anne Sexton's 'The Divorce Papers'." *The Modern Poetic Sequence: The Genius of Modern Poetry,* 428–43. Oxford: Oxford University Press, 1983.

Rudolf, Anthony, ed. *Theme and Version: Plath and Ronsard: Essays by Yves Bonnefoy, Audrey Jones, Daniel Wiessbort.* London: Menard Press, 1995.

Salomon, Lynda B. "'Double, Double': Perception in the Poetry of Sylvia Plath." *Spirit* 37 (1970): 34–39.

Salop, Lynne. *Suisong.* New York: Vantage Press, 1978.

Sanazaro, Leonard. "The Transfiguring Self: Sylvia Plath a Reconsideration." In *Critical Essays on Sylvia Plath,* edited by Linda W. Wagner, 87–97. Boston: G. K. Hall, 1984.

———. "Icons of the Apocalypse: The Poetry of Sylvia Plath and Edith Sitwell." *Halcyon* (1983): 54–70.

Scheerer, Constance. "The Deathly Paradise of Sylvia Plath." In *Sylvia Plath: The Woman and the Work,* edited by Edward Butscher, 166–76. London: Peter Owen, 1979.

Schullman, Grace. "Sylvia Plath and Yaddo." In *Ariel Ascending: Writings about Sylvia Plath,* edited by Paul Alexander, 165–77. New York: Harper & Row, 1985.

Schwartz, Murray M., and Christopher Bollas. "The Absence at the Center: Sylvia Plath and Suicide." In *Sylvia Plath: New Views on the Poetry,* edited by Gary Lane, 179–202. Baltimore and London: Johns Hopkins University Press, 1979.

Sexton, Anne. "The Barfly Ought to Sing." In *The Art of Sylvia Plath,* edited by Charles Newman, 174–81. London: Faber, 1970.

Shapiro, David. "Sylvia Plath: Drama and Melodrama." In *Sylvia Plath: New Views on the Poetry,* edited by Gary Lane, 45–53. Baltimore and London: Johns Hopkins University Press, 1979.

Sigmund, Elizabeth. "Sylvia in Devon: 1962." In *Sylvia Plath: The Woman and the Work,* edited by Edward Butscher, 100–107. London: Peter Owen, 1979.

Simpson, Louis. "Black, Banded with Yellow." *A Revolution in Taste: Studies of Dylan Thomas, Allen Ginsberg, Sylvia Plath and Robert Lowell,* 85–127. New York: Macmillan, 1978.

Smith, Pamela. "Architectonics: Sylvia Plath's *Colossus.*" In *Sylvia Plath: The Woman and the Work,* edited by Edward Butscher, 111–24. London: Peter Owen, 1979.

Smith, Stan. "Waist-Deep in History: Sylvia Plath." *Inviolable Voice: History and Twentieth-Century Poetry*, 200–225. Dublin: Gill & Macmillan, 1982.

Spender, Stephen. "Warnings from the Grave." In *The Art of Sylvia Plath*, edited by Charles Newman, 199–203. London: Faber, 1970.

Srivastava, K. G. "Plath's Daddy." *The Explicator* 50 (1992): 126–28.

Stade, George. "Afterword." In *A Closer Look at Ariel: A Memory of Sylvia Plath* by Nancy Hunter Steiner, 61–88. London: Faber, 1974.

Steiner, George. "Dying is an Art." In *The Art of Sylvia Plath*, edited by Charles Newman, 211–18. London: Faber, 1970.

———. "In Extremis." In *The Cambridge Mind: Ninety Years of the Cambridge Review: 1879–1969*, edited by Eric Homberger, William Janeway, and Simon Schama, 303–7. London: Cape, 1970.

Steiner, Nancy Hunter. *A Closer Look at Ariel: A Memory of Sylvia Plath*. London: Faber, 1974.

Stevenson, Anne. *Bitter Fame: A Life of Sylvia Plath*. Boston: Houghton Mifflin, 1989.

Stillwell, Robert L. "The Multiplying of Entities: D. H. Lawrence and Five Other Poets." *Sewanee Review* 76 (1968): 520–35.

Tabor, Stephen. *Sylvia Plath: An Analytical Bibliography*. London: Mansell, 1987.

Tomalin, Claire. "Everything But the Truth." *Independent on Sunday* books section, 9 October 1994: 32–33.

Uroff, Margaret Dickie. "Sylvia Plath's Narrative Strategies." In *Critical Essays on Sylvia Plath*, edited by Linda W. Wagner, 170–82. Boston: G. K. Hall, 1984.

———. *Sylvia Plath and Ted Hughes*. Urbana: University of Illinois Press, 1979.

Van Dyne, Susan R. "'More Terrible Than She Ever Was': The Manuscripts of Sylvia Plath's Bee Poems." In *Critical Essays on Sylvia Plath*, edited by Linda W. Wagner, 154–70. Boston: G. K. Hall, 1984.

———. "Fueling the Phoenix Fire: The Manuscripts of Sylvia Plath's 'Lady Lazarus'." In *Modern Critical Views: Sylvia Plath*, edited by Harold Bloom, 133–48. New York: Chelsea House, 1989.

Vendler, Helen. "Sylvia Plath." *The Music of What Happens*, 272–83. Cambridge, MA: Harvard University Press, 1988.

Wagner, Linda W., ed. *Critical Essays on Sylvia Plath*. Boston: G. K. Hall, 1984.

———. "Plath's *Ladies' Home Journal* Syndrome." *Journal of American Culture* 7 (1984): 32–38.

———. "Plath's *The Bell Jar* as Female Bildungsroman." *Women's Studies* 12.1 (1986): 55–68.

Wagner-Martin, Linda. *Sylvia Plath: A Biography*. London: Sphere-Macdonald, 1990.

———. ed. *Sylvia Plath: The Critical Heritage*. London: Routledge, 1988.

Wakeling, Patrick. "Sylvia Plath, a Balance of Loss and Gain." *Contemporary Review* 259 (1991): 142–46.

Walder, Dennis. *Ted Hughes and Sylvia Plath*. Outline and workbook for Open University course, Milton Keynes, Buckinghamshire, 1976.

Young, James E. "'I may be a bit of a Jew': The Holocaust Confessions of Sylvia Plath." *Philological Quarterly* 6 (1987): 127–47.

Zajdel, Melody. "Apprenticed in a Bible of Dreams: Sylvia Plath's Short Stories."

In *Critical Essays on Sylvia Plath,* edited by Linda W. Wagner, 182–93. Boston: G. K. Hall, 1984.

Zivley, Sherry. "Plath's Will-less Women." *Literature and Psychology* 31.3 (1981): 4–14.

Zollman, Sol. "Sylvia Plath and Imperialist Culture." *Literature and Ideology* 2 (1969): 11–22.

OTHER WORKS

Abrams, M. H. *The Mirror and the Lamp: Romantic Theory and the Critical Tradition.* London: Oxford University Press, 1971.

Alexander, Edward. "Stealing the Holocaust." *Midstream* (1980): 46–51.

Alvarev, Al. "The Literature of the Holocaust." *Commentary* 64 (1964): 65–69.

———. *Under Pressure: The Writer in Society: Eastern Europe and the U.S.A.* Harmondsworth, Middlesex: Penguin, 1965.

Applefeld, Aharon. "After the Holocaust." In *Writing and the Holocaust,* edited by Berel Lang, 83–92. New York: Holmes & Meier, 1988.

Arendt, Hannah. *Eichmann in Jerusalem: A Report on the Banality of Evil.* 1963. Harmondsworth, Middlesex: Penguin, 1977.

Aubrey, Crispin, ed. *Nukespeak: The Media and the Bomb.* London: Comedia, 1982.

Barreca, Regina. "Writing as Voodoo: Sorcery, Hysteria and Art." In *Death and Representation,* edited by Sarah Webster Goodwin and Elisabeth Bronfen, 174–91. Baltimore: Johns Hopkins University Press, 1993.

Bate, W. Jackson. *The Burden of the Past and the English Poet.* 1970. London: Harvard University Press, 1991.

Beauvoir, Simone de. *The Second Sex.* 1949. London: Pan-Picador, 1988.

Behrendt, Stephen C., ed. *History and Myth: Essays on English Romantic Literature.* Detroit: Wayne State University Press, 1990.

Blake, William. *Complete Writings.* Edited by Geoffrey Keynes. Oxford: Oxford University Press, 1957.

Bloom, Harold. *The Anxiety of Influence.* London: Oxford University Press, 1975.

———. *A Map of Misreading.* London: Oxford University Press, 1980.

Boose, Lynda E., and Betty S. Flowers, ed. *Daughters and Fathers.* Baltimore and London: Johns Hopkins University Press, 1989.

Bourke, Richard. *Romantic Discourse and Political Modernity: Wordsworth, the Intellectual and Cultural Critique.* Hemel Hempstead, Hertfordshire: Harvester, 1993.

Bowra, C. M. *Poetry and Politics 1900–1960.* Cambridge: Cambridge University Press, 1966.

Breslin, James, E. *From Modern to Contemporary: American Poetry 1945–65.* Chicago: University of Chicago Press, 1983.

Bronfen, Elisabeth. *Over Her Dead Body: Death, Femininity and the Aesthetic.* Manchester: Manchester University Press, 1992.

Brontë, Emily Jane. *The Complete Poems.* Edited by Janet Gezari. Harmondsworth, Middlesex: Penguin, 1992.

————. *Wuthering Heights.* Edited by David Daiches. Harmondsworth, Middlesex: Penguin, 1965.

Butler, Judith. *Gender Trouble: Feminism and the Subversion of Identity.* London: Routledge, 1990.

Butler, Marilyn. "Against Tradition: The Case for a Particularized Historical Method." In *Historical Studies and Literary Criticism,* edited by Jerome McCann, 25–47. Wisconsin: University of Wisconsin Press, 1985.

Caute, David. *The Great Fear: The Anti-Communist Purge Under Truman and Eisenhower.* London: Secker & Warburg, 1978.

Chilton, Paul. "Language and the Nuclear Arms Debate." In *Nukespeak Today,* edited by Paul Chilton. London: Frances Pinter, 1985.

————. "Nukespeak: Nuclear Language, Culture and Propaganda." In *Nukespeak: The Media and the Bomb,* edited by Crispin Aubrey, 94–112. London: Comedia, 1982.

Chodorow, Nancy. *Feminism and Psychoanalytic Theory.* New Haven and London: Yale University Press, 1989.

Coleridge, Samuel Taylor. *The Oxford Authors: Samuel Taylor Coleridge.* Edited by H. J. Jackson. Oxford: Oxford University Press, 1985.

Davies, Stevie. *Emily Brontë.* Brighton, East Sussex: Harvester, 1988.

————. *Emily Brontë: The Artist as a Free Woman.* Manchester: Carcanet Press, 1983.

De Laurentis, Teresa. *Alice Doesn't: Feminism, Semiotics, Cinema.* London: Macmillan, 1984.

De Quincey, Thomas. *Confessions of an English Opium-Eater and Other Writings.* Edited by Grevel Lindop. Oxford: Oxford University Press, 1985.

Douglas, Mary. *Purity and Danger: An Analysis of the Concepts of Pollution and Taboo.* London: Routledge & Kegan Paul-Ark, 1984.

Eagleton, Mary, ed. *Feminist Literary Theory: A Reader.* Oxford: Blackwell, 1986.

Eagleton, Terry. *Literary Theory: An Introduction.* Oxford: Blackwell, 1983.

————. "Myth and History in Recent Poetry." In *British Poetry Since 1960,* edited by Micheal Schmidt and Grevel Lindop. Oxford: Carcanet, 1972.

Eliot, T. S. *Selected Prose of T.S. Eliot.* Edited by Frank Kermode. London: Faber, 1975.

Empson, William. *Seven Types of Ambiguity.* 1930. London: Hogarth-Chatto, 1991.

Feit-Diehl, Joanne. "'Come Slowly-Eden': An Exploration of Women Poets and Their Muse." *Signs: Journal of Women in Culture and Society* 3.3 (1978): 572–87.

Felman, Shoshana. *Jacques Lacan and the Adventure of Insight: Psychoanalysis in Contemporary Culture.* London: Harvard University Press, 1987.

Fletcher, John, and Andrew Benjamin, ed. *Abjection, Melancholia and Love: The Work of Julia Kristeva.* London: Routledge, 1990.

Fowler, Roger, ed. *A Dictionary of Modern Critical Terms.* London: Routledge & Kegan Paul, 1987.

Frazer, J. G. *The Golden Bough: A Study in Magic and Religion,* abridged ed. 1922. London: Macmillan-Papermac, 1987.

Freud, Sigmund. *Totem and Taboo.* 1912–13. Translated by James Strachey. London: Ark-Routledge, 1960.

————. "Dostoevsky and Parricide." In *Penguin Freud Library, vol. 14: Art and Literature,* 441–60. London: Penguin, 1990.

Friedan, Betty. *The Feminine Mystique.* 1963. London: Penguin, 1992.

Frosh, Stephen. *The Politics of Psychoanalysis.* London: Macmillan, 1987.

Gibaldi, Joseph, and Walter S. Achtert. *MLA Handbook for Writers of Research Papers.* New York: Modern Language Association of America, 1991.

Gilbert, Sandra M., and Susan Gubar. *The Madwoman in the Attic.* New Haven and London: Yale University Press, 1979.

————. *No Man's Land: Vol 1—The War of the Words.* New Haven and London: Yale University Press, 1988.

————. *No Man's Land: Vol 2—Sexchanges.* New Haven and London: Yale University Press, 1989.

————. *No Man's Land: Vol 3—Letters From the Front.* New Haven and London: Yale University Press, 1994.

Goodwin, Sarah Webster, and Elisabeth Bronfen, ed. *Death And Representation.* Baltimore: Johns Hopkins University Press, 1993.

Graves, Robert. *The White Goddess.* 1948. London: Faber, 1961.

Gray, Richard. *American Poetry of the Twentieth Century.* Harlow, Essex: Longman, 1990.

Grosz, Elizabeth. *Sexual Subversions.* Sydney: Allen & Unwin, 1989.

————. "The Body of Signification." In *Abjection, Melancholia and Love: The Work of Julia Kristeva,* edited by John Fletcher and Andrew Benjamin, 80–103. London: Routledge, 1990.

————. "Julia Kristeva." In *Feminism and Psychoanalysis: A Critical Dictionary,* edited by Elizabeth Wright, 194–200. Oxford: Blackwell, 1992.

Grove, Robin. "'It would not do': Emily Brontë as Poet." In *The Art of Emily Brontë,* edited by Anne Smith, 33–66. London: Vision Press, 1976.

Guttmann, Allen. "Love and Death and Dachau: Recent Poets." *Studies on the Left* 4 (1964): 98–109.

Hallberg, Robert von. *American Poetry and Culture 1945–1980.* London: Harvard University Press, 1985.

Hardy, Barbara. "The Lyricism of Emily Brontë." In *The Art of Emily Brontë,* edited by Anne Smith, 94–118. London: Vision Press, 1976.

Harris, Jon. "An Elegy for Myself: British Poetry and the Holocaust." *English* (1993): 213–33.

Hegel, G. W. F. "Independence and Dependence of Self-Consciousness: Lordship and Bondage." In *Hegel's Phenomenology of Spirit,* translated by A. V. Miller, 111–19. Oxford: Oxford University Press, 1977.

Homans, Margaret. *Women Writers and Poetic Identity.* Cambridge: Princeton University Press, 1980.

Howe, Irving. "Writing and the Holocaust." In *Writing and the Holocaust,* edited by Berel Lang, 175–99. New York: Holmes & Meier, 1988.

Huxley, Aldous. *Brave New World.* New York: Bantam Books, 1953.

————. *The Doors of Perception and Heaven and Hell.* London: Grafton-HarperCollins, 1977.

Insdorf, Annette. *Indelible Shadows: Film and the Holocaust.* 2d. ed. Cambridge: Cambridge University Press, 1989.

Jung, C. G. *Selected Writings*. Edited by Anthony Storr. London: Fontana, 1983.

Kaplan, Cora. "Speaking/Writing/Feminism." *Seachanges: Culture and Feminism*, 219–28. London: Verso, 1986.

Kermode, Frank. *Romantic Image*. London: Routledge & Kegan Paul, 1957.

Kitson, Peter, ed. *Romantic Criticism 1800–1825*. London: Batsford, 1989.

Kolodny, Annette. *The Land Before Her: Fantasy and Experience of the American Frontiers, 1630–1860*. Chapel Hill and London: University of North Carolina Press, 1984.

———. *The Lay of the Land: Metaphor as Experience and History in American Life and Letters*. Chapel Hill and London: University of North Carolina Press, 1975.

Kristeva, Julia. *Powers of Horror: An Essay on Abjection*. New York: Columbia University Press, 1983.

———. *The Kristeva Reader*. Edited by Toril Moi. Oxford: Blackwell, 1986.

Lang, Berel, ed. *Writing and the Holocaust*. New York: Holmes & Meier, 1988.

Langer, Lawrence L. *The Holocaust and the Literary Imagination*. New Haven and London: Yale University Press, 1975.

Lawrence, D. H. *Selected Poems*. Edited by Mara Kalnins. London: Dent-Everyman, 1992.

———. *Selected Essays*. Edited by Richard Aldington. Harmondsworth, Middlesex: Penguin, 1950.

Leavis, F. R. *Revaluation: Tradition and Development in English Poetry*. 1936. Harmondsworth, Middlesex: Peregrine-Penguin, 1964.

———. *D. H. Lawrence: Novelist*. 1955. Harmondsworth, Middlesex: Pelican-Penguin, 1973.

Lechte, John. *Julia Kristeva*. London: Routledge, 1990.

Lehman, David. *Signs of the Times: Deconstruction and the Fall of Paul de Man*. London: Andre Deutsch, 1991.

Leighton, Angela. *Elizabeth Barrett-Browning*. Brighton, East Sussex: Harvester, 1986.

Lentricchia, Frank. *After the New Criticism*. London: University Paperback-Methuen, 1983.

Lifton, Robert Jay, and Eric Markusen. *The Genocidal Mentality: Nazi Holocaust and Nuclear Threat*. London: Macmillan, 1991.

Mellor, Anne K., ed. *Romanticism and Feminism*. Bloomington and Indianapolis: Indiana University Press, 1988.

Miles, Rosalind. "A Baby God: The Creative Dynamism of Emily Brontë's Poetry." *The Art of Emily Brontë*. Edited by Anne Smith. London: Vision Press, 1976, 68–93.

Millett, Kate. *Sexual Politics*. London: Virago, 1977.

Mitchell, Juliet. *Psychoanalysis and Feminism*. 1974. Harmondsworth, Middlesex: Penguin, 1990.

Moi, Toril. *Sexual/Textual Politics*. London: Methuen, 1985.

Montefiore, Jan. *Feminism and Poetry: Language, Experience, Identity in Women's Writing*. London: Routledge-Pandora, 1987.

Murdoch, Brian. "Transformations of the Holocaust: Auschwitz in Modern Lyric Poetry." *Comparative Literature Studies* 11 June 1974: 123–50.

Nelson, Cary. *Repression and Recovery: Modern American Poetry and the Politics of Cultural Memory 1910–1945.* Wisconsin: University of Wisconsin Press, 1989.

Norris, Christopher, and Ian Whitehouse. "The Rhetoric of Deterrence." In *Styles of Discourse,* edited by Nikolas Coupland, 293–322. London: Croom Helm, 1985.

Nuclear Criticism. *diacritics* 14, no. 2 (1984).

Ortega y Gasset, Jose. *The Revolt of the Masses.* 1930. London: Unwin, 1961.

Ostriker, Alicia. *Stealing the Language: The Emergence of Women's Poetry in America.* London: Women's Press, 1987.

Owen, Ursula, ed. *Fathers: Reflections by Daughters.* London: Virago, 1983.

Parrinder, Patrick. *Authors and Authority: English and American Criticism 1750–1990.* London: Methuen, 1991.

Prickett, Stephen, ed. *The Romantics.* London: Methuen, 1981.

Rich, Adrienne. *On Lies, Secrets and Silence.* London: Virago, 1980.

———. *Of Woman Born: Motherhood as Experience and Institution.* London: Virago, 1977.

Richards, I. A. *Practical Criticism: A Study of Literary Judgement.* 1929. London: Routledge, 1964.

———. *Principles of Literary Criticism.* 1924. London: Routledge, 1960.

Richardson, Alan. "Romanticism and the Colonization of the Feminine." In *Romanticism and Feminism,* edited by Anne K. Mellor, 13–23. Bloomington and Indianapolis: Indiana University Press, 1988.

Salusinszky, Imre, ed. *Criticism in Socitey.* London: Methuen, 1987.

Sartre, Jean-Paul. *What Is Literature?* Translated by Bernard Frechtman. London: Methuen-University Paperbacks, 1967.

———. *Existentialism and Humanism.* Translated by Philip Mairet. London: Methuen, 1989.

Segal, Lynne. *Is the Future Female?* London: Virago, 1987.

Smith, Anne, ed. *The Art of Emily Brontë.* London: Vision Press, 1976.

Trilling, Lionel. *Sincerity and Authenticity.* London: Oxford University Press, 1972.

Watson, J. R. *English Poetry of the Romantic Period 1789—1830.* London and New York: Longman, 1992.

Whitford, Margaret. *Luce Irigaray: Philosophy in the Feminine.* London: Routledge, 1991.

Wright, Elizabeth, ed. *Feminism and Psychoanalysis: A Critical Dictionary.* Oxford: Blackwell, 1992.

Yeats, W. B. *Selected Criticism.* Edited by A. Norman Jeffares. London: Pan-Macmillan, 1976.

Young, James. *Writing and Rewriting the Holocaust.* Bloomington and Indianapolis: Indiana University Press, 1988.

Index